# MOMENTS
# WITH FRIENDS

From THE WORD
1906–1916

# Books by Harold W. Percival

THINKING AND DESTINY

MASONRY AND ITS SYMBOLS
In the Light of *Thinking and Destiny*

MAN AND WOMAN AND CHILD

DEMOCRACY IS SELF-GOVERNMENT

MONTHLY EDITORIALS
FROM THE WORD 1904–1917
Part I

MONTHLY EDITORIALS
FROM THE WORD 1904–1917
Part II

MOMENTS WITH FRIENDS
FROM THE WORD 1906–1916

# MOMENTS
# WITH FRIENDS

## From THE WORD

## 1906–1916

Harold W. Percival

The Word Foundation, Inc.
P.O. Box 17510
Rochester, NY 14617
USA
thewordfoundation.org

# TABLE OF CONTENTS

How can we tell what we have been in our last incarnation?
Can we tell how many times we were born before?
Are we conscious between our reincarnations?
What are the theosophical views of Adam's and Eve's reincarnations?
What is the length of the time appointed between reincarnations, if
    there is any specified time?
Do we change our personality when we return to earth?

Does a Theosophist believe in superstitions?
What basis is there for the superstition that one born
    with a "caul" may possess some psychic faculty or
    occult power?
If a thought may be transmitted to the mind of another, why is this
    not done as accurately and with as much intelligence as ordinary
    conversation is carried on?
Have we anything which is analogous to the process of thought
    transference?
How can we converse by thought intelligently?
Is it right to read the thoughts of others whether they would that we
    should or not?

Why is it better to have the body cremated after death instead of
    having it buried?
Is there any truth in the stories that we read or hear about, concerning
    vampires and vampirism?

What is the reason of the sudden death of people whether young or in the prime of life, when it would appear that many years of usefulness and growth, mental and physical, are before them?

If the astral arm, leg, or other member of the body is not severed when the physical member is amputated, why is the astral body not able to reproduce another physical arm or leg?

Is a Theosophist a vegetarian or a meat eater?

How can a real theosophist consider himself a theosophist and still eat meat when we know that the desires of the animal are transferred from the flesh of the animal to the body of the one who eats it?

Is it not true that the yogis of India, and men of divine attainments, live on vegetables, and if so, should not those who would develop themselves avoid meat and also live on vegetables?

What effect does the eating of vegetables have on the body of man, as compared with the eating of meat?

How can vegetarianism prevent concentration of the mind when vegetarianism has been advised in order to attain concentration?

What is the exact meaning of the term elementals, used in so many connections by theosophists and occultists?

What is meant by the "human elemental"? Is there any difference between it and the lower mind?

Is there an elemental controlling the desires, another controlling the vital forces, another controlling the bodily functions, or does the human elemental control all these?

Does the same elemental control both the conscious acts and the unconscious functions of the body?

Are elementals in general evolving entities, and will they all or any of them in the course of evolution become men?

Is it really possible for one to see into the future?

Is it not possible for one to see actual occurrences of the past and occurrences as they will be in the future as clearly and distinctly as he sees the present?

How is it possible for one to see clairvoyantly when such seeing is opposed to all our experience?

What are the organs used in clairvoyance, and how is one's vision transferred from the objects near at hand to those at great distances, and from the known visible to the unknown invisible?

Can an occultist look into the future whenever he so wills, and does he use a clairvoyant faculty to do it?

If an occultist can pierce the veil why do not occultists, individually or collectively benefit from their knowledge of coming events?

What is the "third eye" and does the clairvoyant and the occultist use it?

Who uses the pineal gland, and what is the object of its use?

How does the third eye or pineal gland open, and what happens at such opening?

Does Christmas have any particular meaning to a theosophist, and if so, what?

Is it probable that Jesus was an actual person, and that he was born on Christmas Day?

If Jesus was an actual man why is it that we have no more historical record of the birth or life of such a man than the bible statement?

Why do they call this, the 25th of December, Christmas instead of Jesusmass or Jesusday, or by some other name?

Why are so many mental healers prosperous if they do not effect cures, and if they are not what they represented themselves to be, would their patients not discover the fact?

Did not Jesus and many of the saints cure physical ills by mental means and if so was it wrong?

If it is wrong to receive money for curing physical ills by mental processes, or for giving "science teaching," is it not also wrong for a school teacher to receive money for instructing pupils in any of the branches of learning?

*(In a letter to the editor, the March 1907 "Moments with Friends" is critiqued, followed by a response from Mr. Percival.—Ed.)*

The Christian says that Man has a Body, Soul and Spirit. The Theosophist says that Man has Seven Principles. In a few words what are these Seven Principles?

In a few words can you tell me what takes place at death?

Most spiritualists claim that at their seances the souls of the departed appear and converse with friends. Theosophists say that this is not the case; that what is seen is not the soul but the shell, spook or desire body which the soul has discarded. Who is correct?

If the soul of man may be held a prisoner after death by its desire body, why may not this soul appear at seances and why is it wrong to say that it does not appear and converse with the sitters?

If the appearances at seances are only the shells, spooks or desire bodies, which have been discarnated by the human souls after death, why is it that they are able to communicate with the sitters on a subject known only to the person concerned, and why is it that the same subject will be brought up over and over again?

The fact cannot be denied that spirits do sometimes tell the truth and also give advice which if followed will result to the benefit of all concerned. How can the theosophist, or any other opposed to spiritualism, deny or explain away these facts?

If it is true that none but shells, spooks and entities devoid of manas appear, according to theosophical teachings, at seances, whence comes the information and teachings of a philosophical and often theosophical nature, which some mediums have undoubtedly received?

Do the dead work individually or collectively to attain a certain end?

How do the dead eat, if at all? What sustains their life?

Do the dead wear clothes?

Do the dead live in houses?

Do the dead sleep?

Do the dead live in families, in communities, and if so is there a government?

Is there a punishment or reward for the deeds done by the dead, either while in life or after death?

Do the dead acquire knowledge?

Do the dead know what is going on in this world?

How do you explain cases where the dead have appeared either in dreams, or to people who were awake, and have announced that death of certain persons, generally other members of the family, was near?

Are the dead attracted to members of what was their family while on earth, and do they watch over them; say a departed mother over her young children?

How does the moment of birth determine one's destiny in the world?

How do the influences at birth, or one's destiny, cooperate with the karma of the ego?

Are the planetary influences employed to administer human karma, or fate? If so, where does free will come in?

Why is it sometimes said that Jesus was one of the saviours of mankind and that the peoples of antiquity had also their saviours, instead of saying he was The Saviour of the world, as is held by all Christendom?

Can you tell us if there are any people who celebrate the birth of their saviours on or around the twenty-fifth day of December (at the time that the sun is said to enter the sign Capricorn?

It is said by some that the birth of Christ is a spiritual birth. If this is so, why is it that Christmas is celebrated for the physical body by the eating and drinking, in a material way, which is the very opposite of our conceptions of spirituality?

In "Moments with Friends," of Vol. 4, page 189, it is said Christmas means "The birth of the invisible sun of light, the Christ Principle," which, as it continues, "Should be born within man." If this is so, does it follow that the physical birth of Jesus was also on the twenty-fifth of December?

If Jesus or Christ did not live and teach as he is supposed to have done, how is it that such an error could have prevailed for so many centuries and should prevail today?

Do you mean to say that the history of Christianity is nothing but a fable, that the life of Christ is a myth, and that for nearly 2,000 years the world has been believing in a myth?

If astral intelligences are capable of seeing through matter, why is it
that no spirit control of a medium is able to meet the now famous
orange counting test?

What explanation can Theosophy offer for the terrific earthquakes
which so frequently occur, and which may destroy thousands of
people?

What is a divine incarnation or incarnation of the Supreme Being?
What is the use or function of the pituitary body?
What is the use or function of the pineal gland?
What is the use or function of the spleen?
What is the use or function of the thyroid gland?

Have animals minds and do they think?
Will any evil influence be brought to human beings by the presence of
domestic animals?

Is there any ground for the claim of those who say that the souls of
departed men incarnate in birds or animals?

Can you explain more fully how the different thoughts of man act on
the matter of the physical world so as to produce different kinds
of animals such as the lion, bear, peacock, rattlesnake? (This
question refers to Percival's editorial *Thought.*—Ed.)

Can one look inside his body and see the workings of the different
organs, and if so how can this be done?

Are the individuals who are trying to solve the problem of aerial navigation, reincarnated Atlanteans?

If the Atlanteans had solved the problem of aerial navigation, and if those who are now concerned with the same problem were Atlanteans, then why have these individuals not reincarnated since the sinking of Atlantis and before the present time, and if they have reincarnated before the present age, why have they not been able to master the air or to fly before the present time?

Are we or are we not in union with atma-buddhi?

Is it not true that all that we can become is already in us and that all we have to do is to become conscious of it?

Is darkness the absence of light, or is it something separate in itself and which takes the place of light? If they are distinct and separate, what is darkness and what is light?

What is radium and how is it possible for it to throw off continuously a great energy without any apparent waste and loss of its own power and body, and what is the source of its great radioactivity?

Is it possible to develop a new species of vegetable, fruit or plant, totally different and distinct from any other known species? If so, how is it done?

Is it possible and is it right to look into the future and predict future events?

Is man a microcosm of the macrocosm, the universe in miniature? If
so, the planets and the visible stars must be represented within
him. Where are they located?

What is meant by health in general? If it is the equilibrium of man's
physical, mental and spiritual strength, then how is the balance
maintained?

Is it best for a man to leave his physical body unconsciously, that the
soul may enter its dream state?

What height do souls reach who leave their physical bodies
consciously and who remain conscious after death?

Please give a definition of immortality and state briefly how
immortality can be attained?

Are man's likes and dislikes reflections of his own soul? If so, how are
they reflected? If not, whence come these likes and dislikes?

Is it best that a man should suppress his sexual desires, and should he
strive to live a life of celibacy?

What is the rationale of the doctrine of the atonement, and how can it
be reconciled with the law of karma?

# CONTENTS

# PREFACE

"Moments With Friends" is a question-and-answer feature of *The Word* magazine. Between 1906 and 1916, the questions listed below were posed by readers of *The Word* and answered by Mr. Percival under the appellation "A Friend."

In 1986, The Word Foundation created a second series of *The Word* that is still in publication as a quarterly magazine. It also features a "Moments With Friends" section with questions from our readers.

The Word Foundation

HAROLD W. PERCIVAL
1868 – 1953

# MOMENTS WITH FRIENDS

## MARCH 1906

[From *The Word*, Vol. 2 No. 6]

*How can we tell what we have been in our last incarnation?* asked a visitor the other night after a lecture.

The only way to tell is to know positively as who we lived before. The faculty by which this knowledge comes is memory, of a higher order. In the absence of that, each may form estimates of what he was before by what he really likes now. It is only reasonable to suppose that, if we have any choice in the matter, we would not select as the condition or environments into which we were to come, such as were unsuited to our tastes or development and, on the other hand, if we have no choice, then, the law which governs reincarnation would not put us into conditions unsuited for development.

We feel in sympathy with or are opposed to certain ideals, characters, classes of people, types of people, crafts, professions, arts and occupations, and this would indicate whether we had worked for or against these before. If we feel at home or ill-at-ease in good or bad society, that would indicate to what we had been accustomed before. A tramp, accustomed to sunning himself idly on an old wharf or along a dusty country road, would not feel comfortable in polite society, a chemist's laboratory, or on the rostrum. Nor would one who had been an active industrious man, mechanically or philosophically inclined, feel comfortable and at ease sunning himself, unwashed, in ragged clothes.

We may with fair accuracy infer what we were in the past life not by wealth or position in the present, but to what our impulses, ambitions, likes, dislikes, controlling passions, draw us in the present.

༄

*Can we tell how many times we were born before?*

The body is born and the body dies. The soul is neither born nor dies, but incarnates into the body which is born and leaves the body at the body's death.

To know how many lives a soul has spent in this world, take a glance at the different races now in the world. Consider the moral, mental and spiritual development of an African, or South Sea Islander; and then that of a Newton, Shakespeare, Plato, Buddha, or Christ. Between these extremes think of the different grades of development which humanity presents. After this ask where do "I" stand between these extremes.

After averaging the position see how much "I" have learned from the experiences of the present life—the ordinary man learns but little— and how do "I" *act* what "I" have learned. After this interesting question, we may perhaps form some idea of the number of times it must have been necessary to have lived in order to have reached even the present state.

There is no way for any one person to tell how many times he has lived before except by actual knowledge and a continued consciousness from the past. If he were told he lived twice or fifty thousand times the information would not benefit him, and he would not be able to verify it except by knowledge which comes from his own soul. But by the illustration given we may perhaps form some idea of the millions of years through which we must have come to have reached the present state.

৪৶

*Are we conscious between our reincarnations?*

We are. We are not conscious in the same manner as we are during life in the body. This world is the field of action. In it man lives and moves and thinks. Man is a composite being made up or composed of seven men or principles. At death the divine portion of man separates itself from the grossly material portion, and the divine principles or men then dwell in a state or condition which has been determined by the thoughts and actions through the entire life. These divine principles are the mind, soul, and spirit, which, with the higher desires, pass into the ideal condition which the life on earth has determined. This condition can be no higher than were the thoughts or ideals during life. As these principles are disconnected from the grossly material portion they are not conscious of the evil of the life. But they are conscious, and live out the ideals which have been formed during the life just ended. This is a period of rest, which is as necessary to the soul's progress as a rest at night is necessary to fit the body and mind for the activities of the coming day.

At death, the separation of the divine from the mortal principles allows the bliss of the living out of ideals to be experienced. This is a conscious state between reincarnations.

ॐ

*What are the theosophical views of Adam's and Eve's reincarnations?*
Whenever this question has been asked of a theosophist it has caused a smile, for even though the idea of Adam and Eve being the first two human beings who lived in this world has been shown in its absurdities by modern scientific investigations, yet the question quite frequently comes up.

The well informed man will at once say that evolution shows this tale to be a fable. The theosophist agrees with this, but saying that the early history of the human race has been preserved in this myth or fable. The Secret Doctrine shows that the human family in its early and primeval state were not as they are now, made up of men and women, but that in fact there was no sex. That gradually in the natural development a dual sex or hermaphroditism, was developed in each human being. That still later were developed the sexes, into which humanity at present is divided.

Adam and Eve does not mean one man and one woman, but the whole humanity. You and I have been Adam and Eve. The reincarnations of Adam and Eve is the reincarnation of the human soul in many different bodies, in many lands, and through many races.

ॐ

*What is the length of the time appointed between reincarnations, if there is any specified time?*

It has been said that the period between incarnations, or from the time of the death of one body until the soul takes up its abode in another which is born into the world, is about fifteen hundred years. But this by no means applies to all people, and especially not to the active-minded modern western man.

The good man who longs for heaven, who performs good works in this world and has ideals and a vivid imagination, one who longs for an eternity in heaven, may have a heaven for an immense period, but it is safe to say that such is not the average man in the present day.

Life in this world is the field of action in which seeds are sown. Heaven is a state or condition of rest where the mind rests from its labors and works in life that it may be again reincarnated. The period after which the mind is drawn back depends on what it has done in life and where it has placed its thought, for wherever the thought or the aspiration is to that place or condition the mind will go. The period is not to be measured by our years, but rather by the mind's capacity for enjoyment in activity or rest. A moment at one time seems to be an eternity. Another moment passes like a flash. Our measurement of time, therefore, is not in the days and years which come and go, but in the capacity for making these days or years long or short.

The time is appointed for our stay in heaven between reincarnations. Each one appoints it himself. Each human being lives his own life. Inasmuch as each differs in detail from every other no definite statement as to time can be made other than that each makes his time himself by his own thoughts and actions, and it is long or short as he makes it. It is possible for one to reincarnate in less than a year, though this is unusual, or to extend the period for thousands of years.

ॐ

*Do we change our personality when we return to earth?*

We do in the same manner that we change a suit of clothes when it has served its purpose and no longer is necessary. The personality is made up of elemental matter combined into form, animated by the principle of life, directed and promoted by desire, with the lower phases of the mind acting therein through the five senses. This is the combination which we call the personality. It only exists for the term of years from birth to death; serving as the instrument with and through which the mind works, comes into contact with the world, and experiences life therein. At death, this personality is laid aside and returns into the occult elements of earth, water, air, and fire, from which it was drawn and combined. The human mind then passes on to its state of rest after the enjoyment of which it builds up and enters another personality to continue its education and experiences in the world.

A FRIEND

# APRIL 1906

[From *The Word*, Vol. 3 No. 1]

*Does a Theosophist believe in superstitions?* was asked one of a party of friends not long ago.

A Theosophist accepts all facts, and never loses his reason. But a Theosophist does not stop and rest content with the fact; he endeavors to trace it to its origin and see its consequences. Superstition is the belief in or the practice of some thing without actually knowing why. In a broader light, superstition is a consent of the mind to an instinct or tendency concerning some practice without other reason for belief. The superstitions of a people are the dim reflections of forgotten knowledge. The knowledge gone, and those who had the knowledge, the people continue the practice of the forms; and so the forms and beliefs are handed down by tradition from generation to generation. As they become farther removed from knowledge they cling the closer to their superstitions and may even become fanatic. The practice without the knowledge is superstition. Visit the churches in a large city on a Sunday morning. See the formalities of worship; watch the procession of choristers; notice the insignia of office of those who conduct the service; observe the statues, sacred ornaments, instruments, and symbols; listen to the repetition and formula of worship to—what? Could we blame one unfamiliar with all this for calling it superstition, and saying that we were a superstitious people? We are thus inclined to regard the beliefs of others which are seldom more superstitious than our own people. The superstitions held by those whom we call "the ignorant" and "the credulous," must have had an origin. Those who would know must trace the traditions or superstitions to their origin. If they will do this they will get knowledge, which is the opposite of its unintelligent reflection—superstition. An unprejudiced study of one's own superstitions will reveal a woeful ignorance of one's self. Continue the study and it will lead to the knowledge of self.

ॐ

*What basis is there for the superstition that one born with a "caul" may possess some psychic faculty or occult power?*

This belief comes down through the ages from antiquity, when humanity held intercourse with beings within and around the earth. Then man's sight, hearing and other inner occult senses, were clouded over by growing into a more sensuous and material life. There is no part of man's body that is not related to some force and power in one or more of the invisible worlds of nature. That which is called the "caul" is related to the astral world. If, when man is born into this physical world, the caul remains with him it stamps or impresses the astral body with certain tendencies and attunes it to the astral world. In later life these tendencies may be overcome, but never entirely effaced, as the linga sharira, the astral design body, is attuned to receive impressions from the astral light. The superstition which seafaring men attach to this relic, as to its being an omen of "good luck" or as a preservative against drowning, is based on the fact that as it was a protection to the embryo from adverse elements in the pre-natal world, so it may now in the physical world protect from the dangers of the water which corresponds with the astral light and the elements which, though they are called physical, are none the less occult and originates in the astral world.

ॐ

*If a thought may be transmitted to the mind of another, why is this not done as accurately and with as much intelligence as ordinary conversation is carried on?*

It is not done because we do not "talk" in thought; nor have we yet learned the language of thought. But still, our thoughts are transferred to the minds of others more often than we suppose, though it is not done as intelligently as we would converse because we have not been compelled by necessity to communicate with each other through thought only, and, because we will not take the trouble to educate the mind and the senses to do it. One born among cultured people is cared for, trained, disciplined and educated into the ways of the parents or the circle into which he is born. Stop but to think, and it will at once be seen that it requires long years of patience on the part of the teacher and persistent effort on the part of the pupil to learn the art of speaking and reading and writing a language, and to learn the habits, customs and the modes of thought in that language. If it requires such effort and training in this physical world to learn one language, it is not strange that few persons are able to transfer thoughts correctly without the use of words. It is no more occult to transfer thought without words than it is to transfer thought by the use of words. The difference is that we have learned how to do it in the world of talk, but still remain as ignorant as speechless children in the world of thought. Transference of thought by word requires two factors: the one who speaks, and the one who listens; the transmission is the result. This we know how to do, but the actual manner in which we speak and understand is as occult to us as is the transference of thought without words. We do not know how and in what manner the different organs in the body operate in order to produce the sound uttered; we do not know by what process the sound uttered is transmitted through space; we do not know how the sound is received by the tympanum and the auditory nerve; nor by what process it is interpreted to the intelligence within who understands the thought conveyed by the sound. But we do know that all this is done, and that we do understand each other after some such fashion.

ॐ

*Have we anything which is analogous to the process of thought transference?*

Yes. The telegraphic and photographic processes are very similar to that of thought transference. There must be the operator who transmits his message, there must be the receiver who understands it. So then there must be two persons who are disciplined, trained or educated to transmit and receive each other's thoughts if they would do so intelligently and with the same accuracy with which ordinary intelligent conversation is carried on, just as two persons must be able to speak the same language if they would converse. It is said that many people are able to do this, but they do it only in a very unintelligent manner, because they are not willing to submit the mind to a rigid course of training. This training of the mind should be as orderly, and conducted with as much care, as is the life of the scholar in a well-disciplined school.

੨੩

*How can we converse by thought intelligently?*

If one will carefully observe his own mind and the minds of others, he will come to realize that his thoughts are conveyed to others by some mysterious process. The one who would converse by thought without the use of words must learn to control the functions of his mind. As the functions of the mind are controlled, and one is able to hold the mind steadily on any one subject, it will be perceived that the mind carves out the form, takes the shape and character of the subject which is under consideration, and at once conveys this subject or thought to the object to which it is directed, by willing it there. If this is done properly, the person to whom the thought is directed, will surely receive it. If it is not done properly there will be an indistinct impression as to what is intended. As to reading or knowing of thoughts, the functions of the mind must also be controlled if the thought of another is to be received and understood. This is done in the same manner that an ordinarily intelligent person listens to the words of another. To understand properly one must listen attentively to the words uttered. To listen attentively the mind should be held as still as possible. If irrelevant thoughts enter the mind of the listener the necessary attention is not given, and the words, even though heard, are not understood. If one would read the thought of another his mind must be held in an attentive

blank so that the impression of the thought transmitted may be preserved clearly and distinctly. Then if that thought is clear and distinct
there will be no difficulty whatever in the understanding of it. We thus
see that the mind of the transmitter of the thought and the mind of the
receiver of the thought must both be trained to the practice, if thought
transference is to be conducted accurately and intelligently.

‎ॐ

*Is it right to read the thoughts of others whether they would that we
should or not?*

Certainly not. To do this is as unpardonable and dishonest as it is to
enter another's study and ransack and read his private papers. Whenever
one sends out a thought it is stamped with the individuality of the sender
and bears an impress or signature. If the thought is of a nature that the
sender does not desire it to be known, the impress or signature of the
sender marks it much the same as we would mark an envelope "private"
or "personal." This causes it to be invisible to the would-be dishonest
meddler unless the thought is loose in its formation and is related to the
meddler. By the true occultist, such a thought would not be read or interfered with. Were it not for this barrier all the would-be teachers of
occult powers would be able to become millionaires over night, and,
perhaps, they would do away with the necessity of earning money at so
much per lesson or sitting. They would upset the stock market, form an
occult trust with the markets of the world, then attack each other and
come to a timely end, such as that of the "Kilkenny cats."

A Friend

# MAY 1906

[From *The Word*, Vol. 3 No. 2]

In a letter recently received, a friend asks: *Why is it better to have the body cremated after death instead of having it buried?*

There are many reasons advanced in favor of cremation. Among them one that cremation is cleaner, more sanitary, requires less room, and breeds no diseases, such as often come from cemeteries, among the living. But the most important is that advanced by Theosophists, namely, that death is the passing out of the higher principles, and means leaving the body an empty house. After the human soul has disconnected itself from the remains, there is left the astral body, which gave and kept the physical in form, and the body of desire. The astral or form body lingers around, and lasts as long as, the physical, fading away as the physical decomposes. The desire body, however, is an active force capable of doing damage in proportion as the desires were vicious or inimical during life. This desire body may last for hundreds of years if the desires of which it is composed be strong enough, whereas the physical body lasts comparatively few years. This desire body is a vampire which draws its strength, first from the remains and secondly from any living body who will give it audience, or admits its presence. The desire body draws sustenance from the dead form and astral body, but if the physical body is cremated that avoids all of the foregoing. That destroys the forces of the physical body, dissipates its astral body, resolves these into the elements from which they were drawn before birth and while living in the world, and enables the mind to disentangle itself more easily from the desire body and pass into the rest which religionists call heaven. We cannot do a greater service to those whom we love and who have passed out of this life than to have their bodies cremated and thus relieve them of the necessity of shaking off the mortal coil and the terrors of the grave.

಄

*Is there any truth in the stories that we read or hear about, concerning vampires and vampirism?*

We live in an age altogether too scientific to allow of there being any truth in such mediaeval nursery tales as those of vampires. But, nevertheless, the truth still exists, and many scientific men, who have outlived the years of superstition, have become more superstitious than the most credulous when they have had experience with a vampire; then it was their turn to experience the taunts and jibes of their fellow scientists. One advantage of the prevalent materialistic incredulity concerning sub-mundane and super-mundane existences, is that it takes the popular thought away from the tales of goblins, ghouls, and vampires, by ridiculing such things. Therefore there is less vampirism than in the Middle Ages when everyone believed in sorcery and witchcraft. Vampires still exist and will continue to be formed and kept alive as long as human beings live fiendish lives, in which they do *in thought and desire* murder their enemies, defraud the poor and helpless, ruin the lives of their friends, and sacrifice others to their selfish and bestial desires. When a human being having strong desires and intellectual power with a dwarfed or throttled conscience, lives the life of selfishness, has no compassion for others when his desires are concerned, takes every possible advantage in business, ignores the moral sense, and subjects others to his desires in every way that his intellect can discover: then when the time of death for such a man has come there is formed after death what is called a desire body, of strength and fiendish power. This is quite distinct from the astral form which hovers around the physical remains. Such a desire body is stronger than that of the average person and is more powerful, because the thoughts while in life were concentrated in the desires. This desire body is then a vampire in that it preys on all persons who will open a door by the life, thoughts, and desires, and who are sufficiently weak in will to allow the vampire to overcome their moral sense. Horrible tales could be told of the experiences of many who were the prey of a vampire. The body of those of such as have lived the life of a vampire will often be found fresh, intact, and the flesh will even be warm years after it has been in the grave. This simply means that the desire body is sometimes strong enough to keep in touch with the physical through the astral body, and to keep intact the physical form, through life supplied it with the life drawn from the bodies of living human beings by the vampire or desire body. The burning of the body by cremation does away with the possibility of a human vampire preserving its physical body with the life drawn from the living. The human body, in as much as it is the reservoir or storage house, has been destroyed and the desire body is unable either to immediately take the life of those living and is prevented from coming so nearly in contact with them.

ᘒ

*What is the reason of the sudden death of people whether young or in the prime of life, when it would appear that many years of usefulness and growth, mental and physical, are before them?*

When the soul comes into life, it has a definite lesson to learn, at the learning of which it may pass out if desired. The period in which the lesson of a particular life is to be learned, may be a few years or be extended over a hundred, or the lesson may not be learned at all; and the soul returns to school again and again until it learns that lesson. One may learn more in twenty-five years than another may learn in one hundred. Life in the world is for the purpose of gaining intimate knowledge of eternal verities. Each life should promote the soul one degree nearer to self-knowledge. What are usually called accidents are simply the carrying out in detail of a general law. The accident or happening is only one small arch of a cycle of action. The accident known or seen, is only the continuation and completion of the invisible cause of action. Strange as it may seem, accidents are almost always caused by the thoughts which one generates. Thought, action, and accident form the complete cycle of cause and effect. That part of the cycle of cause and effect which connects cause with the effect is action, which may be visible or invisible; and that part of the cycle of cause and effect which is the effect and the result of the cause, is the accident or happening. Every accident might be traced to its cause. If we find the immediate cause of any accident it simply means that the cause has been recently generated, which means that it is only the small cycle of thought, action, and effect, which is recent; but when the accident or effect stands isolated and one is not able to at once see it preceded by a cause, this simply means that the cycle of thought is not a small cycle, and therefore recent, but is extended into a larger cycle, the thought and action of which may be found in the prior or any preceding life.

꒰

*If the astral arm, leg, or other member of the body is not severed when the physical member is amputated, why is the astral body not able to reproduce another physical arm or leg?*

This question would appear to be asked on the assumption that the astral body does not exist, as if it existed it could reproduce any physical member when lost, especially as it is claimed by all Theosophists that the physical matter is built into the human body according to the design of the inner or astral body. But the explanation is very simple. There must be a physical medium through which physical matter is transformed into other physical matter and there must also be a body for each of the planes on which it is to function. The physical medium is the blood, through which food is transformed into the body. The linga sharira is molecular in structure, whereas the physical body is composed of cellular tissue. Now although the astral arm is not usually severed when the physical member is amputated, there is no physical medium by which physical matter can be linked to and built on physical matter. Therefore, although the astral arm exists, it is not able to convey the physical matter into itself because there is no longer a physical medium to transfer the physical matter. So the molecular astral counterpart of the cellular physical arm which has been amputated has no means of building physical matter into itself. The best that can be done is to build new tissue at the extremity of the stump and thus close up the wound. This will also explain how wounds are healed, and why deep scars remain if the flesh has not been brought together close enough for tissue to knit with tissue.

A FRIEND

# JUNE 1906

[From *The Word*, Vol. 3 No. 3]

At a gathering some evenings ago the question was asked: *Is a Theosophist a vegetarian or a meat eater?*

A theosophist may be a meat eater or a vegetarian, but vegetarianism or meat eating will not make one a theosophist. Unfortunately, many people have supposed that the sine qua non for a spiritual life is vegetarianism, whereas such a statement is contrary to the teachings of true spiritual instructors. "Not that which goeth into the mouth defileth a man, but that which cometh out of the mouth, this defileth a man," said Jesus. (Matt. xvii.)

"Believe thou not that sitting in the dark forests, in proud seclusion and apart from men; believe thou not that life on roots and plants. . . . Oh devotee, that this will lead thee to the goal of final liberation," says the Voice of the Silence. A theosophist should use his best judgment and always be governed by reason in the care of his physical psychic and mental health. As regards the matter of food the first question which he should ask himself is "What food is necessary for me to keep my body in health?" When he finds this out by experiment then let him take that food which his experience and observation show him to be best adapted to his physical and mental requirements. Then he will be in no doubt as to what food he shall eat, but he will surely not speak or think of meatariasm or a vegetablearianism as being qualifications of the theosophist.

ॐ

*How can a real theosophist consider himself a theosophist and still eat meat when we know that the desires of the animal are transferred from the flesh of the animal to the body of the one who eats it?*

A real theosophist never claims to be a theosophist. There are many members of the Theosophical Society but very few real theosophists;

because a theosophist is, as the name implies, one who has attained to divine wisdom; one who has united with his God. When we speak of a real theosophist, we must mean one having divine wisdom. Generally, though not accurately, speaking, however, a theosophist is a member of the Theosophical Society.

The one who says he knows the desires of the animal to be transferred to the body of one who eats it proves by his statement that he does not know. The flesh of the animal is the most highly developed and concentrated form of life which may be ordinarily used as food. This represents desire, certainly, but the desire of the animal in its natural state is much less baneful than desire in the human being. Desire in itself is not bad, but only becomes bad when an evilly disposed mind unites with it. It is not the desire itself which is bad, but the evil purposes to which it is put by the mind and to which it may induce the mind, but to say the desire of the animal as an entity is transferred to the human body is an incorrect statement. The entity called the kama rupa, or desire-body, which actuates the body of the animal, is in no way connected with the meat of that animal after death. The desire of the animal lives in the blood of the animal. When the animal is killed, the desire-body passes out of its physical body with the life blood, leaving the flesh, made up of the cells, as the concentrated form of life which has been worked up by that animal from the vegetable kingdom. The meat eater would have quite as much right to say, and be more reasonable if he did say, that the vegetarian was poisoning himself with prussic acid by eating lettuce or any of the other poisons which abound in vegetables, than the vegetarian could truly and correctly say that the meat eater was eating and absorbing the desires of the animals.

౨๛

*Is it not true that the yogis of India, and men of divine attainments, live on vegetables, and if so, should not those who would develop themselves avoid meat and also live on vegetables?*

It is true, that most yogis do not eat meat, nor do they who have great spiritual attainments, and who usually live apart from men, but it does not follow that because they did, all others should abstain from meat. These men have not spiritual attainments because they live on vegetables, but they eat vegetables because they can do without the strength of the meat. Again we should remember that those who have attained are quite different from those who are trying to begin to attain, and the food of the one cannot be the food of the other because each body requires the food most necessary to it to maintain health. It is pathetic as it is amusing to see that the moment an ideal is perceived the one who perceives it is likely to suppose that it is within his reach. We are like children who see an object far away but who ignorantly reach out to grasp it, unmindful of the distance intervening. It is too bad that would-be aspirants to yogiship or divinity should not imitate the divine characteristics and the spiritual insight of divine men instead of aping the most physical and material habits and customs, and thinking that by so doing, they also shall become divine. One of the essentials to spiritual progress is to learn what Carlyle calls "The Eternal Fitness of Things."

ॐ

*What effect does the eating of vegetables have on the body of man, as compared with the eating of meat?*

This is largely determined by the digestive apparatus. Digestion is carried on in the mouth, stomach and intestinal canal, aided by the secretions of the liver and pancreas. Vegetables are digested chiefly in the intestinal canal, whereas the stomach is principally a meat digesting organ. The food taken into the mouth is there masticated and mixed with saliva, the teeth indicating the natural tendency and quality of the body as to its being herbivorous or carnivorous. The teeth show that man is two-thirds carnivorous and one-third herbivorous, which means that nature has provided him with two-thirds of the entire number of his teeth for eating meat and one-third for vegetables. In the natural healthy body this should be the proportion of its food. In a healthy condition the use of one kind to the exclusion of the other will cause an unbalancing of health. The exclusive use of vegetables causes fermentation and yeast production in the body, which bring in all manner of diseases that the human is heir to. As soon as fermentation begins in the stomach and bowels then there are yeast formations in the blood and the mind becomes unsettled. The carbonic acid gas which is developed affects the heart, and so acts on the nerves as to cause attacks of paralysis or other nervous and muscular disorders. Among the signs and evidences of vegetarianism are irritability, lassitude, nervous flushes, impaired circulation, palpitation of the heart, lack of continuity of thought and concentration of the mind, a breaking down of robust health, an oversensitiveness of body, and a tendency to mediumship. The eating of meat supplies the body with the natural force which it requires. It makes of the body a strong, healthy, physical animal, and builds up this animal body as a fortress behind which the mind can withstand the onslaughts of other physical personalities which it meets and has to contend with in every large city or gathering of people.

A FRIEND

# JULY 1906

[From *The Word*, Vol. 3 No. 4]

*How can vegetarianism prevent concentration of the mind when vegetarianism has been advised in order to attain concentration?*

Vegetarianism has been advised for a certain stage of development, the aim being to subdue the passions, control the desires of the body and thus prevent the mind from being agitated. In order to control desires one must first have desire and in order to concentrate the mind, one must have a mind. That portion of the mind which is incarnated in the body, affects that body by its presence and is in turn affected by the body. The mind and body react on each other. The body is made up of the gross food taken into the body, and the body serves as a background or lever for the mind. The body is the resistance with which the mind works and becomes strong. If the body is a vegetable body instead of an animal body it will react on the mind according to its nature and the mind will be unable to find the resisting power or leverage necessary to work with and develop its strength and faculties. A body which feeds on mush and milk cannot reflect the strength of the mind. The mind which acts on a body built up on milk and vegetables becomes discontented, irritable, melancholic, pessimistic and sensitive to the wickedness of the world, because it lacks the power to hold and dominate, which power a strong body would afford.

The eating of vegetables weakens the desires, it is true, but it does not control desires. The body is only an animal, the mind should use it as an animal. In controlling an animal the owner would not weaken it, but would, in order to get the greatest use out of it, keep it healthy and in good training. First get your strong animal, then control it. When the animal body is weakened the mind is unable to grasp it through the nervous system. Those who know have advised vegetarianism for those only who already had a strong, healthy body and a good healthy brain, and then, only when the student could absent himself gradually from densely populated centres.

A FRIEND

---

# OCTOBER 1906

[From *The Word*, Vol. 4 No. 1]

In speaking of elementals a friend asks: *What is the exact meaning of the term elementals, used in so many connections by theosophists and occultists?*

An elemental is an entity below the stage of man; the body of an elemental is composed of one of the four elements. Hence the word elemental, meaning of or belonging to the elements. The mediaeval philosophers known as the Rosicrucians divided the elements into four classes, relating each class to one of the four elements treated of by them as earth, water, air, and fire. Of course it is to be remembered that these elements are not the same as our gross elements. Earth, for instance, is not what we see around us, but the primal element on which our solid earth is based. The Rosicrucian's named the elementals of the earth, gnomes; those of the water, undines; those of the, air, sylphs; and those of the fire, salamanders. Whenever a portion of one of the elements is given direction by an intense thought of a human being, this thought takes its form in the element characteristic of its nature and appears as an entity separate from the element, but whose body is of that element. Those elementals which are not created by human thought in this period of evolution assumed their being, due to the impressions in a former period of evolution. The creation of an elemental is due to the mind, human or universal. The elementals known as earth elementals are in themselves of seven classes, and are those which live in caverns and mountains, in mines and all the places of the earth. They are the builders of the earth with its minerals and metals. The undines live in springs, rivers, seas, and in the moisture of the air, but it takes a combination of water, air and fire elementals to produce rain. In general it takes a combination of two or more classes of elementals to produce any natural phenomenon. So crystals are formed by a combination of earth, air, water, and fire elementals. So it is with precious stones. The sylphs live in the air, in trees, in the flowers of the fields, in shrubs, and in all the vegetable kingdom. The salamanders are of the fire. A flame comes into existence through the presence of a salamander. Fire makes a salamander visible. When there is a flame we see one part of the salamander. The fire elementals are the most immaterial. These four combine with each other in producing fires, storms, floods, and earthquakes.

ॐ

*What is meant by the 'human elemental'? Is there any difference between it and the lower mind?*

The human elemental is that entity with which man associated when he first incarnated and with which he associates with each incarnation at the building up of his body. It persists through all the incarnations of the mind until it, through long association with the mind, receives the spark or ray of self consciousness. It is then no longer the human elemental, but the lower mind. From the human elemental comes the linga sharira. The human elemental is what is in Madame Blavatsky's "Secret Doctrine" called the "bharishad pitri," or "lunar ancestor," whereas man, the Ego, is of the agnishwatta pitri, of solar lineage, the son of the Sun.

ॐ

*Is there an elemental controlling the desires, another controlling the vital forces, another controlling the bodily functions, or does the human elemental control all these?*

The human elemental controls all these. The linga sharira is the automaton which carries out the desires of the human elemental. The bharishad pitri does not die with the death of the body, as does the linga sharira. The linga sharira, its child, is produced from it for each incarnation. The bharishad is as the mother which is worked on by the reincarnating mind or Ego, and from this action is produced the linga sharira. The human elemental controls all the functions mentioned in the question, but each function is carried out by a separate elemental.

The elemental of each organ of the body knows and controls only the lives which go to make up that organ, and perform its function, but knows nothing of any function of any other organ, but the human elemental sees that all of these functions are performed and related to each other harmoniously. All involuntary actions of the body such as breathing, digesting, perspiring, all are controlled by the human elemental. This is the buddhic function in the physical body of the human elemental. In the Editorial on "Consciousness," The Word, Vol. I, page 293 [*p. 24 in* Monthly Editorials From THE WORD Part I], it is said: "The fifth state of matter is the human mind or I-am-I. In the course of innumerable ages, the indestructible atom which guided other atoms into the mineral, through the vegetable, and up to the animal, at last attains the high state of matter in which is reflected the one Consciousness. Being an individual entity and having the reflection of Consciousness within, it thinks and speaks of itself as I, because I is the symbol of the One. The human entity has under its guidance an organized animal body. The animal entity impels each of its organs to perform a particular function. The entity of each organ directs each of its cells to do a certain work. The life of each cell guides each of its molecules to growth. The design of each molecule confines each of its atoms into an orderly form, and Consciousness impresses each atom with the purpose of becoming self-conscious. Atoms, molecules, cells, organs, and animal, are all under the direction of the mind—the self-conscious state of matter—the function of which is thought. But the mind does not attain self-consciousness, which is its complete development, until it has subdued and controlled all desires and impressions received through the senses, and centered all thought on Consciousness as reflected in itself." The bharishad is the thread soul of the body just as the agnishwatta pitri is the thread soul of the mind. "Is there an elemental controlling the desires?" No. The kama rupa bears a similar relation to the Ego as does the linga sharira to the human elemental. Only whereas the linga sharira is the automaton of the body, the kama rupa is the automaton of the turbulent desires which move the world. The world's desires move the kama rupa. Every passing elemental strikes into the kama rupa. So the linga sharira is moved and moves the body according to the impulses or commands of the human elemental, the kama rupa, or the Ego.

&

*Does the same elemental control both the conscious acts and the unconscious functions of the body?*

There is no such thing as an unconscious function or act. For though the human being may not be conscious of the functions or acts of its body, the presiding elemental of the organ or function certainly is conscious, else it could not function. The same elemental does not always perform all the functions or acts of the body. As for instance, the human elemental presides over the body as a whole though it may not be conscious of the separate and individual action of a red blood corpuscle.

&

*Are elementals in general evolving entities, and will they all or any of them in the course of evolution become men?*

The answer is yes to both questions. The body of man is the school house for all elementals. In the body of man all classes of all elementals receive their lessons and instruction; and the body of man is the great university from which all elementals graduate according to their degrees. The human elemental takes the degree of self-consciousness and in its turn then, as the Ego, presides over another elemental which becomes human, and all the lower elementals, even as the Ego in the body now does.

A FRIEND

# NOVEMBER 1906

[From *The Word*, Vol. 4 No. 2]

In speaking of clairvoyance and occult matters, a friend asks: *Is it really possible for one to see into the future?*

Yes. It is possible. Time is divided by the past, present and future. We look into the past, when we remember a thing by seeing in our mind's eye what has occurred. This seeing in the past everybody can do, but not everybody can see into the future, because few use the knowledge of the past intelligently to see into the future. If one took all the factors and bearings of a past event into consideration his knowledge would enable him to predict certain future events, for though the future is that division of time which has not yet come in fact, still, the actions of the past create, fashion, determine, limit the future, and, therefore, if one is able, like a mirror, to reflect knowledge of the past, he may predict future events.

ॐ

*Is it not possible for one to see actual occurrences of the past and occurrences as they will be in the future as clearly and distinctly as he sees the present?*

It is possible, and many have done it. To do this one uses what is called clairvoyance, clear seeing, or second sight. To see clairvoyantly, a second set of faculties or the inner sense of seeing is used. The eye may be used, though it is not essential to clairvoyance, for that faculty which functions through the sense of sight may transfer its action from the eye to some other organ or part of the body. Objects may then be seen, for instance, from the tips of the fingers or the solar plexus. Where the clairvoyant looks on what we call distant objects that have passed or on events which are to come, the part of the body from which this is done is usually in the skull just above the eyebrows. There as on a panoramic screen the scene or object appears which is oftentimes seen as distinctly as though the clairvoyant were at that very place. All that is then necessary so as to communicate what is seen, is the faculty of speech.

໑

*How is it possible for one to see clairvoyantly when such seeing is opposed to all our experience?*

Such seeing is not within the experience of all. It is within the experience of some. Many of those who have not had the experience doubt the testimony of those who have had it. It is not opposed to natural laws, for it is quite natural, and is possible to those whose linga sharira, astral body, is not too firmly knit into its physical cells. Let us consider the objects which we see, and what we see those objects through. Vision itself is a mystery, but the things with which vision is concerned we do not consider a mystery. Thus, we have physical eyes through which we look into the air and there see physical objects. We think this quite natural, and so it is. Let us consider the different kingdoms into which sight is possible. Suppose that we were in the earth as worms or insects; we should there have the sense of sight, but our faculties would be very limited. The organs which we know as eyes could not be used to see great distances, and the physical sight would be limited to very short spaces. Advance one stage and suppose that we were fishes. The distance through which we could then see in the water would be very much greater and the eyes would be attuned to registering the light vibrations coming through the water. As fishes, however, we should deny the possibility of seeing in any other way than through the water or, in fact, that there was such an element as air. If perchance we poked our noses out and got our eyes above the water into the air then we should not be able to breathe, and the eyes would not be serviceable because out of their element. As animal or human beings we are one stage in advance of the fishes. We see through our atmosphere and are capable of perceiving objects through the eyes at much greater distances than through the water. But we know that our atmosphere, being thick and murky, limits our vision. Everybody knows that in the atmospheres of Chicago, Cleveland

and Pittsburg objects can be seen at a distance of a few miles only. In cities where the air is clearer, one may see thirty or forty miles, but from the mountains of Arizona and Colorado distances of several hundred miles may be covered, and all this with the physical eyes. Just as one may see clearer by rising into clearer atmospheres, so one may see clairvoyantly by rising into another element higher than the air. The element which is used by the clairvoyant to see in is the ether. To the clairvoyant who sees in the ether our idea of distance loses its value even as the idea of distance of the worm or of the fish would lose its meaning to a dweller in high altitudes, whose keen eye could detect objects invisible to those who live in lower strata on the plains.

                                     ॐ

*What are the organs used in clairvoyance, and how is one's vision transferred from the objects near at hand to those at great distances, and from the known visible to the unknown invisible?*

    Any organ in the body can be used for clairvoyant purposes, but those parts or organs of the body which are instinctively or intelligently used by the clairvoyant are the visual center on the cortex of the brain, the frontal sinuses, the optic thalami, and the pituitary body. Nearby physical objects are reflected by the atmospheric light waves on the eye, which converges these light waves or vibrations to the optic nerve. These vibrations are borne along the optic tract. Some of these are conveyed to the optic thalami, while others are thrown on the brain cortex. These are reflected in the frontal sinus, which is the picture gallery of the mind. The pituitary body is the organ through which the ego perceives these pictures. They are no longer physical when they are there seen, but rather the astral images of the physical. They are physical objects reflected into the astral world of the ego, to see which the lower vibrations of physical objects have been raised to a higher rate of vibration. One's vision may be transferred from the physical to the astral world in several ways. The most physical is by the focussing of the eye. The etheric or astral world permeates, penetrates, and passes beyond our physical world. The physical eye is so constructed that it registers only such vibrations from the physical world as are slow when compared with the etheric or astral world. The physical eye cannot receive or register etheric vibrations unless it is trained or unless one is a natural clairvoyant. In either case it is then possible for one to change the focus of the eye from the physical world to the etheric or astral world. When this is done, the organs or parts of the body before mentioned are connected with the etheric world and receive the vibrations from it. As one sees the object of his wish by turning his eyes to that object, so the clairvoyant sees a distant object by desiring or being directed to see it. This may seem wonderful to some, but the wonder ceases when the facts are known. By a perfectly natural process the one who sees clairvoyantly rises or is raised to a clearer world of greater distances, even as the deep sea diver may be raised from his limited vision in the water to vision in a foggy atmosphere, and then into high altitudes from which he beholds objects at a still greater distance. One who has learned to see clairvoyantly by a long course of study and training need not follow this method. He need think only of a place and sees it if he wills. The nature of his thought connects him with the strata of the ether corresponding to the thought, even as one turns his eyes on the object which he would see. The understanding of the object seen depends on his intelligence. One may transfer his vision from the known visible to the unknown invisible and understand what he sees by the law of analogy. Starting with the known he rises into what was, but is no longer, the unknown, and so, following the law of analogy, he rises steadily and sees intelligently.

ॐ

*Can an occultist look into the future whenever he so wills, and does he use a clairvoyant faculty to do it?*

A clairvoyant is not an occultist, and although an occultist may be clairvoyant, he is not necessarily so. An occultist is one who has a knowledge of the laws of nature, who lives in conformity with those laws, and who is guided from within by his highest intelligence.

Occultists vary in degree of knowledge and power even as the laborer varies in understanding and ability from the engineer or astronomer. One may be an occultist without having developed clairvoyance, but the occultist who has developed this faculty uses it only when he is dealing with subjects belonging to the astral world. He does not use it for pleasure or to gratify his own or another's whims. It is not necessary for the occultist to use the clairvoyant faculty to see into the future, though he may do so, if he desires, by intently holding his thought on a particular period in the future and willing to see and know what is transpiring at that time.

ॐ

*If an occultist can pierce the veil why do not occultists, individually or collectively benefit from their knowledge of coming events?*

An occultist who would look into the future and benefit personally from his knowledge would cease to be an occultist in the true sense. An occultist must work in conformity with natural law and not opposed to nature. Nature forbids the benefiting of one individual to the detriment of the whole. If an occultist, or anyone who works with higher powers than those possessed by the ordinary man, uses those powers against the others or for his individual benefit he opposes the law which he should work with, not against, and so he either becomes a renegade to nature and a selfish being or else loses the powers which he may have developed; in either case he ceases to be a true occultist. An occultist is only entitled to what he needs as an individual and for his work, and the feeling of selfishness or the love of gain would blind him to the law. If he is so blinded, he is then unable to understand and comprehend the laws which govern and control life, which pass beyond death, and which relate and bind all things together into a harmonious whole for the good of all.

ॐ

*What is the 'third eye' and does the clairvoyant and the occultist use it?*

The "third eye" referred to in some books, particularly the "Secret Doctrine," is that little organ in the center of the head which physiologists call the pineal gland. The clairvoyant does not use this third eye or pineal gland to see distant objects or to look into the future, though some clairvoyants who have lived good and pure lives may for a brief second have had the third eye open. When this occurs their experiences are quite different from any before. The occultist does not ordinarily use the pineal gland. It is not necessary to use the pineal gland or third eye to see into the future, because the future is one of the three divisions of time, and organs other than the pineal gland are used for looking into the past, seeing the present, or peering into the future. The pineal gland or third eye is above the divisions of mere time, though it comprehends them all. It has to do with eternity.

એﮞ

*Who uses the pineal gland, and what is the object of its use?*

Only a highly developed person, a high occultist or master, can use the "third eye" or pineal gland at will, though many of the saints, or men who have lived unselfish lives and whose aspirations have been exalted, have experienced the opening of "the eye" in moments of their highest exaltation. This could only be done in this natural way, as a flash in the rare moments of their lives and as a reward, the fruition of their thoughts and deeds. But such men could not open the eye themselves, because they have not been trained, or because they were not able to maintain a long continued course of the training of body and mind necessary to the attainment. An occultist, knowing the laws of the body, and the laws controlling the mind, and by living a morally pure life, at last calls into use long disused functions of the body and faculties of the mind, and finally is able to open his "third-eye," the pineal gland, by his will. The object of the use of the pineal gland or "third eye" is to see the relationships as they exist between all beings, to see the real through the unreal, to perceive truth, and to realize and become one with the infinite.

ॐ

*How does the third eye or pineal gland open, and what happens at such opening?*

Only an occultist of a high order could answer this question with certainty. Without pretending to any such actual knowledge, we may with benefit, however, speculate about as well as anticipate the manner in which this is accomplished, and also the result. One who lives the ordinary worldly life cannot open or use his "third eye." This physical organ is the bridge between body and mind. The power and intelligence which operates through it is the bridge between the finite and the infinite. He who lives in the finite thinks in the finite and acts in the finite cannot grow into and comprehend the infinite while he so lives and thinks and acts. The initial step to be taken toward opening the "third eye" is to control the thoughts, to cleanse the mind, and make the body pure. This strikes at the roots of life, and covers the whole range of human development. All duties must be performed faithfully, all obligations be lived up to strictly, and the life must be guided by one's inherent sense of justice. One must change the habits of thought on the baser things to the consideration of the higher objects of life, and thence of the highest. All the forces of the body must be turned upward in thought. All marital relations must have ceased. One so living will cause the long disused occult organs of the body to become active and awakened. The body will thrill with a new life, and this new life will rise from plane to plane in the body until all of the finer essences of the body carry the power to the head and finally, either of itself naturally, or by an effort of the will, the flower of eternity will bloom: the Eye of God, the "third eye," will open. The radiance of a thousand suns is not to be compared to the light of truth which then fills and surrounds the body and penetrates all space. Objects, as objects, disappear and are resolved into the principle which they represent; and all principles as representing the real are in turn resolved into the immensity of the whole. Time disappears. Eternity is the ever-present. The personality is lost in the individuality. The individuality is not lost, but it expands into and becomes one with the whole.

A FRIEND

---

# DECEMBER 1906

[From *The Word*, Vol. 4 No. 3]

*Does Christmas have any particular meaning to a theosophist, and if so, what?*

The meaning which Christmas has to a theosophist depends a great deal on his racial or religious beliefs. Theosophists are not exempt from prejudices, they are still mortal. Theosophists, that is to say, members of the Theosophical Society, are of every nation, race and creed. It would therefore depend somewhat as to what the prejudices of the particular theosophist might be. There are few people, however, whose opinions are not broadened by an understanding of theosophical doctrines. The Hebrew understands Christ and Christmas in a much different light than before he became a theosophist. So does the Christian, and all others of every race and creed. The particular meaning attached to Christmas by a theosophist is that Christ is a principle rather than a person, a principle which frees the mind from the great illusion of separateness, brings man closer in touch with the souls of men and unites him to the principle of divine love and wisdom. The sun is the symbol of true light. The sun passes into the sign of capricorn on the 21st day of December at the end of his southern course. Then there are three days when there is no increase of their length and then on the 25th day of December the sun begins his northern course and is therefore said to be born. The ancients celebrated this occasion by festivals and rejoicing, knowing that with the advent of the sun the winter would pass, the seeds be fructified by the rays of Light and that the earth under the influence of the sun would bring forth fruit. A theosophist regards Christmas from many standpoints: as the birth of the sun in the sign capricorn, which would apply to the physical world; on the other hand and in the truer sense it is the birth of the invisible sun of light, the Christ Principle. The Christ, as a principle, should be born *within* man, in which case man is saved from the sin of ignorance which brings death, and should begin the period of life leading to his immortality.

&

*Is it probable that Jesus was an actual person, and that he was born on Christmas Day?*

It is more than probable that some one appeared, whether his name was Jesus or Apollonius, or any other name. The fact of the presence in the world of millions of people who call themselves Christians testifies to the fact, that there must have been someone who taught the great truths—such for instance, those in the Sermon on the Mount—and which are called Christian doctrine.

&

*If Jesus was an actual man why is it that we have no more historical record of the birth or life of such a man than the bible statement?*

It is true that we have no historical record either of the birth of Jesus or of his life. Even the reference in Josephus to Jesus is said by authorities to have been an interpolation. The absence of such record is of minor importance as compared with the fact that a set of teachings have been grouped around a character, whether or not it is a fanciful or actual character. The teachings exist and one of the greatest religions of the world bear testimony to the character. The actual year in which Jesus was born, not even the most bigoted theologian can name with certainty. The "authorities" are disagreed. Some say it was prior to A. D. 1; others claim it was as late as A. D. 6. Notwithstanding the authorities the people continue to hold to the time now recognized by the Julian calendar. Jesus may have been an actual man and still unknown to the people as a whole, during his life. The probability is that Jesus was a teacher who instructed a number of those who became his pupils, which pupils received his teaching and preached his doctrines. Teachers often come among men, but they are seldom known to the world. They select such as are most suited to receive the new-old doctrines and instruct them, but do not themselves go into the world and instruct. If such was the case with Jesus it will account for the historians of the time not having known of him.

ᐒ

*Why do they call this, the 25th of December, Christmas instead of Jesusmass or Jesusday, or by some other name?*

Not until the fourth or fifth century was the title Christmas given to the ceremonies which were performed on the 25th of December. A Christmas means Christ's mass, a mass held for, of, or to Christ. Therefore the more appropriate word would be Jesus-mass, because the services which were held and the ceremonies called "mass" which were performed on the morning of the 25th of December were to Jesus, the infant who was born. This was followed by the great rejoicings of the people, who burned the Yule log in honor of the source of fire and light; who ate plum pudding, betokening the spices and gifts which the wise men from the East brought to Jesus; who passed around the wassail bowl (and who often became disgustingly intoxicated thereby) as a symbol of the life-giving principle from the sun, which promised the breaking up of ice, the flowing of rivers, and the starting of the sap in the trees in spring. The Christmas tree and evergreens were used as the promise of the renewal of vegetation, and presents were generally exchanged, betokening the good feeling present among all.

ᐒ

*Is there an esoteric way of understanding the birth and life of Jesus?*

There is, and it will appear as the most reasonable to any who will consider it without prejudice. The birth, the life, the crucifixion, and the resurrection of Jesus represent the process through which every soul must pass who comes into life and who in that life attains to immortality. The teachings of the church concerning the history of Jesus lead away from the truth concerning him. A theosophical interpretation of the biblical story is here given. Mary is the physical body. The word Mary is the same in many of the great religious systems, who have claimed divine beings as their founders. The word comes from Mara, Mare, Mari, and all of which mean bitterness, sea, chaos, the great illusion. Such is every human body. The tradition amongst the Jews at that time, and some still hold it to the present day, was that a Messiah was to come. It was said that the Messiah was to be born of a virgin in an immaculate manner. This is absurd from the standpoint of the beings of sex, but in perfect keeping with esoteric truths. The facts are that when the human body is properly trained and developed it becomes pure, virgin, chaste, immaculate. When the human body has reached the point of purity and is chaste, it is then said to be Mary, the virgin, and is ready to conceive immaculately. The immaculate conception means that one's own god, the divine ego, fructifies the body which has become virgin. This fructification or conception consists of an illumination of the mind, which is its first real conception of immortality and divinity. This is not metaphorical, but literal. It is literally true. The purity of the body maintained, there begins a new life within that human form. This new life develops gradually, and a new form is called into being. After the course has been passed through, and the time come, this being is actually born, through and from that physical body, its virgin Mary, as a separate and distinct form. This is the birth of Jesus who was conceived by the Holy Ghost, the light of the ego, and born of the virgin Mary, its physical body. As Jesus passed his early years in obscurity, so must such a being be obscure. This is the Jesus body, or he who comes to save. This body, the Jesus body, is the immortal body. Jesus is said to have come to save the world. So he does. The Jesus body does not die as does the physical, and that which was conscious as a physical being is now transferred to the new body, the Jesus body, which saves from death. The Jesus body is immortal and one who has found Jesus, or for whom Jesus has come, no longer has breaks or gaps in memory, as he is then continually conscious under all circumstances and conditions whatever. He is without lapses in memory through day, through night, through death, and future life.

৵

*You spoke of Christ as a principle. Do you make a distinction between Jesus, and Christ?*

There is a difference between the two words and that which they are intended to represent. The word "Jesus" was often used as a title of honor and to be conferred on him who deserved it. We have shown what the Esoteric meaning of Jesus is. Now as to the word "Christ," it comes from the Greek "Chrestos," or "Christos." There is a difference between Chrestos and Christos. Chrestos was a neophyte or disciple who was on probation, and while on probation, preparatory to his symbolical crucifixion, he was called a Chrestos. After initiation he was anointed and called Christos, the anointed. So that one who had passed through all trials and initiations and attained knowledge of or union with God was called "a" or "the Christos." This applies to an individual attaining to the principle Christ; but Christ or Christos without the definite article is the Christ principle and not any individual being. As related to the title Jesus, the Christ, it means that the principle Christ had operated through or taken up its abode with the Jesus body, and the Jesus body was then called Jesus the Christ to show that the one who had become immortal by having the Jesus body was not only immortal as an individual, but that he was also compassionate, godlike, divine. As to the historical Jesus, we will remember that Jesus was not called the Christ until he had been baptized. As he was coming up from the river Jordan it is said the spirit descended on him and a voice from heaven said: "This is my beloved son, in whom I am well pleased." Then and thereafter Jesus was called Jesus the Christ, or Christ Jesus, thereby meaning the man-god or the god-man. Any human being may become a Christ by uniting himself to the Christ principle, but before the union can take place he must have had a second birth. To use the words of Jesus, "Ye must be born again before ye can inherit the kingdom of heaven." This is to say, his physical body was not to rebecome an infant, but that he, as a human being, must be born as an immortal being from or through his physical body, and that such birth would be the birth of Jesus, his Jesus. Then only would it be possible for him to inherit the kingdom of heaven, for though it is possible for Jesus to be formed within a virgin body, it is not possible for the Christ principle to be so formed, as it is too far removed from the flesh and needs a more highly evolved or developed body to manifest through. It is therefore necessary to have the immortal body called Jesus or by any other name developed before Christ as the Logos, The Word, can manifest to man. It will be remembered that Paul exhorted his colleagues or disciples to work and pray until Christ should be formed within them.

ᔐ

*What particular reason is there for celebrating the 25th day of December as being that of the birth of Jesus?*

The reason is that it is the natural season and can be celebrated at no other time; for whether taken from an astronomical standpoint, or as the birth of an historical human physical body, or as the birth of an immortal body, the date must be on the 25th day of December, or when the sun passes into the sign capricorn. The ancients well knew this, and celebrated the birthdays of their saviours on or about the 25th of December. The Egyptians celebrated the birthday of their Horus on the 25th day of December; the Persians celebrated the birthday of their Mithras on the 25th day of December; the Romans celebrated their Saturnalia, or golden age, on the 25th day of December, and on this date the sun was born and was the son of the invisible sun; or, as they said, "dies natalis, invicti, solis." or the birthday of the invincible sun. The relation of Jesus to Christ is known by his alleged history and the solar phenomenon, because he, Jesus, is born on the 25th of December, which is the day on which the sun begins his northern journey in the sign of capricorn, the beginning of the winter solstices; but it is not until he has passed the vernal equinox in the sign of aries that he is said to have attained his strength and power. Then the nations of antiquity would sing their songs of rejoicing and praise. It is at this time that Jesus becomes the Christ. He is resurrected from the dead and is united with his god. This is the reason why we celebrate the birthday of Jesus, and why the "pagans" celebrated the birthday of their respective deities on the 25th day of December.

ॐ

*If it is possible for a human being to become a Christ, how is it accomplished and how is it connected with the 25th day of December?*

To one brought up in the orthodox Christian home such a statement might seem sacrilegious; to the student acquainted with religion and philosophy it will not seem impossible; and Scientists, least of all, should consider it impossible, because it is a matter of evolution. The birth of Jesus, the second birth, is connected with the 25th of December for many reasons, among which are that a human body is built on the same principle as the earth and conforms to the same laws. Both the earth and the body conform to the laws of the sun. On the 25th day of December, or when the sun enters the sign of capricorn, the human body, providing it has passed through all previous training and development, is best suited for such a ceremony to take place. The previous preparations necessary are that a life of absolute chastity should be lived, and that the mind should be well trained and skilled, and be able to continue any line of work for any length of time. The chaste life, the sound body, the controlled desires and the strong mind enable that which was called the seed of Christ to take root in the virgin soil of the body, and within the physical body to build up an inner ethereal body of a semi-divine nature. Where this was done the processes necessary were passed through. The time arrived, the ceremony took place, and for the first time the immortal body which had for a long period of time been developing within the physical body at last passed out of the physical body and was born through it. This body, called the Jesus body, is not the astral body or linga sharira spoken of by theosophists, nor is it any of the bodies which manifest at seances or which mediums use. There are many reasons for this, among which are that the linga sharira or astral body is connected with the physical body, by a thread or umbilical cord, whereas the immortal or Jesus body is not so connected. The linga sharira or astral body of the medium is non-intelligent, whereas the Jesus or immortal body is not only separate and distinct from the physical body, but it is wise and powerful and is quite conscious and intelligent. It never ceases to lose consciousness, nor has it any break in life or from life to life or gap in memory. The processes necessary for having the life and attaining the second birth are along the lines and principles of the zodiac, but the details are too long and cannot be given here.

A FRIEND

# MARCH 1907

[From *The Word*, Vol. 4 No. 6]

A friend from the Central States asked: *Is it wrong to use mental instead of physical means to cure physical ills?*

The question covers too large a field to unqualifiedly answer "yes" or "no." There are instances where one is justified in using the power of thought to overcome physical ills, in which case we would say that it was not wrong. In the great majority of cases it is decidedly wrong to use mental instead of physical means to cure physical ills. How then shall we decide which instances are right and which wrong? This can only be seen according to the principle involved. If we feel sure of the principle the means employed will be in accord with it and therefore right. So that the question can be answered in a general way and not as to a particular case, that if the principle is perceived the individual will be able to apply it to any particular case and determine whether it is right or wrong to cure physical ills by mental processes. Let us discover the principle: Are physical ills facts, or are they delusions? If physical ills are facts they must be the result of causes. If so-called physical ills are delusions they are not physical ills at all, they are delusions. If delusion is said to be a disease of the mind and that the ill exists in the mind and not in the physical body then the delusion is not a physical ill, it is insanity. But we cannot now deal with insanity; we are concerned about physical ills. Allowing then that physical ills are facts, we say that these facts are effects. The next step is to seek the causes of these effects. If we are able to locate a cause of the physical ill we shall be able to cure the physical ill by removing its cause and helping nature to repair the damage. Physical ills may be the result of physical causes or of mental causes. The physical ills which are caused by physical means should be cured by physical means. The physical ills which have mental causes, should have the mental cause of the ill removed and then nature should be allowed to reestablish the physical harmony. If the foregoing be correct, we can now say that any physical ill which has a physical cause should not be treated mentally, and that any physical ill which arises from a mental cause should have the causes removed and nature will repair the physical ill. The next difficulty to be removed in order to discover our way is to decide what physical ills have physical causes, and what physical ills have mental causes. Cuts, wounds, broken bones, sprains and the like, are caused by direct contact with physical matter and should receive physical treatment. Diseases such as consumption, diabetes, gout, locomotor ataxia, pneumonia, dyspepsia and Bright's disease, are caused by improper food and neglect of the body. These should be cured by the proper care of the body and by supplying it with wholesome food, which will remove the proximate cause of the physical ill and give nature a chance to restore the body to its healthy state. The physical ills which are the result of mental causes, such as nervousness, and diseases brought on by the use of narcotics, drugs and alcohol, and the diseases resulting from immoral thoughts and acts, should be cured by removing the cause of the disease, and assisting nature to restore the equilibrium of the body by wholesome food, pure water, fresh air and sunlight. Having distinguished between the physical ills as being due to physical causes and to mental causes, and having shown that those due to physical causes should be cured by physical means, and that those of mental origin should have the mental cause removed, we would answer the question by saying, that it is not wrong to use the mind to cure physical ills if these physical ills are due to mental causes, provided one knows the mental cause, and how to remove it, and if the motive of the healer is good.

❧

*Is it right to attempt to cure physical ills by mental treatment?*

No! It is not right to attempt to cure the physical ills of another by "mental treatment," because one will inflict more lasting harm than good. But one has the right to attempt to cure any nervous trouble of his own and the effort may meet with beneficial results providing he does not try to make himself believe he has no ill.

৯৬

*If it is right to cure physical ills by mental means, providing the physical ills have a mental origin, why is it wrong for a mental or christian scientist to cure those ills by mental treatment?*

It is wrong because Christian and mental scientists do not know the mind or the laws which govern and control the action of the mind; because in the majority of cases the mental scientist, not knowing the mental cause of the physical ill, and often denying the existence of the ill, attempts to effect a cure by mentally commanding the mind of his patient or by suggesting to the mind of the patient that he is superior to the ill or that the ill is only a delusion; therefore, not knowing the cause nor the positive effect of his mind on the mind of his patient in relation to the ill, especially if the ill be ignored or considered as a delusion, he is not justified in the treatment. Again, if his motive were right in the attempted treatment of a patient and the results appeared to be beneficial, still such treatment would be wrong if the mental scientist either accepted or exacted money for the treatment.

৯৬

*Why is it wrong for mental scientists to receive money for the treatment of physical or mental ills while physicians charge their regular fees?*

It would be much better were the State to pay or maintain physicians for the people, but inasmuch as this is not so the physician is justified in asking fees; because, in the first place he makes no pretense of occult power by mental processes, whereas he does recognize physical ills to be facts, and does treat them by physical means, and treating them by physical means he has a right to physical remuneration. It is not so in the case of the mental or other scientist, because he claims to cure by means of the mind, and money should not be concerned with the mind in the cure of disease, as money is used for and applied to physical purposes. If, therefore, the physical ill was called a delusion, he would have no right to take physical money for the treatment of that which did not exist; but if he did admit the physical ill and cure it by mental processes he would still have no right to receive money because the benefit received should be of the kind as the benefit given, and the benefit being from the mind the only pay should be the satisfaction of knowing that benefit had been given. The benefit received should be received on the same plane in which benefit is given and vice versa.

೩๑

*Why is it not right for a mental scientist to receive money for the treatment of disease when he devotes all his time to this work and must have money to live?*

Because one who receives money cannot restore perfect health to one mentally diseased while the would-be mental healer's mind is polluted by the thought of money. One would not employ a dissolute, disorderly and immoral man to teach and improve the morals of himself or his children; and no more should one employ a mental or Christian scientist to cure him or friends when the "scientist's" mind is inoculated with and diseased by the money microbe. It is well enough to say that the mental healer heals for the love of healing and benefiting his fellow men. If this is true, and the question of money does not enter into his mind he will revolt at the thought of accepting money; because the thought of money and the love of one's fellow are not on the same plane and are quite dissimilar in their attributes. Therefore, when money is suggested in payment for benefits received, the healer will refuse it if he heals only from love for his fellow. This is the true test of healing. But it is asked how can he devote all his time to his work and live without receiving money? The answer is very simple: Nature will provide for all those who truly love her and who devote their lives to aid her in her work, but they are tried by many tests before they are accepted and provided for. One of the requirements which nature demands of her minister and physician is that he shall have a pure mind, or that his mind shall be free from the love of gain for self. Supposing that the would-be healer has a natural good-will for mankind and desires to assist by mental healing. If he has any natural ability and meets with any success, his patients naturally desire to show their gratitude, and offer him money, even though he did not demand it. If he demands it or accepts it this at once proves that he is not the one that nature chooses; if he at first refuses nature tries him again, and he finds that he is in need of money, and when urged to take it necessity often seems to force him to do so; and the acceptance of the money however good his intention might otherwise be, is the first means of inoculating his mind with the money microbe—as has proven to be the case with the most successful healers. The money microbe infects his mind, and the money disease grows with his success, and even although he may appear to benefit his patients in one part of their nature he will damage them in another part for, even though unconsciously, he has become immoral and diseased mentally and he cannot fail to inoculate his patients with his own diseases. It may take a long time, but the germs of his disease will take root in the minds of his patients, and the disease will break out in the weakest sides of their natures. So that it is not right for one who would effect permanent cures to receive money, because he cannot cure permanently if he does receive money, however results appear on the surface of things. On the other hand, if his sole desire is to benefit others instead of making money by healing then nature will provide for him. If he does not know the truth he is not one of nature's physicians—he is only a commercial healer.

࿇

*How can nature provide for one who really desires to benefit others, but who has no means of supporting himself?*

In saying that nature will provide we do not mean that she will shower money into his lap or that unseen forces will nourish him or birds feed him. There is an unseen side of nature, and there is the side which is seen. Nature does her real work on the unseen side of her domain, but the results of her work appear on the surface in the visible world. It is not possible for every man to become a healer, but if one among many should feel that he had the natural faculty and decide that he would like to make healing his life's work, then such a man would do his work spontaneously. In nearly every such case he would discover that his finances would not allow him to devote all his time to healing unless he received money. If he accepted money nature would not accept him. He would fail at the first test. If he refused money and devoted only such time to healing as his circumstances would permit, then if he had the natural ability and his duties to the world and to his family did not prevent, he would find his position in life to be gradually changing. With continued desire to devote his time gratuitously to work for humanity, his circumstances and relation to humanity would continue to change until he finds himself in such a position, financially and otherwise, as to allow of his giving his entire time to his work. But, of course, if he had the thought in his mind that nature was thus intending to provide for him, that very thought would have disqualified him for his work. The knowledge must grow gradually with his development. Such are the facts, which can be seen in the lives of many of nature's ministers. But to see the proceedings of nature in developing the facts, one must be able to work with nature and to observe her workings below the surface of things.

ॐ

*Are the christian and mental scientists not doing good if they effect cures where physicians fail?*

The one who looks on the immediate results without knowing the principle involved would naturally say, yes. But we say, no! Because no one can effect a permanent good without any evil consequences if his premises are wrong and if he does not know the principle involved. Aside from the question of money, the mental or other healer almost invariably begins his operations with wrong premises, and without knowing the principle involved in his mental operations. The fact that they do treat certain diseases prove that they know nothing of the operations of the mind, and prove that they are unworthy of using the title of "scientist" which they claim. If they could show that they know how the mind operates in relation to certain diseases they would be mentally qualified to treat others, even though they may not be qualified morally.

ॐ

*What criterion have we as to what mental requirements a mental scientist should have?*

To be mentally qualified to treat another mentally one should be able to set himself a problem or to have some problem given him which he proceeds to and does solve. He should be able then to watch his mental operations in the processes of thought during the solving of the problem and not only to see these mental processes as clearly as the movements of a bird in full flight, or the painting of a canvass by an artist, or the designing of a plan by an architect, but he should also understand his mental processes even as he would feel and know the sensations of the bird and the cause of its flight, and feel the emotions of the artist and know the ideal of his picture, and follow the thought of the architect and know the purpose of his design. If he is able to do this, his mind is capable of acting salutary with the mind of another. But there is this fact: If he can thus act he will never attempt to cure by mental processes physical ills which have physical causes, nor will he ever attempt to cure physical ills by "treating the mind of another," for the reason that no one can cure another's mind. Each mind must be its own physician if it is to effect a mental cure. All that he could do would be to make clear the truth of the nature of the ill to the mind of the other, and show the origin of the ill and the manner in which its cure might be effected. This can be done by word of mouth and needs no mental treatment or mysterious pretenses. But if the truth is seen it strikes at the root of both Mental and Christian Science for it disproves the theories of both.

ॐ

*In what way does the ability to follow one's own or another's mental operations, and to truly see causes, disprove the claims of mental and christian scientists?*

The claims of both kinds of "scientists" are in the form of denials and affirmations. Taking the position of teachers and healers they assert their ability to teach the mysteries of the world of thought as a science. They assert the non-existence of matter and the supremacy of mind, or they deny the existence of evil, disease and death. Yet they establish themselves as leaders in the world of physics to prove that matter does not exist, that there is no evil, and there is no disease, no death, that disease is error, death a lie. But without the existence of matter, disease and error, they could not live as they do by receiving fees for the treatment of disease which does not exist, nor could they establish costly churches and schools to teach the non-existence of disease, matter and evil. The name of science, which scientists have earned and applied to laws verifiable under predetermined conditions, they take, and then they deny these laws. Deluding themselves, they delude others, and so they live in a world of delusion, created by themselves. The ability to see mental operations, disillusions the mind from fancy because it shows the derivation of physical effects from mental causes, such as the action of hatred, fear, anger, or lust. The ability to see the working of one's own mind also brings with it the faculty of examining one's physical body as a thing apart from the mind, and all this proves the facts on each plane of action and the action of the mind on any plane. A mind so developed can never acknowledge the claims of the mental or christian scientists because those claims would be known to be wrong, and if one of their "scientists" should be able to see the facts on each plane he could no longer remain a "scientist" and at the same time see the facts.

ஓ

*What are the results of the acceptance and practice of the teachings of the christian or mental scientists?*

The results, for a time being, appear to be most beneficial in the majority of cases because the delusion created is new and the living of the delusion can last for a time and for a time only. But there must come a reaction from every delusion, which will bring with it disastrous results. The teaching and practice of their doctrines is among the most terrible and far-reaching crimes against humanity as it compels the mind to deny facts as they exist on any plane. The mind so treated is rendered incapable of distinguishing fact from fancy, and thus incapacitated for perceiving truth on any plane. The mind becomes negative, uncertain, and will deny or affirm whatever it is bidden and its evolution thus arrested, it may become a wreck.

ஓ

*Why are so many mental healers prosperous if they do not effect cures, and if they are not what they represented themselves to be, would their patients not discover the fact?*

All healers are not intentional frauds. Some of them believe that they are doing good, even though they may not examine too closely into their motives. A successful mental healer is prosperous because he has allied himself to and become a servant of the great Spirit of the Earth, and the Earth Spirit rewards him. That they do effect cures no one who knows of them or their work will deny. But the means and processes by which the cures are effected, the healers themselves do not know. A healer would naturally not be expected to represent himself in an unfavorable light to a patient, but all patients do not see the healer in the light in which he would have them see him. If we believed some of the patients who have been treated by healers, these would be seen in an unfavorable light. One of the questions arising as to the treatment of patients, is what an unprincipled healer might suggest to his patient when that patient is either under mental control or at least sufficiently en rapport to receive his suggestions. It would not be astonishing to know that there are dishonest healers in the mental profession, as there are in every trade or profession. The opportunity and temptation offered to an unprincipled man is great, in that by mental suggestion or control it is an easy matter to affect the mind of a generous and grateful patient to insist on the healer's acceptance of a large fee or gift, especially when the patient believes that he has been benefited.

მ

*Did not Jesus and many of the saints cure physical ills by mental means and if so was it wrong?*

It is claimed, and we believe it possible and true, that Jesus and many saints did cure physical ills by mental means and we have no hesitation in saying that it was not wrong, if they knew what they were doing. That Jesus knew what he was doing in effecting cures we have no doubt, and many of the saints were also possessed of much knowledge and great good will for mankind, but Jesus and the saints received no money for their cures. When this question is brought up by those who favor the work of the healers they do not always stop to think of this fact. How unlike Jesus and unsaintly it would seem for either Jesus or his disciples or any of the saints to charge so much per visit to every patient, cure or no cure, or to charge from five to upwards of one hundred dollars a lesson, in classes, to teach the disciples how to heal. Because Jesus healed many ills is no license for one to set himself up in the business of mental healing. Anyone who is willing to live a life as nearly like that of Jesus as he can, will have the right to heal, but he will heal with love for his fellow, and never accept remuneration. Jesus cured with knowledge. When he said "Thy sins be forgiven thee," it simply meant that the sufferer had paid the penalty of his offence. Knowing this Jesus used his knowledge and his power to relieve him from further suffering, thus working in conformity with rather than against the law. Jesus, nor any other with knowledge, would not cure everyone who came to him, but only those whom he could cure within the law. He, himself, did not come under the law. He was above the law; and being above it he could see all those who came under the law and suffered from it. He could relieve physical, moral, or mental disease. The moral culprits were cured by him when they had endured the suffering necessary to make them see their wrong, and when they really desired to do better. Those whose ills originated from a mental cause could be cured only when the demands of physical nature had been complied with, when their moral habits had been changed, and when they were willing to assume their individual responsibilities and perform their individual duties. When such came to Jesus he used his knowledge and power to relieve them from further suffering because they had paid the debt to nature, were repentant of their wrong-doing, and in their interior natures were willing to assume and perform their obligations. After curing them he would say: "Go, and sin no more."

ঽ৺

*If it is wrong to receive money for curing physical ills by mental processes, or for giving 'science teaching,' is it not also wrong for a school teacher to receive money for instructing pupils in any of the branches of learning?*

There is little comparison to be made between the teacher or healer of mental or Christian Science and a teacher in the schools of learning. The only point in which they are similar is that the teaching of both has to do with the minds of their patients or pupils. Otherwise they are different in their claims, purpose, processes, and in results. The pupil of the schools learns that figures have certain values; that the multiplication of certain figures has always the same certain result, and never, under any circumstance does the teacher tell a pupil that three times four are two, or that twice one make twelve. Once the pupil learns to multiply he can always prove the truth or falsity of another's statement in the multiplication of figures. In no case is the healer able to instruct his patient-pupil with anything like exactness. The scholar learns grammar and mathematics for the purpose and convenience of the correct arrangement and easy expression of his thoughts to others who are intelligent. The mental healer or Christian Scientist does not teach his pupil by rules or example to prove or disprove the statements of others, or to arrange his own thoughts and to express them in a manner intelligible to others who are not of his belief, or to allow his beliefs and assertions to stand on their merits for what they are worth. The schools of learning exist for the purpose of enabling the pupil to understand the facts of the plane in which he is living, to be a useful, and an intelligent member of society. The "scientist" healer does not prove or demonstrate the claims of another "scientist" by his own processes, nor does the pupil of a healer prove the truth of the claims of his own or of another teacher with any degree of exactness; but the pupil of the schools can and does prove what he learns to be true or false. The teacher of the schools does not pretend to teach the cure of physical ills by mental means, but the "scientist" does, and is therefore not in the same class with the teacher in the schools. The teacher in the schools trains the mind of his pupil to understand the things which are evident to the senses, and he receives his pay in money which is in evidence to the senses; but the mental or christian scientist trains the mind of his patient-pupil to contradict, deny, and disbelieve facts which are evident to the senses, and at the same time exacts his pay in money, and according to the evidence of the senses. So that it does seem that there is no wrong in the school teacher's receiving money as payment for his services according to the plane in which he lives and teaches; whereas it is not right for a mental scientist or a christian scientist to claim to heal or to teach against the evidences of the senses, and at the same time take or exact pay according to the senses which he denies, but which he nevertheless enjoys. But suppose that it is wrong for the teacher of the schools to receive money for his services. That wrong would not make it right for the healer to be guilty of the same wrong, nor would it in any way relieve him from the responsibility of his own wrong act.

A FRIEND

---

# OCTOBER 1907

[From *The Word*, Vol. 6 No. 1]

The subjects dealt with in these columns are such as are of general interest and suggested by readers of THE WORD. MOMENTS WITH FRIENDS, we desire to remain all that the title suggests. They are not intended in any way to be controversial. Questions propounded by friends are endeavored to be answered by one of them and in the manner of friends. Arguments, for the sake of argument, are seldom conducive to friendship.

The following article, received soon after the issue of the March WORD, may not seem to the reader to be exactly as the former questions and answers under MOMENTS WITH FRIENDS, but owing to the general interest of the subjects discussed and to the correspondent's earnest request to have his objections published in THE WORD, A FRIEND will reply to his objections as requested, it being understood that the objections are to the principles and practices of Christian science, and not to personalities—Ed. THE WORD

New York, March 29, 1907.

To the Editor of THE WORD.

Sir: In the March issue of THE WORD, "A Friend" asks and answers a number of questions about Christian Science [*p. 42 in this book*]. These answers show that the writer has adopted certain premises unfavorable to Christian Science, which, if carried to their logical conclusions, are alike unfavorable to the practice of all religious bodies. The first question, "Is it wrong to use mental instead of physical means to cure physical ills?" is answered practically "yes." It is stated that "there are instances where one is justified in using the power of thought to overcome physical ills, in which case we would say that it was not wrong. In the great majority of cases it is decidedly wrong to use mental instead of physical means to cure physical ills."

If by the use of mental means the writer refers to the operation of one human mind upon another human mind, to remove physical ills, then I agree with him that it is wrong in every case. Christian Scientists do not employ the human mind in any case to remove physical ills. Therein lies the difference between Christian Science and mental science, which is overlooked by "A Friend."

Christian Scientists employ spiritual means, through prayer only, to cure disease. The Apostle James said, "The prayer of faith shall save the sick." Christian Science teaches how to make "the prayer of faith," and, since the sick are healed through Christian Science prayer, it is proof that it is "the prayer of faith." "A Friend" has unwittingly confused Christian Science treatment and mental treatment. Christian Science relies wholly upon God, through prayer, whereas so-called mental science, whether it operates through mental suggestion, hypnotism, or mesmerism, is the operation of one human mind upon another human mind. The results in the latter case are transitory and harmful, and fully merit the condemnation put upon such practice by "A Friend." No one, however, can object to prayer to God, nor can anyone say that sincere prayer for another can ever be injurious.

Another question is, "Did not Jesus and many of the saints cure physical ills by mental means, and if so, was it wrong?"

In answering this question "A Friend" admits they did heal the sick, and that it was not wrong for them to do so. He says, however, "Jesus and the saints received no money for their cures," and he also says, "How unlike Jesus and unsaintly it would seem for either Jesus or his disciples or any of the saints to charge so much per visit to every patient, cure or no cure."

The facts are that Jesus healed the sick, and taught his disciples how to do likewise. These disciples in turn taught others, and for three hundred years the power to heal was regularly exercised by the Christian church. When Jesus first sent out a band of his disciples with the command to preach the gospel and to heal the sick, he bade them not to accept pay for their services. When he sent them out the next time, however, he told them to take their purses along, and declared that "the laborer is worthy of his hire." This text has been accepted for nearly two thousand years as sufficient authority for the clergy and others engaged in Christian work to accept compensation for their services, and there can be no reasonable ground for making an exception in the case of Christian Scientists. Clergymen are employed by churches to preach and pray, and in almost all cases are paid a fixed salary. Christian Science practitioners both preach the gospel and pray, but they receive no fixed salary. Their charge is so small as to be trivial, and is paid voluntarily by the individual who seeks their aid. There is no compulsion about it, and in any event it is a personal matter between the patient and the practitioner with which outsiders are not concerned. In order to be a Christian Science practitioner, one must give up secular business and devote his or her entire time to the work. In order to do this, they must at least have some means for ordinary necessities. If no provision were made for compensation it is apparent that the poor would be excluded entirely from this work. This question has been settled by the Christian Science church on a basis that is eminently proper and satisfactory to the parties themselves. There is no complaint from those who turn to Christian Science for help that they are overcharged. Such complaint usually comes from those who have had nothing to do with Christian Science. In any event, it must be admitted by all who wish to treat the subject fairly, that if it is right to pay clergymen to preach, and to pray for the recovery of the sick, it is equally right to pay a Christian Scientist for such services.

Very truly yours.

(Signed) V. O. STRICKLER.

The questioner says that we have "adopted certain premises unfavorable to Christian Science, which, if carried to their logical conclusions, are alike unfavorable to all religious bodies."

That the premises are unfavorable to Christian science is true, but we do not see how from their logical conclusions these premises would be unfavorable to the practice of all religious bodies. Christian science maintains that its teachings are unique among modern faiths, and that is no doubt true. Because those premises are unfavorable to Christian science, it by no means follows that the same premises apply to all religious bodies; but if all religious bodies were to deny facts and teach falsehoods, then we should unhesitatingly be unfavorable to them in our premises to their doctrines and practices, when the occasion required that our views be expressed.

Referring to the first question and answer thereto, which appeared in the March WORD, 1907, the writer of the above letter says in the second paragraph that he agrees with us that "the operation of one human mind upon another human mind, to remove physical ills, is wrong in every case."

On reading this, the question naturally arises, what then the need for further objection or argument; but we are astonished at the statement which follows: "Christian Scientists do not employ the human mind in any case to remove physical ills."

If it is true that the human mind is not used by the Christian scientist in his efforts and practices to remove physical ills, then the case is removed from the courts of the world, and is not then for any court of inquiry. Therefore the Christian scientist need not be concerned with any unfavorable comment on his practices, and it is out of the sphere of MOMENTS WITH FRIENDS to attempt to deal with a subject not concerning the human mind. But it hardly seems possible that such a statement can truthfully be made. If it is claimed that it is the divine mind (or any other kind of mind) which removes physical ills, and not the human mind, then how without the human mind can the divine mind take action? If the divine mind, or whatever principle the "scientist" claims, does act, how is that action induced without the suggestion or employment of the human mind? But should the divine mind be capable of acting and removing physical ills without the employment or use of the human mind, then why is it that the intervention of a Christian scientist is necessary to remove physical ills of any kind? On the other hand, the only alternative is that neither any divine nor human mind is employed in the removal of physical ills. If that is so, how are we human beings, without the use of the human mind, to know or fancy that physical ills, or a divine mind, or the human mind, exist. The writer of the letter concludes the second paragraph by saying: "Therein lies the difference between Christian Science and mental science, which is overlooked by 'A Friend.'"

We acknowledge that we did not know this distinction between Christian science and mental science. The distinction made by the Christian scientist is in favor of the mental scientist, in that, according to the statement in the letter, the mental scientist still uses the human mind, whereas the Christian scientist does not.

In the beginning of the third paragraph the writer of the letter says: "Christian Scientists employ spiritual means through prayer only to cure disease. The Apostle James said, 'The prayer of faith shall save the sick.'"

These statements confuse rather than elucidate the foregoing quotations. The question naturally arises, what distinction does the Writer intend to infer between spiritual means and mental means? To the psychic, the mesmerist, and amateur psychologist, all action not believed to be due to a physical cause is lumped under a common head and called either psychic, mental, or spiritual; preferably spiritual. It is not clear how the Writer intends to employ his phrase "spiritual means," except that he holds that prayer is not a mental operation. But if prayer is not a mental operation, or has not to do with the human mind, what then is prayer? Who is the one who prays? What does he pray about, and to whom does he pray, and for what?

If the one who prays is a Christian scientist, how can he start his prayer without the human mind? But if he is no longer human and has become divine, then he need not pray. If one prays, we take it that his prayer is directed to a power higher than his own, hence the prayer. And if he is human he must use his mind to pray. The one who prays must pray about something. The inference is, that he prays about physical ills, and that these physical ills shall be removed. If the import of the prayer is for the removal of physical ills, the human being who prays must use his humanity and his mind to know of the physical ill and to ask for its removal for the benefit of the human sufferer. Prayer is the message or request addressed to the person, power or principle who is to remove the physical ill. It is said that the prayer is addressed to God; but one who wishes to address effectively a message or petition to an inferior, equal, or superior, must know how to address such message or petition in a manner which will obtain the desired ends. One who prays or petitions would not petition a power inferior to himself, as it could not grant his request, nor would he ask of one his equal to do what he himself could do. It is reasonable, therefore, to suppose that the one to whom he appeals is superior. If he is superior in power and all-wise in action, then the petition must be to apprise the one to whom it is addressed of something which he does not know. If he does not know it, he is not all-wise; but if he does know it, it is an act of insolence and impudence on the part of the petitioner to request an all-wise and all-powerful intelligence to perform an action, inasmuch as the request suggests that the all-wise intelligence either neglected to perform that which he should have done, or did not know that it should be done. If allowing, on the other hand, that the intelligence is all-wise and all-powerful, but did not concern himself with human affairs, then the one who intercedes or prays for the removal of physical ills must be aware of those physical ills, and uses his human mind in some initial way to make known the physical ills through prayer to God, the intelligence. The petition must be for the removal of the ills, and so in any case the mind is used for physical ends. The beginning is physical, the process must be mental (whatever else may follow); but the end is physical.

As to the prayer of faith the question arises: what is faith? Every being in human form has faith, but the faith of one is not the faith of another. The faith of a sorcerer in the successful results of his practices differs from the faith of the Christian scientist who may succeed in his practices, and both these differ from the faith of a Newton, a Kepler, a Plato, or a Christ. A fanatic who has blind faith in his wooden god obtains results as do any of the above mentioned who also have faith. What is termed successful action may be based on blind belief, on confident speculation, or on actual knowledge. The results will be according to the faith. The principle of faith is the same in each, but faith differs in the degree of intelligence. Therefore, if the Christian scientists claim to heal through the prayer of faith, then the cures effected must be according to the degree of faith in its intelligent use. It may be infernal or divine; but in any case, because the Apostle James said "the prayer of faith shall save the sick," does not make it so. The facts are the witnesses and not the Apostle James.

The Writer continues: "'A Friend' has unwittingly confused Christian Science treatment and mental treatment."

If this is the case, "A Friend" acknowledges his mistake; yet he does not see how Christian scientists can learn to make, and "make 'the prayer of faith,'" without the use of their human minds. This doubt seems to be supported by the following statement: "Christian Science relies wholly on God through prayer, whereas so-called mental science, whether it operates through mental suggestion, hypnotism or mesmerism, is the operation of one human mind upon another human mind. The results in the latter case are transitory and harmful, and fully merit the condemnation put upon such practice by 'A Friend.'"

While we do not here speak as to the mental scientists and say that the above statements are correct, still in their books the mental scientists claim together with Christian scientists to rely wholly upon God, or by whatever term they might designate God. This does not make plain the difference claimed by the Writer, for the reasons already advanced. The cures effected by mental scientists are claimed by them to be as effective and as numerous in proportion to the practitioners as the cures of the Christian scientists. Whatever the principle of cure involved may be, cures are effected by the two kinds of "scientists." The claims, however, of the writer of the above letter for Christian science are very pronounced, as accentuated by his denouncement of the mental scientists on whom he looks with displeasure. This is made apparent by the use and absence of capital letters in the terms "Christian Science" and "mental science." Throughout the letter the words "Christian Science" or "Scientists" are capitalized, whereas in speaking of mental science or scientists, capitals are noticeably absent. At the close of the above paragraph we read: "No one, however, can object to prayer to God, nor can anyone say that sincere prayer for another can ever be injurious."

"A Friend" endorses this statement, but must add that prayer for another, to be sincere and beneficial, must be unselfish; prayer even though it be for the apparent benefit of another, if there is to be personal remuneration or the receipt of money, cannot but be tainted and ceases to be unselfish, because personal benefits are to be received other than the benefit which comes from the knowledge of performing service.

In the paragraph beginning: "The facts are that Jesus healed the sick, and taught his disciples how to do likewise," our Correspondent attempts to prove the legitimacy of the action of Christian science in taking pay, by the following: "When Jesus first sent out a band of his disciples with the command to preach the gospel and to heal the sick, he bade them not to accept pay for their services. When he sent them out the next time, however, he told them to take their purses along, and declared that 'the laborer is worthy of his hire.' "

The first reference in the New Testament applying to the statement of our Correspondent is found in Matt., chap. x., vs. 7, 8, 9, 10: "And, as ye go, preach, saying, The kingdom of heaven is at hand. Heal the sick, cleanse the lepers, raise the dead, cast out devils: freely ye have received, freely give. Provide neither gold, nor silver, nor brass, in your purses; nor scrip for your journey, neither two coats, neither shoes, nor yet staves; for the workman is worthy of his meat."

We can see nothing in the above to warrant the Christian scientist for exacting compensation. In fact the statement "freely ye have received, freely give," argues against it.

In Mark, chap. vi., vs. 7–13, we find: "And he called unto him the twelve, and began to send them forth by two and two, and gave them power over unclean spirits; and commanded them that they should take nothing for their journey, save a staff only; no scrip, no bread, no money in their purse. But be shod with sandals: and not put on two coats. . . . And they went out, and preached that men should repent. And they cast out many devils and anointed with oil many that were sick, and healed them."

The above does not argue in favor of the practices of Christian scientists, and in fact Christian scientists cannot claim to follow any of the above instructions.

The next reference we find in Luke, chap. ix., vs. 1–6: "Then he called his twelve disciples together, and gave them power and authority over all devils, and to cure diseases. And he sent them to preach the kingdom of God, and to heal the sick. And he said unto them, Take nothing for your journey, neither staves, nor scrip, neither bread, neither money; neither have two coats apiece. And whatsoever house ye enter into, there abide, and thence depart. . . . And they departed, and went through the towns preaching the gospel, and healing everywhere."

There is no mention in the above of compensation, and the same instructions concerning the absence of pay, the plainness of dress, is noticeable. The above does not support our Correspondent in his claims.

The next reference is in Luke, chap. x., vs. 1–9, where it is said: "After these things the Lord appointed other seventy also, and sent them two and two before his face into every city and place whither he himself would come. . . . Carry neither purse, nor scrip, nor shoes; and salute no man by the way. And into whatsoever house ye enter, first say, Peace be to this house. And if the son of peace be there, your peace shall rest upon it: if not, it shall turn to you again. And in the same house remain, eating and drinking, such things as they give: for the laborer is worthy of his hire. Go not from house to house. And into whatsoever city ye enter and they receive you, eat such things as are set before you: And heal the sick that are therein, and say unto them, The Kingdom of God is come nigh unto you."

The above contains the quotation in the letter "that the laborer is worthy of his hire"; but this hire is plainly the "eating and drinking such things as they give." Certainly from this reference our Correspondent cannot claim the right to receive compensation other than the simple eating and drinking given him in the patient's house. All of the references thus far have been against the receipt of any compensation other than the food and shelter which is given the healer. And as shown in

MOMENTS WITH FRIENDS, nature always provides this for the true healer.

We now turn to the last reference, Luke. chap. xxii., vs. 35–37: "And he said unto them, when I sent you without purse, and scrip, and shoes, lacked ye anything? And they said, Nothing. Then said he unto them, but now, he that hath a purse, let him take it, and likewise his scrip: And he that hath no sword let him sell his garment, and buy one. For I say unto you, that this that is written must yet be accomplished in me. And he was reckoned among the transgressors: for the things concerning me have an end."

The meaning in the foregoing passages seems to be that Jesus would be no longer with the disciples, and that they would have to fight their own way; but there is absolutely no reference to compensation for the curing of disease. In fact, the instruction to take their purses and their scrip along with them would suggest the opposite of compensation: *that they would have to pay their own way.* In this fact, what our Correspondent advances as proof in support of the claims and practices of Christian science, turns out to be against them. Our Correspondent has injured his case by what he advances in favor of it. The instructions which are given by Jesus are not followed either in the spirit nor in the letter. Christian scientists are neither Christians in their teachings nor are they the disciples of Jesus; they are disciples of Mrs. Eddy, and the promulgators of her doctrines, and they have no right to advance the teachings of Jesus either as their or Mrs. Eddy's teachings or in the support of their claims and practices.

The Correspondent continues: "This text has been accepted for nearly two thousand years, as sufficient authority for the clergy and others engaged in Christian work, to accept compensation for their services, and there can be no reasonable ground for making an exception in the case of Christian Scientists."

It does not seem right for Christian scientists to follow certain practices of the clergy of the Christian church, and excuse themselves for accepting compensation because the clergy do it, and at the same time to entirely ignore the Christian church in its principal doctrines, and to attempt to supplant Christianity by Christian Science. The Christian church observes certain practices and teaches certain doctrines, which hundreds of thousands of the people of Christendom condemn, and the leaders of the Christian church of every denomination act against the teachings of Jesus, though they hold the doctrines; but this has nothing to do with the wrong, if it is wrong, for Christian scientists to accept money for removing physical ills by mental means, or, if the phrase is preferable, by spiritual means, because if God or spiritual means, effects the cure, then the cure is of God, and it is a gift of the spirit, and the Christian scientist has no right to accept physical money where he did not effect the cure, and he is obtaining money under false pretenses.

The Writer continues: "Clergymen are employed by churches to preach and pray, and in almost all cases are paid a fixed salary. Christian Science practitioners both preach the gospel and pray, but they receive no fixed salary."

This is no doubt true, but, good business men, they collect pay for their time and work. Continuing on the question of compensation, the Writer says: "Their charge is so small as to be trivial, and is paid voluntarily by the individual who seeks their aid."

That the charge is small and trivial and is paid voluntarily may possibly be so in the same sense that a man may give up his purse when he thinks he had better, or that a hypnotized subject will voluntarily deed his possessions and give his money to his hypnotist. The claim that the Christian scientists have no fixed salary and that the charges made are so small as to be almost trivial, is exceedingly naive and must appeal to the ingenuousness of the reader. The income of some of the practitioners and readers in the Christian science church is "so small as to be trivial" only when future possibilities of the Christian scientist's income are considered.

Referring to the statement of our Correspondent that "their charge is so small as to be almost trivial," and "this Question has been settled by the Christian Science Church on a basis that is eminently proper and satisfactory to the parties themselves. There is no complaint from those who turn to Christian Science for help that they are overcharged."

We relate the following from the many cases to which our attention has been called. An engineer on a local railroad had a nervous affection of the right arm which threatened to incapacitate him for work. Help was vainly sought from many physicians. Advices of his physicians were followed whenever possible, and his fellow employees even furnished the means for him to take a sea voyage as advised. But this did not result in any benefit. He then tried a Christian science practitioner and was somewhat relieved. This caused him to join the cult and he became an ardent believer, and endeavored to convert such of his friends as would listen to him. But he was not cured. One day he was asked, why, if he had been so much helped, his Christian science practitioner could not cure him. His reply was: "I cannot afford to have him cure me." When asked for an explanation, he said that it had taken all the money he could scrape together to be relieved as much as he then was, and that he could not get money enough together to be cured entirely. He further explained that the Christian scientist could not afford to give enough of his time to effect a thorough cure unless he was paid for it; that the Christian scientist must live, and as he depended for his living on the pay received for his cures, he could only cure those who could afford to pay for the cures. This votary of Christian science seemed to think that it was eminently proper not to be cured unless he had the money to pay for his cure.

Continuing on the subject of receiving money from the patient for benefits given, the Correspondent says: "There is no compulsion about it, and in any event it is a personal matter between the patient and the practitioner, with which outsiders are not concerned."

Apparently, there is no compulsion as to receiving pay or giving it. This is a question which is left to inference, but the Correspondent cannot so easily dispose of the matter of the latter part of the sentence. That outsiders are not concerned with personal matters between man and man is true; but this does not apply to the practice of Christian science. Christian science endeavors to make its doctrines known, and its practices are not merely a matter of private and personal interest between man and man. The practices of Christian science are a public matter.

They affect the interests of the community, the nation, and of the world. They strike at the vitals of humanity; they deny facts, assume falsehoods, attack the moral sense of right or wrong, affect the sanity and integrity of the mind; they claim practical omniscience and omnipotence for the founder of their cult, a woman addicted to most of the frailties of her human kind; they would make and reduce the spiritual world to be the servant of this physical earth; their ideal of religion appears to be, in its chief purpose, merely the cure of disease, and the luxury of the physical body. The church of the Christian scientist is founded and built up on the cure of physical ills, with an eye to physical conditions. The whole religion of Christian science turns on worldly success and the living in physical life; though it claims to be spiritual in origin, in purpose, and in practice. Success in life and the health of the physical body are right and proper; but all of that on which the Christian science church is built, leads away from a worship of the principle of Christ and of the true God. With the Christian scientists, judging from their claims, God exists primarily for the purpose of answering their prayers. Christ exists but as a figure to be pointed at to prove that the Christian scientist is warranted in his practice, and in place of God or Christ and of religion, Mrs. Eddy is by them deified and enshrined in a halo of glory and turned by them into an oracle, whose decree is inviolate and infallible, from which there is no redress or change.

The three sentences following in the letter were answered in MOMENTS WITH FRIENDS. The following sentence, however, presents a different aspect, though it still deals with the subject of compensation. "This question has been settled by the Christian Science church on a basis that is eminently proper and satisfactory to the parties themselves."

Just so; but this is only what any corrupt political or so-called religious body might say concerning their practices. Though it may be considered eminently proper and satisfactory to Christian scientists, it is not so to the public any more than it would be if the inmates of an insane asylum should be allowed to do what they might perchance have a notion is eminently fit and proper.

The Writer of the letter concludes it by saying: "In any event it must be admitted by all who wish to treat the subject fairly, that if it is right to pay clergymen to preach and to pray for the recovery of the sick, it is equally right to pay a Christian Scientist for such services."

Once more we draw attention to the unfairness to attempt to throw the blame, if blame there be, on the clergyman of the Christian church, and to excuse the actions of Christian scientists by the practice of the Christian clergy. It is not a practice in the Christian church for the clergyman to receive pay for praying for the sick. He, as pointed out by the Christian scientist, receives a fixed salary for preaching the gospel as the minister of the church, and not as a healer. But the question involved is not whether it is right or wrong to pay clergymen to preach and to pray for the recovery of the sick, and therefore to excuse the Christian scientists for a like service.

The attempt to throw the argument on the Christian clergy weakens the argument of the Christian scientist. The question is: Is it right or wrong to take money for the gift of the spirit? If it is wrong, then whether the clergyman does it or not, is no excuse for false pretenses or claims made by the Christian scientists.

As to the basis of Christian science, it would seem that if all possibility of making money either from the teaching of Christian science doctrines or from the curing, or the attempted curing, of physical ills were removed the cult would cease to exist, because the Christian science money-makers would either lose respect for it, or have no use for it. As to the believers in Christian science, if the curing of physical ills were done away with, the foundation of their belief in Christian science doctrines would be shattered, and their "spirituality" would disappear with the physical basis.

A FRIEND

# NOVEMBER 1907

[From *The Word*, Vol. 6 No. 2]

*The Christian says that Man has a Body, Soul and Spirit. The Theosophist says that Man has Seven Principles. In a few words what are these Seven Principles?*

The theosophist views man from two standpoints. From one he is mortal, from the other he is immortal. The mortal part of man is made up of four distinct principles. First, the physical body, which is built up from solids, liquids, air and fire, which are altogether the material of the physical body. Second, the linga sharira, which is the form, or design body of the physical. This form body is of ether, a less changeable matter than the constantly changing physical. The design or form body is the principle which moulds the unformed foods of solids, liquids, gases and light taken into the body, and which preserves its form throughout life. Third, is prana, or the principle of life. This principle of life causes the form body to expand and grow, otherwise the form would always remain the same. By the principle of life the foods of the physical body are kept in constant circulation. The principle of life tears down and sluffs off the old and replaces it in the form with the new matter. Thus the old physical is carried away and replaced with new physical matter, and the life matter is built into a physical body, and that physical body is given shape and held together by the design or form body. Fourth, is kama, the principle of desire. Desire is the turbulent craving animal in man. It is the inherent instincts and animal tendencies in man, and it uses and gives direction to the life and form of the physical body. These four principles constitute that part of man which dies, is separated, disintegrated and returns to the elements from which it is drawn.

The immortal part of man is threefold: First, manas, the mind. The mind is the distinctive principle which makes man a human being. The mind is the reasoning principle in man, that which analyzes, separates, compares, which identities itself and considers itself separate from others. It unites with desire and during physical life it conceives desire to be of itself. Mind reasons, but desire wants; the instincts crave, as opposed to what reason dictates. From the contact of mind with desire come all our experiences in life. Owing to the contact of mind and desire we have the duality of man. On the one hand, a craving, furious, rampant brute; on the other, a reasonable, peace loving being whose origin is divine. The mind is the principle by which the face of nature is changed; mountains are levelled, canals built, sky-towering structures raised and the forces of nature harnessed and driven to build up civilizations. The sixth, buddhi, is the divine soul, the principle which knows and feels itself to be in others and others in itself. It is the principle of true brotherhood. It sacrifices itself that all nature might be raised to a higher degree. It is the vehicle through which the pure spirit acts. Seventh, atma, is the spirit itself, pure and undefiled. All things unite in it, and it is the one pervading principle through within and about all things. Mind, soul and spirit, are the immortal principles, whereas the physical, the form, life and desire are mortal.

The christian division of man into body, soul and spirit is not at all clear. If by body is meant the physical form, then how account for the separate life, the permanent form and the animal in man? If by soul is meant the thing that may be lost or may be saved, this requires an explanation different from the christian. The christian uses soul and spirit and synonymously and he seems to be neither able to define soul and spirit nor to be able to show the difference between each. The theosophist by his sevenfold classification gives of man an explanation of man, which at least is reasonable.

৵

*In a few words can you tell me what takes place at death?*
Death means the separating of the physical body from its design, or form body. As death approaches the form body of ether withdraws itself from the feet upwards. Then the mind or ego leaves the body through and with the breath. The breath in departing stops life, leaves the form body, and the form body ascends from the chest and usually rolls out of

the physical from the mouth. The cord which had connected the physical with its form body is snapped, and death has taken place. It is then
impossible to revive the physical body. The desire principle may hold
the sensual mind in bondage for a time, if that mind during life has
thought of its desires as itself, in which case it remains with the animal
desires until such time as it can distinguish between itself and them, then
it passes into the ideal state of rest or activity which conforms to its highest thoughts, entertained by it while living in the physical body. There
it remains until its period of rest is at an end, then it returns to earth life
to continue its work from the point where it was left off.

❧

*Most spiritualists claim that at their seances the souls of the departed
appear and converse with friends. Theosophists say that this is not the case;
that what is seen is not the soul but the shell, spook or desire body which the
soul has discarded. Who is correct?*

We consider the statement of the theosophist to be the more correct,
because the entity with which one may converse at a seance is only an
echo of what was by the entity thought during life and such conversation applies to material things, whereas the divine part of man would
speak of things spiritual.

❧

*If the soul of man may be held a prisoner after death by its desire body,
why may not this soul appear at seances and why is it wrong to say that it
does not appear and converse with the sitters?*

It is not impossible for the human soul to appear at seances and
converse with friends, but it is highly improbable that it does, because
the "sitters" do not know how to evoke the temporary prisoner and
because such appearance would either have to be summoned by one
who knows how, or else by the intense desire of one who is living as well
as of the discarnated human soul. It is wrong to say that the appearances

are the souls of the departed because the human soul who cannot distinguish between itself and its desires usually goes through a metamorphosis similar to that of a butterfly in order that it may realize its condition. While in this condition it is inactive as is the cocoon. That human soul who is able of its own volition to distinguish itself from the animal would refuse to have more to do with that animal which causes it such torment.

The reason for such an unusual occurrence as the appearances of a discarnated human soul at a seance would be to communicate with some one present on certain topics, such, for instance, as information of spiritual importance or a philosophical value to the one most concerned. The communications of the entities who do masquerade under the title of some departed person, chatter and prattle about unimportant things with an occasional speculation on some matter suggested by one of the sitters. If our departed friends had been guilty of such driveling conversation while with us during their earth life, we would, as friends, have grieved for them, but nevertheless we should have been compelled to have had them placed in an insane asylum, because it would have been apparent at once that they had lost their minds. This is just what has occurred to the beings who appear at seances. They have actually lost their minds. But the desire which we speak of remains, and it is the desire with only a bare reflection of the mind which it had been connected with that appears at the seance. These appearances jump from one topic to another with no showing of reason nor any apparent lucidity of thought or expression. Like the insane, they appear to be suddenly interested in a subject, but they as suddenly lose the subject, or their connection with it, and jump to another. When one visits an insane asylum he will meet with some exceptional cases. A few will converse with apparent ease on many topics of interest, but when certain matters are introduced the lunatic becomes violent. If the conversation is continued long enough the point at which they ceased to be human will be discovered. It is just so with the spooks or desire forms who appear at seances. They echo the old instincts and longings of and for earth life and express themselves according to those longings, but they invariably fall into nonsensical chattering when other matters are introduced that are not suited to their particular desire. They have the cunning of the animal and, like the animal, will play about the field and cross and recross their tracks to elude the one who pursues them with consecutive questions. If the hunt is carried on, the departed either bids farewell to the questioner because his "time is up and he must go" or else he will say that he does not know how to reply to what he is asked. If a discarnated human soul should appear he would be direct and lucid in his statements and what he said would be of value to the person addressed. The nature of his communication would be of moral, ethical, or spiritual worth, it would not be of commonplace matters, as is almost always the case at seances.

ֆ

*If the appearances at seances are only the shells, spooks or desire bodies, which have been discarnated by the human souls after death, why is it that they are able to communicate with the sitters on a subject known only to the person concerned, and why is it that the same subject will be brought up over and over again?*

If the spooks or desire forms were connected during earth life with the names with which they claim to be, they are aware of certain topics, as in the case of a madman, but they are only automatons, they repeat over and over again the loose thoughts and desires of life. Like a phonograph they speak out what was spoken into them, but unlike the phonograph they have the desires of the animal. As their desires were connected with the earth, so they are now, but without the restraint due to the presence of the mind. Their answers are suggested and oftentimes indicated by the questions put to them, and which are by them seen in the questioner's mind even though he may not be aware of it. As for instance, one may see a light reflected on the wearer's hat or other object of which he may not be aware. When the questioner is informed of something of which he has not before known, he considers it wonderful and of course thinks that it could only have been known by himself and his informant, whereas it is only the reflection seen in the mind of the questioner or else it is the impression of an occurrence caused by the desire-form and given expression whenever the occasion allowed it.

જી

*The fact cannot be denied that spirits do sometimes tell the truth and also give advice which if followed will result to the benefit of all concerned. How can the theosophist, or any other opposed to spiritualism, deny or explain away these facts?*

No theosophist or other person respecting the truth ever tries to deny facts, nor to dodge the truth, nor would he attempt to hide the facts, or to explain them away. The endeavor of any truth loving person is to get at the facts, not to hide them; but his love for facts does not require that he should accept as true the claims of an unreasoning person, or those of a spook, or shell, or elemental, masquerading at a seance as a dear departed friend. He listens to the claims made, then proves the claims to be true or false by the evidence advanced. The facts always prove themselves. Out of their mouths, saints prove themselves to be saints, philosophers to be philosophers; the talk of unreasoning people proves them to be unreasoning and spooks prove themselves to be spooks. We do not believe that theosophists are opposed to the facts of Spiritualism, though they deny the claims of most spiritualists.

The first part of the question is: do "spirits" sometimes tell the truth. They do—sometimes; but so does the most hardened criminal for the matter of that. Inasmuch as no particular instance of the truth stated by a "spirit" has been given, we will venture to say that the truth or truths stated by what some people will insist on calling "spirits" is of a commonplace nature. Such, for instance, as a statement that within a week you will receive a letter from Mary, or John, or that Maria will fall sick, or get well, or that some good fortune will befall, or that a friend will die, or that an accident will occur. Should any of these things be true it would only go to show that an entity—whether of a high or low character—is capable of a finer sensuous perception than the same being, if incarnated. This is so because each body perceives on that plane on which it is functioning. While living in a physical body, one perceives material things through the physical senses; and events are perceived only at the time of their occurrence, such as getting a cold, or falling, or receiving a letter, or meeting with an accident. But if one is not limited to the physical body and still has the senses, these senses act on the plane next the physical, which is the astral. One who functions on the astral plane can perceive events occurring there; the viewpoint in the astral plane is from a higher ground than the physical. Thus, for instance, the thought or positive intention of one to write a letter could be seen by one capable of seeing such intention or thought, or a cold could be predicted with certainty by seeing the condition of the astral body of the one who would have it. Some accidents may also be predicted when the causes of them have been set in motion. These causes are invariably in the thoughts or the actions of people, and when a cause is given the result follows. To illustrate: if a stone is thrown in the air one may predict its fall long before it touches the ground. According to the force with which it was thrown and the arc of its ascent, the curve of its descent and the distance it will fall may accurately be predicted.

Entities who function on the astral plane may thus see the causes after they are generated and may predict an event with accuracy because they can see in the astral that which will occur in the physical. But a murderer can see the ascent of a stone and predict its descent quite as truly as a saint or a philosopher. These are of material things. The advice given as to how to avoid an accident does not prove that it is given by an immortal soul. A villain might advise one of an impending accident as accurately as a sage. Either might advise one standing in the way of a descending stone and prevent his injury. So might a lunatic. It might be asked how such advice could be given by a spook, if a spook is devoid of mind. We would say that a spook is devoid of mind in the same sense that a hopelessly insane man is devoid of mind. Even though he lose a knowledge of his identity, there is a slight reflection that is implanted on the desire, and it remains with the desire. It is this reflection that gives the semblance of mind in certain cases, but it must be remembered that although the shell has lost the mind that the animal remains. The animal has not lost its cunning and the cunning of the animal with the impression left by the mind enables it to follow, under certain cases, such as those already instanced, the events transpiring in the realm where it functions. The facts are then reflected on itself as a picture may be reflected by a mirror. When an event is reflected on the desire body and this picture is connected with or related to one of the sitters at the seance, the spook or shell responds to the thought picture reflected on it and attempts to voice forth the thought or impression as a piano would voice forth or respond to the person who operated its keys. When a sitter at a seance has lost or mislaid something, this loss remains as a picture in his mind and this picture is stored as an old memory. The picture is often perceived or reflected by the desire body or spook. It then responds to the picture by telling the sitter that at such a time was lost such an article of value, or that this article may be found by him, in the place where he had put it, or where it had been lost. These are instances where the facts are stated and advice given, which proves to be correct. On the other hand, where one fact is given, a hundred falsehoods are said, and where advice is once correct, it is a thousand times misleading or harmful. We therefore say that it is a waste of time and detrimental to ask and follow the advice of the departed. It is a well known fact that all people who prey on the weaknesses of others, engaged in betting, or gambling, or speculations on the market, allow their intended victims to win small sums of money, or they will flatter the victim on his shrewdness in speculation. This is done to encourage the victim to continue his risk, but eventually this results in his utter failure and ruin. Similar is the case with mediums and spook chasers and phenomena hunters. The little facts which they find true entice them to continue their practices until, like the speculator, they are in too deep to get out. The spooks assume control and may finally obsess the victim entirely and then follows failure and ruin. The statistics of mediumship and of phenomena chasers will prove these statements true. And the one who champions the "spirits" can neither "deny nor explain away these facts."

A FRIEND

# MARCH 1908

[From *The Word*, Vol. 6 No. 6]

*If it is true that none but shells, spooks and entities devoid of manas appear, according to theosophical teachings, at seances, whence comes the information and teachings of a philosophical and often theosophical nature, which some mediums have undoubtedly received?*

Teaching of any kind carries its value on or within itself. All teachings should be judged for what they are worth, irrespective of their source or authority. It depends upon the ability of the one who receives a teaching as to whether or not he is able to judge the teaching at its true value. Some teachings bear on their face all there is to them, while others have to be looked into, thought over and assimilated before the true meaning is perceived. Mostly mediums babble and drivel at seances, and the listeners receive these utterances in wonder. Occasionally a medium may receive or repeat a philosophical discourse, which is said to be dictated by some control. When teaching of a philosophical or theosophical nature is given through a medium, it may be said to come from either the medium's higher ego, or from a wise man still living in a body, or from one who has learned to separate himself and live distinct from the physical body, or it may come from one who has departed this life, but has not dissociated himself from his body desire which then connects him with the world and who has not been subject to the state of coma through which the ordinary man passes during and after death.

Teaching which is worth while may come from any of these sources, through a medium, whether at a seance or not. But never should a teaching be valued because it comes from a source which one regards as "authority."

꙾

*Do the dead work individually or collectively to attain a certain end?*

What do we mean by "the dead?" The body dies and is dissipated. It does no work after death and its form is dissipated into thin air. If by "the dead" is meant the personal desires, then we can say that they persist for a time, and such personal desires continue in their efforts to obtain their object or objects. Each of such dead ones must work for his or her personal ends, because as each works for the personal desire they are not concerned with attaining certain ends for others. If on the other hand, by "the dead" is meant that portion of one's self which persists from life to life, then we would say that it may live after death in the world of its ideals built by itself, and for its individual enjoyment, or its ideals may have been such as to include in their aims the lives of others, in which case the departed would live out or assimilate the ideals which it had formed during life on earth. This earth is the place for work. The dead pass into a state of rest preparatory to their return to this world for work. Of the immortal sparks acting through these physical bodies in this world, some work in this world to attain certain ends as individuals, while others work collectively to attain their end. Each of the first class works selfishly for its own individual end. The other class work individually and collectively for the good of all. This applies to both of these classes who have not attained their immortality, meaning by immortality an unbroken and continuous conscious existence through all states and conditions. Such as have attained immortality in the present life may work after the death of the body either for their individual objects or for the good of all. This life is the place for work in this world for the ordinary human being. In the state after death he does not work, as that is the time for rest.

স৶

*How do the dead eat, if at all? What sustains their life?*

Food is necessary to maintain the existence of a body of whatever kind. Rocks, plants, animals, men and gods require food to continue existence. The food of one is not the food of all. Each kingdom uses as food the kingdom below it and in turn serves as food for the kingdom above it. This does not mean that the gross body of one kingdom is the food of the other, but that the essence of these bodies is the food which is either taken from the kingdom below or offered to the kingdom above. Dead bodies of men serve as food for the earth, the plants, the worms and animals. The entity which used the food continues its existence by food, but the food of such entity is not the same food that was used to continue the existence of its physical body. After death the real man passes into a state of rest and enjoyment, only after he has separated himself from the gross desires of his physical life. By his association with these desires through contact with the physical world he gives to these desires a semblance of human being and these desires partake somewhat of thought, but only in the sense that a glass bottle partakes of the fragrance of a perfume which it contained. These are usually the entities which appear after death. They continue their existence by food. Their food is taken in many ways, according to the particular nature of the entity. To perpetuate the desire is to repeat it. This can only be done by experiencing the particular desire through the physical body of a human being. If this food is refused by living human beings the desire burns itself out and is consumed. Such desire forms do not eat physical food, because they have no physical apparatus to dispose of physical food. But desire and other entities, such as nature elementals, perpetuate their existence in form by the smell of foods. So in this sense they may be said to live on the smell of foods, which is the grossest form of food of which they are able to make use. Owing to this fact, certain classes of elementals and discarnated human desire entities are attracted to certain localities by the odors which arise from foods. The grosser the odor the more dense and sensual will be the entity attracted; pre-human entities, elementals, nature sprites are attracted and propitiated by the burning of incense. The burning of incense attracts or repels such classes or entities according to their nature. In this sense "the dead" may be said to eat. In a different sense the departed conscious principle who lives in his ideal heaven or state of rest may also be said to eat in order to continue his existence in that state. But the food which he lives on is of the ideal thoughts of his life; according to the number of his ideal thoughts he furnishes the food which he assimilates after death. This truth was symbolized by the Egyptians in that part of their Book of the Dead in which it is shown that the soul after it has passed through the Hall of the Two Truths and has been weighed in the balance, passes into the fields of Aan Ru, where it finds wheat of the growth of three and five and seven cubits high. The departed can only enjoy the period of rest, the length of which is determined by his ideal thoughts while on earth. When these are exhausted he returns again to earth.

ॐ

*Do the dead wear clothes?*

Yes, but according to the texture of the body that is to wear them, of the thought that formed them and of the character which they are intended to express. The clothes of any man or race are an expression of the characteristics of the individual or the people. Aside from the use of clothes as a protection against climate, they exhibit certain peculiarities of taste and art. This is all the outcome of his thought. But to answer the question directly, we would say that it depends on the sphere in which the dead are as to whether or not they wear clothes. When closely associated in thought with the world the departed entity will retain the habits and customs of the social world in which it moved, and if such departed entity could be seen it would appear in the clothes which were most suited to its liking. It would appear in such costume because whatever its thought is, that it would be, and the clothes which one would wear naturally in his thought are those which he would have used while in life. If, however, the thoughts of the departed should change from one condition to another, then he would appear in the clothes which he would have in thought, to suit the condition. However, owing to the thought of human beings, clothes are intended to conceal defects or improve the form, quite as much as to shield or protect it from inclement weather, but there is a sphere into which one passes after death and where he is seen as he really is and not as clothes would make him appear to be. This sphere is in the light of his inner god, who sees him as he is and who judges according to worth. In that sphere one needs neither clothes nor any protection, as he is not subject to nor affected by the thoughts of other beings. So "the dead" may be said to wear clothes if they need them or want clothes, and may be said to wear the clothes needed to shield, hide or protect their bodies according to the conditions in which they are in.

ॐ

*Do the dead live in houses?*

After death the physical body is tightly housed in its wooden casket, but the form of the body, the astral body, does not remain in that house. It dissipates as the body does about the grave; so much for the physical side. As to the entity inhabiting the body, it lives in such conditions or environments as are most in keeping with its nature. If its dominant thought has been such as to attract it to a particular house or locality, it is there either in thought or in presence. This applies to the desire body, but the entity who lives in its ideal world after death—usually called heaven—may there live in a house, providing it thinks of a house because it may paint any picture that it pleases. The house if any that it would live in would be an ideal house, built by its own thought, and not by human hands.

ॐ

*Do the dead sleep?*

Death itself is a sleep, and it is a long or short sleep as the entity who has worked in this world requires it. Sleep is a period of rest, a temporary cessation from activity on any plane. The higher mind or ego does not sleep, but the body or bodies through which it functions require rest. This rest is called sleep. So the physical body, all its organs, cells and molecules sleep or have a period however short or long, which allows them to readjust themselves magnetically and electrically to their condition.

A FRIEND

# MAY 1908

[From *The Word*, Vol. 7 No. 2]

*Do the dead live in families, in communities, and if so is there a government?*

Those who depart this life take a rest which is long or short, according to their needs. They then continue their existence in the after state as they had lived on earth. But there is this difference, that whereas life on earth required all the constituent principles of a man to be present in this world, the after state requires only a vehicle suitable to the plane on which the mind, the ego, functions.

Has man lived with his family or in a community on earth according to his desire, it will then also be his desire to continue this sort of life in the after-death state. If he has preferred a solitary life, or a life devoted to study or research, then he will not desire a life among others; but in either case, according to what was his desire in physical life, so will his desire continue after death.

After death, man, the ego, the mind, continues with all his faculties, but minus the physical body and the form of that physical body. Wherever his thought and interest lay there will the man be. When, however, the mind is separated from the world by the severance from its physical body, the medium of expression and communication with the physical world is cut off and the man cannot be with the physical bodies of his family or the community which had occupied his thought. If, however, his thought of family or community had been strong he would be in thought with them or hold them in his thought as one may be in thought with his family or friends while living in the world even though he be living in a distant country. He would not have new thoughts, nor derive information concerning the family or community after his death, nor be about them knowing their fate, as is sometimes erroneously supposed. After death man lives in thoughts which he had had while in physical life. He thinks over again what he had thought during life.

There is a world of thought, which is after all the world which man really lives in even while in a physical body, for the world is to him as he translates it into his thought world. But there is another world which lies between the thought world and the physical world which is the desire world (kama loca). In the desire world are the passions and gross desires of man. So that after death there is a desire body of man from which man, the mind, must free himself if he is to have any period of enjoyment or rest in the after death states. In rare instances, man, the mind, is enslaved by his gross desire body, in which case he might frequent the place of his former family or community. In such particular case, however, the mind would appear to be drugged or intoxicated. The desire would be the dominant factor. Such an apparition would act much the same as one under the influence of a drug or intoxicant. Nevertheless, the desire would make itself manifest even as the drunkard makes manifest his desire. Only in few appearances of such desire bodies is the mind present. As the mind conceived of family life or community life as an ideal in its physical world, so will the same mind hold family or community life in the ideal thought world in its after death state. But whereas in this physical world the ideal life seemed to be shadowy and vague and the physical life the real and matter of fact, now the condition is reversed; the ideal world is the real and the physical has entirely disappeared or simply remains an abstract ideal.

Yes, there is a government in the after death states. Each of the states after death has its own government and the laws of each state control that state. The law of the desire state is indicated by its own name: desire. The ideal world is governed by thought. Each state is controlled automatically by desire, or ideal thought, each according to its nature, and all according to justice.

ॐ

*Is there a punishment or reward for the deeds done by the dead, either while in life or after death?*

Yes, and each deed brings its own result, according to the action and according to the motive and thought which prompted the action. Many who act in this world act ignorantly, nevertheless the action brings its reward or punishment. The one who pulls the trigger of a gun that he didn't know was loaded and shoots off his finger, or the hand of a friend, suffers the results physically quite as much as though he had shot with intention to injure. The physical punishment is the same. But he does not suffer the mental punishment which would ensue as remorse, which he would suffer had he performed the action with knowledge of what would take place.

This applies to the question while living in the physical world. But there is another side which is the after death state. Those in the after death state act only as effects following causes. This world is the world of causes as well as of effects, but the after states are only of effects. The desire body continues to act after death according to the impetus permitted it during physical life. Therefore, the deeds performed by the astral entity, or even by the mind in its ideal world, are only results, not causes. They are the consequences as reward or punishment for deeds performed in the physical world. But these deeds are not in turn rewarded or punished.

The terms "reward" and "punishment" are theological terms. They have a personal and selfish meaning. Whether in this or any other world, the true law interprets punishment to mean a lesson given to the performer of wrong action. Reward is the lesson given to the performer of right action. The lesson which has been called punishment is given to the performer to teach him not to do wrong again. Reward teaches the consequences of right action.

In the after death state, the desire body suffers much the same as a man of strong appetites, when he has not the means nor the opportunity of satisfying his appetite. The physical body is the medium through which the desire body satisfies its appetite. When the desire body is deprived of or cut off from its physical body at death, the appetites remain, but it has not the means of gratifying them. So that if the desires have been intense and for physical gratification there is after death the hunger of desire, or the burning of passion, but without the means of gratifying or appeasing it. But the mind whose ideals were high, experiences all the joys attending the fulfillment of these ideals, because it is in the world where ideals are.

Thus we have in the after death states punishment or reward, or more properly called, the lessons of right and wrong action, as the results of the thoughts, deeds and actions performed while living in the physical world.

❧

*Do the dead acquire knowledge?*

No, they do not in the proper sense of the term. All knowledge which the mind acquires must be acquired while living in a physical body in this physical world. Here is where it must acquire knowledge if knowledge is to be acquired. After death we may pass through a process of digesting or assimilating, but only of the things acquired in this world, in the same sense that an ox might chew its cud while in its manger, but only of that which it has carried with it from the field. So the departed lives over or digests those desires, thoughts, or ideals, which it has generated, developed and garnered during life. The real knowledge of all the worlds must be acquired while living in this world. The entity cannot acquire after death what it has not known during life. It may magnify and live over again what it has known during life, but it can acquire no new knowledge after death.

❧

*Do the dead know what is going on in this world?*

Some may, others cannot. It depends on what we mean by "the dead." The earth bound desire bodies are the only class of the many classes of "the dead" who may know what is going on in this world. But then they can know only what is going on as it is related to the desires and cravings which they had experienced during life, and which goings on are related to them. As for example, the desire body of a drunkard would know only what was going on in the world as it related to his desire for drink and even then only when he could find the neighborhood and people who were addicted to drink. He could find the neighborhood by the natural attraction of like to like, but in order to experience what was going on he must do so through the physical body of one who drinks, which he would do by entering and obsessing the one who drinks. But the desire body of a drunkard would not likely know what was going on in the world of politics or of literature or art, nor would it know or understand the discoveries in astronomy or the mathematical sciences. As each person seeks the environment most agreeable in the physical world, so desire bodies would be attracted to physical environments suitable to the nature of their desires.

The question is, could they know what was going on even in those localities? The ordinary desire body could not, as it has no physical organs through which to see physical objects. It may feel the desire and be near the object of its expression, but it could not see the object unless it entered into a human body and used the organs of sight or the other senses to connect it with the physical world. At best, the ordinary desire body can see the astral counterparts only of the desires of the physical world.

The mind which had severed its connection with the body and passed into its ideal world would not know what was going on in the physical world. Its ideal world is to it its heaven. This heaven or ideal world would cease to be such if all of the things in the physical world were known. The ideals of the earth world may be known to the departed in the ideal world, but only as these ideals are the same, such as are being experienced by the mind in its ideal world.

ॐ

*How do you explain cases where the dead have appeared either in dreams, or to people who were awake, and have announced that death of certain persons, generally other members of the family, was near?*

A dream which is not due to a physiological cause comes from the astral world or from the thought world. The death of a person announced in a dream simply means that the one announced to die has already set up or generated the causes which are to bring about his death, and the causes thus set up are reflected into the astral world. There they may be seen as a picture; all the circumstances attending the death may also be seen if sought for. Thus dreams, of the deaths which do take place, as announced, may be seen by anyone coming into contact with the current of thought which caused the picture. In the case where someone appears in the dream it means that such appearance directs the attention of the one in dream to the coming death. This would be done either to attempt to avert the death, or to prepare the one for it, or as an example to be noted by those most concerned.

The same principle would be involved in the case where the dead have appeared and announced the coming death of another to a person who was awake, except that the eyes of the person would be sensitized to the appearance, or the astral sense quickened to perceive the appearance. The same reasons would be applied. But the difference would be that whereas the mind sees in dream more clearly than in waking life, and therefore the astral entity need not be dense, the apparition would have to be more pronounced and the physical senses brought into play in order to perceive it. The dead who thus appeared would be the desire body which was connected or related in some way with the one whose death it announced. But all persons so announced to die do not always die as announced. This means (when the person is not deluded by fancy) that the causes which absolutely require death have not been actually evoked, but that death will follow unless countercauses are set up to avert it. When the proper action is so taken the death may be averted.

৯৬

*Are the dead attracted to members of what was their family while on earth, and do they watch over them; say a departed mother over her young children?*

It is possible that one of the departed members of a family may be attracted to one or others of the family if there is an unfulfilled desire which was strong during life. As, for instance, one who desired to convey a piece of property to another which he had possessed during life by trickery. As soon as the conveyance was made, or the one entitled came into rightful possession, the desire would be fulfilled and the mind freed from the bonds holding it. In the case of a mother watching over her children, this is possible only where the thought is so strong during life and the moments of death as to hold the mind of the mother to the conditions of her children. But this must be loosened in order that the mother be freed and the children be allowed to work out the destiny which they had created in former lives. After passing into her ideal world or heaven, the departed mother has still in thought the children who are dear to her. But her thought of the children cannot be disturbed in her ideal state, else the state will not be ideal. If the children suffer she cannot know it without suffering herself, and suffering has no place in the ideal world. Suffering forms a part of the lessons and experience of life from which the mind so suffering acquires knowledge and learns how to live and think and act. What does happen is that the mother, holding in thought the children who are dear to her, might affect them through thought. She cannot watch over them in their physical welfare, but she may by her high ideals convey such ideals to them when their thoughts and lives will respond. In this way not only may the children of parents be aided by those departed, who are in the ideal world or heaven, but all departed friends may help those now living in this world if the ideals of the departed have been high and noble during their contact and friendship in physical life.

ॐ

*In the world of the dead is there the same sun and moon and stars as in our world?*

No, certainly not. The sun and moon and stars are said to be physical bodies in a physical universe. As such they cannot be, nor be seen as such, after death; for though the thought of them may be carried in the mind after death the thought would be different from the objects. The astronomer whose thought had been entirely taken up by his study while living, may after death be still engrossed with his subject, yet he would not see the physical moon and stars, but only his thoughts or the ideas of them. The sun and moon and stars furnish to the beings on earth three kinds of light of varying power and intensity. The light of our physical world is the sun. Without the sun we are in darkness. After death the mind is the light which illuminates the other worlds as it also may illuminate the physical. But when the mind or ego leaves its physical body the physical is in darkness and death. When the mind separates from the desire body, that body is also in darkness and it must also die. When the mind passes into its ideal state it lights up the obscure thoughts and ideals of life. But the physical sun, or moon, or stars, can throw no light on the after death states.

そ

*Is it possible for the dead to influence the living without the knowledge of the living, by suggesting thoughts or deeds?*

Yes, it is possible and it often does happen that disembodied entities whose desires were strong and whose life had been cut off have by their presence incited persons who were susceptible, to commit crimes which they would not have done without that influence. This does not mean that the action is entirely due to the disembodied entity, nor imply the innocence of the one who committed the crime under such influence. It simply means that the disembodied entity would seek or be attracted to the one most likely to be influenced. The one most likely to be impressed must either be a medium without high ideals or moral strength, or else one whose inclinations are similar to those of the entity that impressed him. This is possible and often is done without the knowledge of the one incited to action. So also is it possible for thoughts, which are of a higher character, to be suggested to others, but in such case it is not necessary to go to the dead for thoughts, because thoughts of the living have far more power and influence than thoughts of the dead.

A FRIEND

# JUNE 1908

[From *The Word*, Vol. 7 No. 3]

*Does any one know where the centre is around which our sun and its planets seem to be revolving? I have read that it might be Alcyone or Sirius.*

Astronomers have not yet determined which star is the centre of the universe in toto. Each of those stars thought to be the centre have on later investigation been found to be themselves moving. As long as astronomers hold merely to the physical side of astronomy, they cannot discover the centre. The fact is, no one of those stars which are seen is the centre of the universe. The centre of the universe is invisible and not to be discovered by telescopes. That which is visible of the universe is but a small portion of the real universe, in the same sense that that which is seen of man, his physical body, is a small portion of the real man. The physical body, whether of man or the universe, has a formative principle which holds the visible physical particles together. Through this formative principle there operates another principle, the principle of life. The principle of life extends beyond the physical and the formative principles and keeps all the particles of the physical body and all bodies in space in movement. The principle of life is itself included in a greater principle which, to the human mind, is as boundless as is space. This principle is apprehended by authors of religions and scriptures as God. It is the Universal Mind, which includes all things in manifestation, visible or invisible. It is intelligent and all-powerful, but has no parts in the same sense that space has no parts. Within it the physical universe as a whole and all things live and move and have their being. This is the centre of the universe. "The centre is everywhere and the circumference nowhere."

꙯

*What makes one's heart beat; is it the vibration of waves from the sun, also what about breathing?*

Vibrations from the sun do not cause the heart to beat, though the sun has to do with the circulation of the blood and with all life on the earth. One of the causes of the heart beat is the action of the breath on the blood as it is contacted in the pulmonary alveoli, the air-chambers of the lungs. This is the physical breath action on the physical blood, the central station of which is the heart. But the physical breath action is not the real cause of the heart beat. The primary cause is the presence in the body of a psychic entity which enters the body at birth and remains during the life of the body. This psychic entity is related to another which is not in the body, but which lives in the atmosphere of the body, surrounds and acts on the body. By the action and interaction of these two entities, the in and out breathing continues through life. The psychic entity in the body lives in the blood and it is directly through this psychic entity living in the blood that the heart is caused to beat.

"One's heart" is a large subject; "breathing" is a large subject; much may be written about them. That we might be able to answer the last part of the question: "also what about breathing" we must be informed "what about it."

ॐ

*What is the relation between the heart and the sex functions—also the breathing?*

The heart of man may properly be said to extend through the entire body. Wherever are the arteries, veins or capillaries, there are the ramifications of the heart. The circulatory system is only the field of action for the blood. The blood is the medium of the breath for communication between the organs and the body. The blood, therefore, is the messenger between the breath and the sex organs. We breathe into the lungs, the lungs transmit the air to the blood, the action of the blood stirs up the organs of sex. In the editorial on The Zodiac, V., which appeared in "The Word," Vol. 3, pp. 264–265 [*pp. 113–114 in* Monthly Editorials From THE WORD Part I], the writer speaks of the gland of Luschka, the particular organ of desire, as sex desire. There it is stated that with each inbreathing the blood is stimulated and acts on the gland of Luschka and that this organ either allows the force playing through it to go downward or upward. If it goes downward it goes outward, acting in conjunction with the opposite organ, which is virgo, but if it goes upward it is made to do so by the will-breath and its path is by way of the spine. The heart is the central station for the blood, and is also the reception hall where all thoughts entering into the body gain audience with the mind. Thoughts of the sex nature enter the body through the sex organs; they arise and apply for entrance into the heart. If the mind grants them audience in the heart and entertains them the circulation of the blood is increased and the blood driven to the parts corresponding to the thought. The increased circulation requires a more rapid breath in order that the blood might be purified by the oxygen breathed into the lungs. It requires about thirty seconds for the blood to pass from the heart through the arteries to the extremities of the body and back to the heart through the veins, making one complete cycle. The heart must pulsate faster and the breath be shorter when thoughts of sex are entertained and the sex organs stimulated by the blood from the heart.

Many organic diseases and nervous complaints are caused by the useless expenditure of the life force through thoughts of sex; or, if there be no expenditure, by the rebound on the whole nervous organism of the life force returning from the parts in question and by the return into circulation of the blood from the sex organs. The generative force is liquefied and killed by the rebound. The dead cells pass into the blood which distributes them through the body. They contaminate the blood and disease the organs of the body. The movement of the breath is an indicator of the state of the mind and a register of the emotions of the heart.

*How much does the moon have to do with man and other life on the earth?*

The moon has a magnetic attraction for the earth and all the fluids of the earth. The intensity of the attraction depends on the phase of the moon, its position towards the earth, and the season of the year. Its attraction is strongest at the equator and weakest at the poles. The influence of the moon controls the rise and fall of the sap in all plants and determines the strength and efficiency of the medicinal properties in most plants.

The moon affects the astral body, the desires in animals and man, and the mind in men. The moon has a good and an evil side in its relation to man. Generally speaking the evil side is indicated by the phases of the moon in its waning period; the good side is connected with the moon from the time of the new to the full moon. This general application is modified by individual cases; for it depends on the particular relationship of man in his psychic and physical make-up as to the degree to which the moon may influence him. All influences, however, may be counteracted by will, reason, and thought.

ॐ

*Does the sun or the moon regulate or govern the catamenial period? If not, what does?*

The sun does not regulate the period; it is a matter of common knowledge that the period of menstruation is coincident with certain phases of the moon. Each woman is differently related to the moon in her physical and psychical make-up; as the lunar influence causes oviation it follows that the same phase of the moon does not bring about the period in all women.

The moon causes the generative germ to mature and to leave the ovary. The moon has a similar influence on the male. The moon influences conception and makes it impossible during certain times, and determines the gestative period and the moment of birth. The moon is the chief factor in regulating these periods, and the moon is also a most important factor in foetal development, because the astral body of the mother and of the foetus is each directly connected with the moon. The sun also has an influence on the functions of generation; its influence is different from that of the moon, in that whereas the moon gives a magnetic quality and influence to the astral body and the fluids, the sun has to do with the electrical or life qualities of the body, and the character, nature and temperament of the body. The sun and moon influence man as well as woman. The solar influence is stronger in man, the lunar in woman.

A Friend

# JULY 1908

[From *The Word*, Vol. 7 No. 4]

*Can you tell me anything about the nature of fire or flame? It has always seemed a most mysterious thing. I can get no satisfactory information from scientific books.*

Fire is the spirit of the flame. Flame is the body of the fire.

Fire is the active energizing driving element in all bodies. Without fire all bodies would be immovably fixed—an impossibility. Fire is that in each body which compels the particles of the body to change. In man, fire acts in various ways. The element of fire enters through the breath and into the blood. It burns up the waste tissues which are carried away by the blood and removed through the excretory channels, such as the pores, lungs and intestinal canal. Fire causes the astral, molecular, form body of the physical to change. This constant change produces heat in the body. Fire and oxygen, the gross body in which fire manifests, stimulate the desires, causing outbursts of passion and anger, which burn up the astral body and use up the nerve force. Such action of fire is elemental and according to natural impulse.

There is another fire, known to some as the alchemical fire. The true alchemical fire is the fire of the mind in thought, which resists the elemental fires and controls and compels them to conform to intelligent design as determined by mind; whereas, when uncontrolled by man, the elemental fires of desire, passion and anger, are controlled by the universal mind, that is, the mind in nature, which is not individualized—called God, nature, or God acting through nature. Man, as an individual mind, acting on the elemental fires and compelling them to conform to intelligent design, causes them to enter into new combinations and the result of the combinations of elemental fires is thought. Through thought and in thought the fires of the body and elemental matter are given form in the invisible worlds. These forms of thoughts in the invisible worlds compel gross matter to adapt itself to the forms.

Some of the characteristics of fire and flame are that they are hot, that neither ever for an instant remains the same, that they are different from any other phenomenon that we know, that they give light, that they produce smoke, that they change forms by reducing them to ashes, that through flame, its body, fire appears as suddenly as it disappears, that they always go upward and are pointed. The fire which we see is that condition in which the spirit of the body, held in bondage by gross matter, is liberated and passes back into its primitive elemental state. On its own plane, in its own world, fire is free and active, but in the course of manifestation by involution the action of fire is reduced and controlled and finally is held within the bodies of which it is the spirit, for fire is the spirit in all bodies. The fire held in bond by gross matter we may call latent fire. This latent fire is in all the kingdoms of nature. Latent fire is, however, more active in some of the departments of each of the kingdoms than in other departments of the same kingdom. This is shown by flint and sulphur in the mineral, by hard wood and straw in the vegetable kingdom and by fat and skin in animal bodies. Latent fire is also in certain fluids, such as oil. An inflammable body requires the presence only of the active fire to evoke and free the latent from its prison. As soon as evoked, the latent fire becomes visible for a moment, then passes into the invisible world from which it came.

Fire is one of the four elements known to all occultists. Fire is the most occult of the elements. Not one of the elements known as fire, air, water and earth is visible to the eye, except in the grossest condition of that element. Therefore we see only the very lowest phases or aspects of the elements which we commonly speak of as earth, water, air and fire. Each of the four elements is necessary in the building up of physical matter, and each of the elements is represented in connection with each of the others. As each particle of physical matter holds the four elements in combination in certain proportions, each of the four elements is returned to its elemental condition as soon as the combination is broken up. Fire is that which usually breaks up the combination and causes the elements which entered into the combination to return to their original states. When fire is evoked, it being the chief factor in inflammable bodies, it appears simply to pass away. In passing away it also causes the elements air, water and earth to return to their several sources. The returning air and water are seen in the smoke. That part of the smoke which is air, and which is noticed usually in the quivering of the smoke, soon becomes invisible. That part of the smoke which is water returns to the element water by the moisture, also suspended in the air, and which becomes invisible. The only portion remaining is the grossest part of the element earth, which is in the soot and the ashes.

Besides latent fire there is chemical fire which is shown by the corrosive action of certain chemicals brought in contact with other chemicals, by the oxygen absorbed by the blood, and by the ferments which cause the digestion of foods. Then there is the alchemical fire which is generated by thought. The action of the alchemical fire of thought causes gross desire to be transmuted into a higher order of desire, which is again refined and sublimated into spiritual aspirations, all by the alchemical fire of thought. Then there is the spiritual fire which reduces all actions and thoughts into knowledge and builds up an immortal spiritual body, which may be symbolized by a spiritual fire-body.

ॐ

*What is the cause of great conflagrations, such as prairie fires and fires that seem to spring simultaneously from different parts of a city, and what is spontaneous combustion?*

There are many contributory causes of conflagrations, but these many causes are represented in the immediate cause of the conflagration, which is the presence of the fire element before the flame appears. It should be understood that fire as an element is capable of combining with other elements, on the plane of fire, or on other planes. By the combination of the different elements we get definite results. When the fire element is present in great force it dominates the other elements present and compels them to ignition by its overpowering presence. The presence of the fire element evokes the fire in neighboring bodies and through the transitional flame the imprisoned fire element passes back into its original source. The flame which leaps up is used by the fire which evokes it to enter into the world through the flame. When the fire element dominates the atmosphere in sufficient force it acts on all inflammable matter; then by the merest provocation, such as friction, this matter springs into flame. Prairie or forest fires may be caused from a traveler's camp fire, or by the rays of the setting sun, and incendiarism may be the cause of the burning of a great city, yet these are by no means the main cause at all times. One may often have noticed that the effort to build a fire under very favorable conditions is quite frequently followed by utter failure, whereas, on the throwing of a glowing match stick on a dock, or on the bare floor of a large building where nothing seems present that will easily burn, yet fire has been engendered by the glowing match stick and has spread so rapidly that it has burned an entire building to the ground, however great the efforts may have been to save it. Conflagrations which have consumed great cities are chiefly due to the presence of the fire element in every such case, however many the other contributory causes may be.

Spontaneous combustion is said to be the too rapidly uniting of inflammable matter with oxygen. But the cause is primarily due to the preparation of conflicting inflammable matter which attracts the fire element. Thus, the friction between two inflammable materials, such as oil and rags, is followed by the sudden uniting of the matter with the oxygen in the air; this induces the fire element, which starts the material into flame.

৵

*How are such metals as gold, copper and silver formed?*

There are seven metals, which are sometimes called the sacred metals. Each of these is the precipitated and imprisoned force, light or quality which emanates from one of the seven bodies of light which we see in space and call planets. The force, or light, or quality, of each of those bodies which we call planets is attracted by the earth with its moon. These forces are living and are called the elemental spirits of the elements or planets. The earth with its moon gives body and form to the elemental forces. The metals represent the seven stages or degrees through which the elemental forces must pass in the mineral kingdom before they can have distinct entity and pass into higher kingdoms of physical nature. There are many uses to which the seven metals may be put. Cures may be effected and diseases brought about by the use or misuse of the metals. The metals possess life giving as well as death-dealing qualities. Either of these may be evoked, consciously or unconsciously, when certain conditions prevail. It would be pedantic to give the order of the progression of the metals and their corresponding virtues, even though we were in possession of the facts, because, while there is an orderly progression from state to state of the elemental forces working through the metals, this order could not be made use of by all persons alike; what would apply to the benefit of one would be disastrous to another. Each person, although built according to the same plan, has in his composition certain qualities which correspond to the elemental spirits of the metals; some of these are beneficial, other are inimical. Generally speaking, however, gold represents the highest stage of development among the metals. The seven metals referred to are tin, gold, mercury, copper, lead, silver and iron. This enumeration should not be taken as the order of progression, or the reverse.

Metals most commonly used in past ages are not the most common at present. Gold is considered by us to be the most valuable of the seven metals, though it is not the most useful. We could more easily dispense with gold today than we can with iron. Of the metals, iron is the most necessary to our civilization, as it enters into all phases of industrial life, such as the erection of high structures, the building operation and use of steamships, of railroads, engines, tools, household utensils and furniture. It is used for decorative purposes, and it is valuable and essential in medicine. Other civilizations have run through their different periods, which are known as the golden, silver, bronze (or copper) and iron ages. The people of the earth, generally speaking, are in the iron age. It is an age which is hard and which changes more quickly than any of the others. What we do now will affect us more positively than at any other age because things move more rapidly in the iron age than in any other. Causes are followed by their consequences more swiftly in the iron than in any other age. The causes which we set up now will pass over into the age to follow. The age to follow is the golden age. In America, where a new race is forming, we have already entered it.

The seven metals here enumerated are numbered among the seventy odd elements postulated and tabulated by modern science. As to how they are formed we have said that the forces, lights, or qualities coming from the seven bodies in space, called planets, are attracted by the earth. The earth sets up a magnetic attraction and, owing to the prevailing conditions, there are precipitated these forces which are gradually built up by accretion, forming particle on particle within the magnetic belt attracting the force. Each of the seven forces is known by its particular color and quality and the manner in which the particles lie together. The time it takes for the formation of any one metal depends on prevailing conditions, as gold may be produced in an exceedingly short time when all the conditions necessary are present.

A FRIEND

# AUGUST 1908

[From *The Word,* Vol. 7 No. 5]

*Do you believe in astrology as a science? If so, how far is it to be consid-ered as relating to human life and interests?*

If astrology is, then astrology is a science. As the word indicates, astrology is the science of the stars. We believe that astrology is one of the greatest of sciences, but we also believe that the large majority of those who talk about astrology, who cast horoscopes or predict future events, know little more than the barest outline of some of the physical aspects of astrology. We believe a great deal in astrology and very little in the known astrologers. An astrologer is one who knows the laws which govern the bodies in space, in their inner and outer working, the influ-ences which come from and act on these bodies in their relation to each other, and the laws which govern and control these influences in their relation to each other and their action on man.

An astrologer is one who knows all this, but an astrologer is not one who talks what he knows. He knows that he cannot remain an astrologer and recount happenings in the past or foreshadow and predict coming events, and, for the service, receive money. An astrologer, in the real sense of the word, must have outgrown the things of the world and risen above the world in order to become a knower of the stars and all that is meant by "stars." For we believe the stars are not really known, even by the followers of so exact a science as astronomy. Astronomy deals with the motions, magnitudes, distances and physical constitution of celestial bodies. Astrology is the occult or secret science of astronomy. We believe that those little points of brilliance in what we call the sky mean far more for us than that which any astronomer or astrologer, writing under that title, has ever told.

The stars relate to human life and interests in so far as we can appreciate and understand them. They will always hold the interest of the human mind.

ᕒᕕ

*Why does the moment of birth into the physical world influence the destiny of the ego for that incarnation?*

The "moment" of birth is important to the future of the ego because at that time it is in a most critical condition, and all impressions received will have lasting effects. What is then done cannot well be undone. The influences prevailing at the moment of birth must have a peculiar effect on the future life because owing to the preponderance of the influence it will affect the sensitive astral body. Before it comes into the world, the body depends for its sustenance on the physical life of its parent. It lives in the world by proxy only. It lives in a world within the physical world. It has not yet breathed its own breath, which is the beginning of its independent sentient life. At the moment of birth the body is separated from its parent and no longer breathes by proxy, but it draws its own breath from its own parent ego. The body is no longer molded or shielded from the outward world and influences by the body of its mother; it lives in the world in its own body, without any other physical protection or covering. All the influences therefore which prevail at that time impress themselves indelibly on the newly-born astral body, which is then like a clean film or plate, ready to receive all impressions and influences, which are carried into life, even as the physical body may carry a scar or brand inflicted in early life. For this reason the moment of birth is important and will influence the after life in the world.

ᕒᕕ

*How does the moment of birth determine one's destiny in the world?*

That the moment of birth into the world may determine one's destiny we believe, but that it always decides destiny we do not believe.

Destiny is determined at birth only when one is willing to live exactly in accordance to the impetus received at the moment of birth. At the moment of birth the astral body of the infant is like a keenly sensitized photographic plate. Immediately it is exposed to the physical world the prevailing influences are impressed upon it. The first breathing of the infant records the influences and impressions on the keenly sensitized body, and these impressions are fastened on the astral body of the newly-born infant in much the same manner as impressions are received and retained on a photographic plate. Living according to one's destiny is therefore to follow out the suggestions indicated and live according to the impressions received at the moment of birth. These impressions are developed with the development of the body and the use of the mind. These impressions stand in the background and throw their pictures on the mind and the mind has its destiny given to it by these pictures. It, the mind, may act according to the impulses and suggestions coming from the impressions or it may map out a path quite different from the impressions received. This all depends on the mind or ego, as to whether it is strong enough and wills to do a work in the world other than that which is suggested by the natal influences.

ॐ

*How do the influences at birth, or one's destiny, cooperate with the karma of the ego?*

Karma is the result of what one has thought and done; what one has thought and done is his destiny, but the action and the destiny only applies to a certain period. The period here suggested is a lifetime. The destiny, therefore, for the period, is one's karma for the period; this period is the life of the body which is born into the world. One's thoughts and actions in one life cause and bring about the conditions for the next succeeding life; the influences prevailing at the birth are the indications of what one has done in the past and what he may expect in the present.

The moment of birth, therefore, must coincide and cooperate with the karma of that life, because it is karma, or the result of actions.

౪

*Are the planetary influences employed to administer human karma, or fate. If so, where does free will come in?*

Yes, planetary influences and all other influences are employed in carrying out and in determining fate. But a man's fate is what he himself has provided. What is his present fate may not be acceptable to him; nevertheless he has provided and must accept it. It might be said that a man would not provide a thing he did not like and, therefore, that he would not provide the fate which he did not wish. Such an objection is shortsighted. That which a man selects and provides either for himself or others must depend on his ability to select and his means to provide. An ignorant young man with much means, or an older man with little means, would each select and provide differently, according to his knowledge and means. What one selects and puts away as a boy for himself may not be at all appreciated in later years, because the boy has advanced with age in knowledge and in his appreciation of things, and the childish toy or trinket receives scant consideration as the result. One who has used little judgment in making a contract, is nevertheless bound to his contract, however many his regrets may be on learning the nature of the contract. He may protest, but protest will not relieve him from the obligation.

Either in the present or in the past life one has contracted for what he calls his fate. This is his own karma, or the contract which he has made. It is just. One's free will depends on not what he would whimsically wish to do, or long to obtain, but what he decides that he shall do. An honest man does not spend his energy in planning how to break a contract or relieve himself of his responsibilities. An honest man busies himself with how to fill his contract and meet his responsibilities. At the same time, if the contract or responsibilities are seen by him as undesirable he will not make another such contract, nor will he obligate himself to like responsibilities. Such contract and responsibilities are the fate or the karma, which one has made for himself.

His free will comes in when he decides how he will deal with his fate or karma. Will he try to escape it, or will he face and work through it? Herein lies his free will. As he acts by choice, so will he determine his future fate and be bound to that as he is bound to the present.

A FRIEND

# DECEMBER 1908

[From *The Word*, Vol. 8 No. 3]

*Why is it sometimes said that Jesus was one of the saviours of mankind and that the peoples of antiquity had also their saviours, instead of saying he was The Saviour of the world, as is held by all Christendom?*

The statement is due to several causes. Some make the statement because they have heard it made by others; some, who are acquainted with the history of the ancients, because the history of ancient peoples records the fact that they have had many saviours. The saviours of different peoples differ according to the needs of the people to whom they come, and the particular thing from which they are to be saved. Thus one saviour appeared to deliver the people from a pestilence, or famine, or from the invasions of an enemy or wild beast. Another saviour appeared to free the people to whom he came from savagery to teach them languages, the arts and sciences necessary to civilization, or to enlighten their minds and understanding. Anyone who has read somewhat of the religious systems of the world will plainly see that saviours appeared centuries or thousands of years before the date when Jesus is said to have been born.

If Jesus is said to be the saviour of the world by all Christendom, such declaration would be a manifesto of the ignorance and arrogance of all Christendom, but fortunately for Christendom this is not so. In late years especially, the western world has become and is becoming better acquainted with the histories and the scriptures of other peoples, and a more friendly feeling and good fellowship is being shown to those of other races and their faiths. The western world has learned to value the stores of wisdom contained within the literary treasures of ancient peoples. The old spirit of a few people being elected by God or self elected to be saved from the countless numbers of the past has disappeared and in its place is coming a recognition of justice and the rights of all.

ॐ

*Can you tell us if there are any people who celebrate the birth of their saviours on or around the twenty-fifth day of December (at the time that the sun is said to enter the sign Capricorn?"*

The twentieth day of December was a time of great rejoicing in Egypt, and a festival was held in honor of the birthday of Horus. Among the rites and ceremonies prescribed in the sacred books of China, the festival of other old religions is closely followed. During the last week in December, at the time of the winter solstice, the shops and the courts are closed. Religious solemnities are then celebrated and are called the festivals of Gratitude to Tie Tien. The Persian Mithras was called the mediator or saviour. They celebrated his birthday on the twenty-fifth of December amid great rejoicings. It was recognized that at that time the sun stands still and then begins to return northward after his long sojourn in the south, and it is said that forty days were set apart for thanksgiving and sacrifice. The Romans celebrated the twenty-fifth of December with a great festival in honor of Bacchus, as it was at that time that the sun began his return from the winter solstice. In later times, when many Persian ceremonies were introduced into Rome, the same day was solemnized as a festival in honor of Mithras, the spirit of the sun. The Hindus have six successive festivals. On the twenty-fifth of December people decorate their houses with garlands and gilt paper and universally make presents to friends and relatives. So it will be seen that at this date the peoples of antiquity as well worshipped and rejoiced. That it was at the time of the winter solstice cannot be mere accidents or coincidents. It is far more reasonable to suppose that, within all the apparent coincidences of the past, there is an underlying truth of deep mystic significance.

ॐ

*It is said by some that the birth of Christ is a spiritual birth. If this is so, why is it that Christmas is celebrated for the physical body by the eating*

*and drinking, in a material way, which is the very opposite of our concep-*
*tions of spirituality?*

The reasons for this dates back to the Christians of the early centuries. In their efforts to square their doctrines with the beliefs of the pagans and heathen, they incorporated the festivals of them into their own
calendar. This answered a double purpose: it satisfied the customs of
those people and led them to suppose that the time should be sacred to
the new faith. But, in adopting the feasts and festivals, the spirit which
prompted these was lost and only the most brutish symbols preserved
from among the men of the north, the Druids and the Romans. Wild
orgies were indulged in and full license was permitted; gluttony and
drunkenness prevailed during that time. With the early people, the cause
of their joy was due to their recognition of the Sun's having passed the
lowest point in his apparent course and from the twenty-fifth of
December began his journey, which would cause the return of spring
and would save them from the cold and desolation of winter. Nearly all
of our observances at the season of Christmas have their origin with the
ancients.

꧁

*In 'Moments with Friends,' of Vol. 4, page 189* [p. 34 in this book],
*it is said Christmas means 'The birth of the invisible sun of light, the*
*Christ Principle,' which, as it continues, 'Should be born within man.' If*
*this is so, does it follow that the physical birth of Jesus was also on the*
*twenty-fifth of December?*

No, it does not so follow. In fact it is stated in "Moments with
Friends" above referred to that Jesus is not the physical body. That it is
a distinct body from the physical—though it is born through and from
the physical. The manner of this birth is there set forth and a distinction
is there made between Jesus and the Christ. Jesus is a body which insures
immortality. In fact, immortality is not attained by any individual until
Jesus or the immortal body is born for him. It is this immortal body,
Jesus, or by what ever name it was known to the ancients, which is the

savior of man and not until its birth was he saved from death. The same law holds good today as it did then. One who dies has not become immortal, else he could not die. But one who has become immortal cannot die, else he is not immortal. Man must therefore attain immortality before death, or else reincarnate and continue to reincarnate, until he is saved from death by his immortal body Jesus. But Christ is not a body, as is Jesus. To us and for us, Christ is a principle and not a person or body. Therefore it has been said that Christ must be born within. This means, for those who are not immortal, that their minds are enlightened by the presence of the Christ principle and they are able to understand the truth of things.

ॐ

*If Jesus or Christ did not live and teach as he is supposed to have done, how is it that such an error could have prevailed for so many centuries and should prevail to-day?*

Errors and ignorance prevail until they are replaced by knowledge; with knowledge, ignorance disappears. There is not room for both. In the absence of knowledge, be it material or spiritual knowledge, we must accept the facts as they are. Wishing the facts to be different will not change them a jot. There are no facts in history concerning the birth of Jesus or Christ. The terms Jesus and Christ existed centuries prior to the reputed birth. We have no record of such a being at the time he is said to have been born. That one who had lived—and who had caused such a disturbance and recognition as an important character—should have been ignored by the historians of that period is absurd. Herod, the king, is said to have caused many infants to be slain to make sure that the "young child" should not live. Pilate is said to have sentenced Jesus, and Jesus is said to have risen after his crucifixion. None of these extraordinary events have been recorded by historians of that time. The only record that we have is that which is contained in the Gospels. In the face of these facts we cannot claim the reputed birth to be authentic. The best that can be done is to give it a place among the myths and legends of the world. That we continue in our error concerning the supposed birth and death of Jesus is not strange. It is a matter of custom and habit with us. The fault, if there is a fault, lies with those early church fathers who made the claim for and established the dogma of the birth and death of Jesus.

॥

*Do you mean to say that the history of Christianity is nothing but a fable, that the life of Christ is a myth, and that for nearly 2,000 years the world has been believing in a myth?*

The world has not believed in Christianity for nearly 2,000 years. The world does not believe in Christianity today. Christians themselves do not believe enough in the teachings of Jesus to live one hundredth part of them. Christians, as well as the rest of the world, oppose the teachings of Jesus in their life and work. No single teaching of Jesus is fully observed by Christians. As to the difference between fact and fable, we have mentioned that there are no facts concerning the historical birth and life of Jesus. Fable and myth are held by many Christians to be the basis of heathen religions, but the Christian faith is in the same class. As a matter of fact, the Christian religion has less basis in fact than have many of the great religions of the world. This does not mean that Christianity is false, nor that all religions are false. There is an old saying that within every mythos there is a logos. A myth is a narrative containing a profound truth. This is true of Christianity. The fact that so many have been benefited in the early history and in our times by the belief in the life and saving power of Jesus must have some secret power; herein lies its strength. The appearance of any great teacher or teaching is according to a certain law, the law of cycles, or of seasons. The time of the reputed birth of Jesus was the cycle or season for the promulgation and development of a newly revealed truth. We believe that at about that time there was among the people one who attained to immortality, the birth of a Jesus body already referred to, that having so attained, he gave out the teaching of immortality to those whom he considered able to receive and understand it, and that there gathered around him a number who were termed his disciples. That there is no history of this is due to his not being known to the people who were unacquainted with the mystery concerning the immortal life. Remaining and teaching his disciples for a time, he then left, and his teachings were promulgated by his disciples. The reason for the persistence in the belief of Christ and his teachings is that there is within man an underlying conviction in the possibility of his immortality. This latent belief finds expression in the teachings which the church distorted into their present form.

A FRIEND

# MARCH 1909

[From *The Word*, Vol. 8 No. 6]

*If astral intelligences are capable of seeing through matter, why is it that no spirit control of a medium is able to meet the now famous orange counting test?*

This question refers to a test to which the Psychical Research Society has put its subjects. It is said that it has offered the sum of five thousand dollars to any medium who can tell the exact number of oranges as they are poured out of a bag into a basket or similar object placed to receive them.

Up to the present time no one has been able to either guess or tell the exact number of oranges on the table or in a basket, though many have made the attempt.

If the correct answer is to be given, it must be given either by the intelligence of the medium or by that intelligence which controls the medium. If the intelligence of the medium were able to solve the problem there would be no need of a control; but neither the medium nor the control has solved the problem. The problem involves not the ability to see through matter, but to compute numbers. Both medium and control may be able to see through matter, as a child might through a glass see the people passing on the opposite side of the street. But if the child has not learned the mental operation of counting, it will not be able to tell the number in front of the window at any given time. It requires a mind trained in counting to be able to add up a large column of figures quickly, and still more trained must be the mind which is able to tell how many coins there are in a group or how many people in a crowd.

As a rule, the mentality of mediums is not of a high order, and the controls of the mediums are below the average of ordinary human beings. A clairvoyant or a control of a medium may, like a child in a library, art gallery or flower garden, see the objects therein. Like the child the control of the medium or the clairvoyant might speak of the strange books in their costly cases, or of the wonderful pieces of art, and of the beautiful flowers, but would be at a woeful loss to deal with the subject matter of the books, to criticize and describe the art treasures or to speak of the flowers in terms other than descriptive. The ability to see through matter does not include the capacity to know what is seen.

A direct answer to the question as to why no medium has been able to qualify for the test is: because no human being has so trained his mind as to be able to compute at a glance the units making up a large number. This is why the medium is not able to clairvoyantly tell the number of oranges in a large bag or basket. A "spirit control" knows no more, where mental operations are concerned, than the mind of that control knew at any time when it was the informing principle of a human being.

If any of those present were able to perform the mental operation of computing the number and would hold the number in his mind, either the control or the medium would be able to give the answer. But inasmuch as none of the minds present can do this, the control is also unable to do it. No control of any medium is able to perform a mental operation that has never been performed by human beings.

ॐ

*What explanation can Theosophy offer for the terrific earthquakes which so frequently occur, and which may destroy thousands of people?*

According to Theosophy all things in the universe are related to each other. Men, plants, animals, water, air, earth and all the elements act and react on each other. Gross bodies are moved by finer bodies, unintelligent bodies are moved by intelligence, and all matter circulates throughout the domains of nature. Every catastrophe as an effect must have been the result of a cause. All phenomena attended by good or disastrous results are the outcome and results of the thoughts of man.

The thoughts of a people surround or ascend and form in groups or clouds as it were above and around that people, and the cloud of thought is of the nature of the people who form it. Each thought of each person adds to the general sum of the thought which is suspended over the people. So each country has hanging over it and about it the thoughts and nature of the people who live on the land. As the atmosphere of the earth has forces playing through it which affect the earth, so the mental atmosphere in clouds of thoughts also affect the earth. As the conflicting elements in the atmosphere, result and find their vent in a storm, so conflicting thoughts in the mental atmosphere must also find their expression through physical phenomena and such phenomena as are of the nature of the thoughts.

The atmosphere of the earth and the mental atmosphere of men react on the forces of the earth. There is a circulation of the forces within and outside the earth; these forces and their action in any particular part of the earth conform to the general laws which control the earth as a whole. As the races of men appear, develop and decay on different parts of the earth, and as the earth, too, must change its structure in the course of ages, the changes necessary to the general development must be brought about, resulting in change of the inclination of the axis of the earth and of the earth's conformation.

An earthquake is caused by an attempt, by the effort of the earth to adjust itself to the forces which affect it and to equalize and to balance itself in its changes. When large numbers of people are destroyed by an earthquake it means that not only is the earth adjusting itself according to a geographical plan, but that the majority of those who suffer death have met it in this way on account of the karmic causes which they have engendered.

A FRIEND

# JUNE 1909

[From *The Word,* Vol. 9 No. 3]

*What is a divine incarnation or incarnation of the Supreme Being?*

The word incarnation means that which has come into a body of flesh. Divine incarnation means deity in a human form of flesh. A Divine incarnation means one of the many appearances of Deity in a human form, which appearances, or Divine incarnations as they are called, have been mentioned in all great religious histories. The appearance of a Divine incarnation is attended by the founding of a new religion, which takes in a human form, which appearances or has its name given to it by later followers. Philosophically, God, Universal Mind, or Deity, is a collective host of Divine Intelligences who are beyond the necessity for reincarnation and beyond all human weaknesses and frailties. This collective host of intelligences who are Divine is sometimes spoken of as the Logos. At periods regulated by law, one of this Divine host, or Universal Mind, or God, appears on earth to assist humanity in its progress and development toward immortality and Divinity. When such an event does take place it is said to be the incarnation of a saviour an avatar, of the Logos, the Demiurgos, the Universal Mind, Deity, the Great Spirit or God, according to the terminology of the people who record the event. There is a considerable philosophy attached to such an event, and there are many degrees and kinds of Divine incarnations. But specifically answering the question regarding a Divine incarnation of the Supreme Being is that one of the Divine host has taken up its abode with a mortal human being who is sufficiently pure and progressed, physically, intellectually and spiritually, to warrant the Divine contact.

⁊♥

*What is the use or function of the pituitary body?*

Physiologically, the most advanced understanding concerning the pituitary body is that it is the governing seat or center of the nervous system. It is composed of two lobes, the posterior lobe being that which receives all impressions of the body from the sensory nerves, and the anterior lobe being that from which the motor nerves are regulated and directed. We would say that the pituitary body is the heart of the nervous system just as the muscular heart is the center of the circulatory system. As the blood flows from the heart through the body by means of the arteries and returns by way of the veins to the heart, so there is a nervous fluid or ether which circulates through the body from the pituitary body by way of the motor nerves and back through the sensory nerves to the pituitary body. The pituitary body is the center in the brain by which the human Ego contacts the physical body, and by which center the human Ego passes through the states known as waking, dreaming, and deep sleep. When the human Ego is acting directly on or with the pituitary body man is said to be awake and to be conscious of his body and the world around him. When the Ego retires from immediate contact or control of the pituitary body, it does so that the body may rest and be recuperated by the life forces of the world which flow in and out of the body, when not interfered with by the tension brought about by the activity of the mind with or on the pituitary body. As the mind or Ego loosens its hold on the pituitary body and retires along the other centers of the brain the dreaming, and deep sleep states with their intermediate conditions are brought about.

*What is the use or function of the pineal gland?*

Both the pituitary body and pineal gland are organs which are centers of contact for the soul of man. But whereas the pituitary body is that center which is used directly by the human mind in all things requiring mental operations, the pineal gland is the organ by which the higher and more divine individuality of man is related. The pituitary body is used in all ratiocinative processes and mental operations requiring the activity of the reasoning faculties. The pineal gland is used when direct knowledge of a thing is to be obtained. The pineal gland is the organ through which is brought to the human understanding that knowledge and wisdom which is complete in itself, self-evident, without the process of reasoning. The pineal gland is the organ which is used consciously and intelligently by one possessed of spiritual understanding and wisdom. This applies to the spiritually wise. To ordinary mankind the pituitary body is used without his immediate knowledge in the same manner that he may think but does not know how he thinks. In the ordinary man the pineal gland is a present witness to the possibilities of the future Divinity of mankind. But at present it is as silent as the tomb.

છ

*What is the use or function of the spleen?*

The spleen is one of the centers of the astral or form body. The spleen serves particularly in early life to establish the relationship between the molecular, astral form body to the cellular structure of physical matter, by means of the process of circulation. It is related both to the circulation of the blood and of the lymphatic system. After the body is set in its habits and the form of the body has been definitely established, the spleen can be dispensed with because the astral form body is then seated in every part of the body.

છ

*What is the use or function of the thyroid gland?*

The thyroid gland is one of the centers in the body on which the entity who is to take possession of the body acts before birth. It is directly related with the pituitary body and is a reservoir or storage battery from which is liberated certain chemical ingredients necessary to the bony structure of the body, and holds also a tincture which acts on the blood. The thyroid gland is an organ with which the mind acts in the body. The thyroid gland, pituitary body and pineal gland all have to do with the bony structure of the body and with the mind. When these glands are affected it interferes with the normal action of the mind and in many cases will cause death or so affect the mind as to bring about temporary idiocy or aberrations of the mind.

A FRIEND

[From *The Word*, Vol. 9 No. 4]

*Have animals minds and do they think?*

Some animals exhibit remarkable ability to understand what is said to them and will do what they are told as if they understood. Animals have not minds as the human being understands the word, nor do they think, though they do appear to understand much that is said to them and will do many of the things which they are told to do. Mind is the individualizing principle in man which causes him and enables him to think of himself as I-am-I. Animals have not this principle and nothing in their actions or behavior would suggest that they have it. Not having mind, they cannot think because thought is possible only by the presence of mind with desire. Animals have desire as their dominant and actuating principle, but they have no mind as have human animal bodies.

In a different sense than in the human, the animal has mind. The sense in which an animal may be said to have mind is that it acts from the impulse of the universal mind, without any such individualizing principle. Every animal, which is not immediately under the influence of man, acts according to its nature. An animal cannot act different than its nature, which is the animal nature. Man can act according to his animal nature strictly, or according to ordinary human instincts and social or business customs, or he may transcend the animal and the ordinary human and act in a saintly and God-like manner. This choice of his action which man has, is possible because he has a mind or is a mind. If the animal had or was a mind it would be possible for some such choice to be noticed in its action. But an animal never acts differently than the species to which it belongs, and which specie determines the animal's nature and action. This all applies to the animal in its natural and native state or condition and when it is not interfered with nor comes under the immediate influence of man. When man brings an animal under his influence he changes that animal to the extent that he exerts his influence upon it. Man is able to exert his mental influence upon the animal in a similar manner in which he exerts the influence of his mind upon the animal in himself. Desire is the principle of the animal, mind the characteristic principle of man. Desire is the vehicle of mind. Desire is the matter with which mind works. The reason that animals can be trained to obey the commands of man is because the principle of desire will respond to the action of mind and obey its dictates when the mind persists in its efforts to rule the animal. The animal therefore does not do the thinking when carrying out the orders of a man. The animal simply obeys automatically the thought of the mind which directs it. In illustration of this it may be said that no animal has been known to understand and obey an order which is different from other orders before given it. Each thing that it does is similar in kind to what it has been taught by man to do. The character of mind is to plan, to compare, to originate. No animal has the ability or capacity either to plan a thing, to compare by argument, or to originate a course of action for itself or another animal. Animals perform tricks or obey orders because they have been taught and trained to perform and obey them and this is due to the mind of man thrown onto the desire of the animal which reflects his thought in action.

ॐ

*Will any evil influence be brought to human beings by the presence of domestic animals?*

That depends on the human being more than it does upon the animal. Each may help the other, but as to how much help may be given or harm done is to be decided by the human. The animal is helped by the association with man if man will teach and control the animal with kindness. The animal in its wild and native state requires no human aid, but when by breeding and domestication man brings the animal under the influence of his mind, the animal is no longer able or has the opportunity to hunt for its own food for itself and young. Then man becomes responsible for the animal; and having assumed such responsibility it is man's duty to care for and protect the animal. Man does this not because he desires the elevation and education of the animal but because he desires to put the animal to his own uses. In this way we have domesticated such animals as the horse, cow, sheep, goat, dog and fowls. The entities which animate the bodies of the animals are being educated to certain uses with the animal bodies preparatory to animating a human body in some future evolution or world. In this way there is an exchange made between the animal, and man. The animal is educated by man for the services which it renders man. The desire principle of the animal is acted on by the mind of man, and by such continual action and reaction the desire principle of the animal is prepared by the human principle of the mind of man, so that in some far distant period the desire principle of the animal may be brought up to a state allowing it to associate immediately and directly with mind. Man will fulfill his duty better if he does his duty intelligently and cheerfully instead of by force of circumstances and grudgingly. Man will help the animals if he regards them in the light just outlined and will treat them kindly and with consideration and will show them a certain affection; they would then respond to his wishes in a manner that would amaze him. In showing them affection, however, care should be exercised. Such affection should not be that of a foolish and whimsical petting, but the affection that one feels for the soul in all living creatures. If man would do this he would develop the animals and they would respond to him in a way that would cause the present man to think positively that the animals had intelligence in the sense of having the reasoning faculty. But even then, if the animal appeared to act far more intelligently than the best do at present they would still not be possessed of the power of thought or of the reasoning faculty.

The association between the human and the animal is evil and pernicious when animals are brought out of their sphere by silly human beings and made to fill a place which is neither animal, human nor divine. This is done by men or women who attempt to make an idol out of some animal pet. Usually a dog or cat is selected for such purpose. The pet is made an object of adoration or worship. The poor human being pours out from an overflowing heart a wealth of silly words on the object of its adoration. The idolization of pets has been carried to such extremes as to have the pet tailored in the latest or special fashions and made to wear jeweled necklaces or other ornaments, and to have specially liveried attendants for cleaning perfuming and feeding it. In one case they took walks with a dog or drove it in a special carriage that it might have the fresh air without being fatigued. The pet was thus nurtured through its life and when death came it was placed in an elaborate casket; ceremonies were performed over it and it was followed by its worshipper and her friends to a cemetery specially prepared for it, where it was laid to rest in pleasant surroundings and a monument placed over it to commemorate the sad event. An animal is not to be blamed for such as this; all blame is to be attached to the human. But the animal is injured by such action because it is taken out of its natural sphere and put into a sphere where it does not belong. It is then unfitted to re-enter the sphere from which it has been taken and is unable to act naturally, usefully and properly in the position given it by the abnormal human being. Such action is an abuse of opportunity of position by the human, who will forfeit all right and claim by such abuse to a like position in a future life. The wasted opportunity of position, the waste of money, the degradation of other human beings in compelling them to be servants of the pet, and in unfitting the animal to the place given it, will all have to be paid for in misery, disappointment and degradation in future lives. There are few punishments too severe for a human being who makes an idol out of an animal and worships that animal. Such action is an attempt to make a potential god the servant of a beast, and such attempt must receive its just deserts.

Under certain conditions the influence of animals is very injurious to certain human beings. For instance, when a person is weak or asleep a cat or an old dog should not be allowed to touch the body, because when the body has not the presence of its mind or the mind is not conscious in the human body, the animal magnetism of the human body will be drawn off by the dog or cat or other animal which touches it. The animal instinctively crouches near or touches the human body because it receives a certain virtue from it. An evidence of this is that a dog, an old dog especially, will always rub up against a human body. This he does for a double purpose; in order to be scratched, but more particularly because he receives a certain magnetic influence from the human body which he appropriates. It may have been frequently noticed that a cat will select some person who lies asleep and will curl itself up on his chest and purr contentedly as it absorbs the magnetism of the sleeping person. If this is continued night after night the person will become weaker and weaker until even death may result. Because animals may absorb magnetism from man, that should not cause man to shun an animal or to be unkind to it, but rather make him use his judgment in dealing with animals, show them all kindness and the affection that man should feel for all living creatures; but he should also train them by the exercise of discipline, which will educate them into useful and dutiful beings, instead of allowing them to do as they please, because he is either too lazy or careless to train them or because he shows foolish and extravagant indulgence of their impulses.

A FRIEND

# AUGUST 1909

[From *The Word*, Vol. 9 No. 5]

*Is there any ground for the claim of those who say that the souls of departed men incarnate in birds or animals?*

There is some ground for the claim, but the statement as a whole is untrue. Human souls do not reincarnate into birds or animals unless these terms are applied to human beings. After the death of a human, the principles of which his mortal part was composed return into the respective kingdoms or realms from which they had been drawn for the building of the body of the mortal man. There are many grounds on which the claim may be made that the human soul may return to life in the body of an animal. The chief cause of such statement is superstition and tradition; but tradition often preserves a deep truth in absurd literal form. Superstition is the form which was the basis of former knowledge. One who holds a superstition without knowing what it means believes in the form, but has not the knowledge. Those who in modern times believe in the tradition that human souls do reincarnate into animals, cling to the superstition or tradition because they have lost the knowledge which the outward and literal statement conceals. The purpose of incarnation and reincarnation of the mind into bodies is that it shall learn what life in the world can teach. The instrument through which it learns is the animal human form. After it has passed from one human form at death and is about to reincarnate it builds up for itself and enters another animal human form. But it does not enter any of the species of animals. It does not enter a body of an animal. The reason is that the strictly animal form will not offer the opportunity for continuing its education. The animal body would only retard the mind. The mistakes of one life could not be rectified by the mind in an animal body if it were possible for the mind to be in an animal body, because the animal organism and brain could not respond to the touch of the individual mind. The human stage in development of the brain is necessary for the mind to contact the human animal form; the animal brain is not a fit instrument for the human mind to work through. If it were possible for the mind to reincarnate into an animal, the mind, while so incarnate, would be unconscious of itself as a mind in the animal body. Such incarnation of the mind in an animal body would be to no purpose, as no mistake could be corrected and atoned for. Mistakes can be corrected, wrongs righted and lessons learned and knowledge acquired only while the mind is in a human body, and can contact a brain which will respond to its touch. It is therefore unreasonable to suppose that anything could be accomplished by a law that a mind which has acted through a human form should incarnate into any of the animal types.

સ

*It is said in the Editorial on Thought, The Word, Vol. 2, No. 3, December, 1905 [p. 62 in Monthly Editorials From THE WORD Part I], that: "Man thinks and nature responds by marshalling his thoughts in a continuous procession while he looks on with wondering gaze unmindful of the cause. . . . Man thinks and fructifies nature by his thought, and nature brings forth her progeny in all organic forms as the children of his thoughts. Trees, flowers, beasts, reptiles, birds, are in their forms the crystallization of his thoughts, while in each of their different natures is a portrayal and specialization of one of his particular desires. Nature reproduces according to a given type, but the thought of man determines the type and the type changes only with his thought. . . . The entities experiencing life in animal bodies must have their character and form determined by the thought of man until they themselves can think. Then they will no longer need his aid, but will build their own forms even as the thought of man now builds his own and theirs." Can you explain more fully how the different thoughts of man act on the matter of the physical world so as to produce different kinds of animals such as the lion, bear, peacock, rattlesnake?*

To answer this question would necessitate writing an article such as one of The Word editorials. This cannot be done in the space devoted to Moments with Friends, and it must be left to the editorial department of this magazine. We shall attempt, however, to outline the principle by which that which is stated in the above quotation is accomplished.

Among all living creatures man is the only being who has the creative faculty (as distinguished from procreative.) The creative faculty is his power of thought and of will. Thought is the product of the action of mind and desire. When mind acts on desire thought is generated and thought takes its form in the life matter of the world. This life matter is on a super-physical plane. The thoughts which take form exist in the super-physical state on the plane of thought. Desire as a cosmic principle acted on by the mind of man produces thoughts according to the nature of the mind and the desire. These thoughts when so produced are the types of forms which appear in the world, and these types of forms are animated by certain entities or phases of life which cannot create forms for themselves.

Man has within him the nature of every animal in the world. Each animal type or species represents a particular desire and is to be found in human beings. But though all animal natures are in man, he, that is, his type, is human, and the animals in him are seen at such times only as he allows passions and desires to take possession of and manifest their nature through him. It is as though all animal creation were of so many strands which were drawn together and wound up within his body and he is the composite animal of all animal creation. Watch the face of a man when he is seized by a paroxysm of passion, and the nature of the then dominant animal will be clearly seen in him. The wolf looks out of his face and can be seen in his manner. The tiger pants through him as if he would rush on his prey. The snake hisses through his speech and glitters through his eyes. The lion roars as anger or lust works through his body. Any one of these gives place to the other as it passes through his body, and the expression of his face changes even in type. It is when man thinks in the nature of the tiger or wolf or fox that he creates the thought of tiger, wolf, or fox, and the thought lives in the life world until it is drawn into the lower psychical worlds to give form to the entities coming into existence through procreation. All of these different animal types pass through the form and are given expression in the face of man as pictures moved behind a screen. However, it is not possible for the wolf to look like a fox or the fox like a tiger or either of these like a snake. Each animal acts according to its nature and never acts like any other kind of animal than itself. This is so because, as stated in the quotation, and as will be later shown, each animal is a specialization, a particular type of desire in man. Thought is the creator of all forms in the world, and man is the only animal which thinks. He stands in relation to the physical world as God, the creator, is said to be related to man. But there is another way in which man is the cause of the appearance of animals in the physical world. This will also explain one of the many meanings of and is the reason for the statement in ancient scriptures that man may reincarnate or transmigrate into the bodies of animals. It is this: During life the desire in man is a manifold animal principle, which has no definite form. During the life of man, the desire in him is ever changing, and no definite type of animal remains in evidence very long with him. The wolf is followed by the fox, the fox by the bear, the bear by the goat, the goat by the sheep and so on, or in any order, and this continues usually through life unless there is a pronounced tendency in a man where one of the many animals dominates the others in his nature and he is a sheep or fox or wolf or bear all his life. But in any case, at death, the changing desire of his nature is fixed into one definite animal type which may still have for a time the human astral form. After the mind has departed from its animal, the animal gradually looses the controlling outline of the human and takes on its true animal type. This animal then is a creature with no vestige of humanity. It is this animal which will coalesce with the thought type created for it and according to the thought type and its animal nature it is born into the world through an animal body of its kind which was previously called into existence in the same manner.

A FRIEND

# SEPTEMBER 1909

[From *The Word,* Vol. 9 No. 6]

*Can one look inside his body and see the workings of the different organs, and if so how can this be done?*

One may look inside his body and see there the different organs in operation. This is done by the faculty of sight, but not sight which is limited to physical things. The eye is trained to see physical objects. The eye will not register vibrations below or above the physical octave, and the mind therefore cannot translate intelligently what the eye cannot transmit to it. There are vibrations which are below the physical octave, and also others above it. To record these vibrations the eye must be trained. It is possible to train the eye so that it may record objects which are invisible to ordinary sight. But a different method is necessary in order that one may see an organ as a physical object inside his own body. The faculty of inner instead of outer vision has to be developed. For one not gifted with such a faculty it is necessary to begin by developing the faculty of introspection, which is a mental process. With the development of introspection would also be developed the power of analysis. By this training the mind distinguishes itself from the organs which it has under consideration. Later, the mind will be able to locate an organ mentally and, by centering the thought on it, feel its pulsations. The addition of the sense of feeling to the mental perception enables the mind to perceive more keenly and then to develop the mental vision concerning the organ. At first the organ is not seen, as are physical objects, but is rather a mental conception. Later, however, the organ may be as clearly perceived as any physical object. The light in which it is seen is not physical light vibration, but rather a light which is furnished by the mind itself and thrown on the organ under examination. Though the organ is seen and its function understood by the mind, this is not physical sight. By this inner sight the organ is perceived more clearly and understood more thoroughly than physical objects usually are.

There is another means of seeing the organs in one's body, which is not, however, arrived at by a course of mental training. This other means is a course of psychic development. It is brought about by changing one's conscious condition from his physical to his psychic body. When this is done, the astral or clairvoyant sight becomes operative, and in this case the astral body usually leaves the physical temporarily or is but loosely connected with it. In this condition the physical organ is seen in its astral counterpart in the astral body as one looking into a mirror does not see his face but the reflection or counterpart of his face. This is to be taken by way of illustration, because one's astral body is the design of the physical body, and each organ in the body has its particular model in detail in the astral body. Every movement of the physical body is an action or reaction or physical expression of the astral body; the condition of the physical body is indicated truly in the astral body. Therefore, one may in a clairvoyant state see his own astral body, as in the physical state he may see his physical body and in that state he will be able to see all parts within and without his body, because the faculty of astral or true clairvoyant vision is not limited to the outside of things as is the physical.

There are many ways of developing the clairvoyant faculty, but only one is recommended to the readers of Moments with Friends. This method is that the mind should be first developed. After the mind becomes mature, the clairvoyant faculty will, if desired, come as naturally as the blossoms of a tree in spring. If the blossoms are forced before their proper season, the frost will kill them, no fruit will follow, and oftentimes the tree itself dies. The clairvoyant or other psychic faculties may be acquired before the mind has reached its maturity and is master of the body, but they will be of as little use as are the senses to an idiot. A half developed clairvoyant will not know how to use them intelligently, and they may be the means of causing misery of the mind.

One of many means for the development of the mind is to do one's duty cheerfully and ungrudgingly. This is a beginning and it is all that can be done at first. It will be found if tried, that the path of duty is the path to knowledge. As one does his duty he gets knowledge, and will become freed from the necessity of that duty. Each duty leads to a higher duty and all duties well done end in knowledge.

A FRIEND

# OCTOBER 1909

[From *The Word,* Vol. 10 No. 1]

*In what essential points does the astral world differ from the spiritual? These terms are often used interchangeably in books and magazines dealing with these subjects, and this use is apt to confuse the mind of the reader.*

"Astral world" and "spiritual world" are not synonymous terms. They cannot be so used by one who is acquainted with the subject. The astral world is essentially a world of reflections. In it the physical world and all doings in the physical are reflected, and within the astral are also reflected the thoughts of the mental world, and, through the mental world, the ideas of the spiritual world. The spiritual world is the realm in which all things are known to be as they are, there no deception can be practiced on those beings who live consciously in it. The spiritual world is the realm in which one when he enters, finds no confusion, but knows and is known. The distinguishing characteristics of the two worlds are desire and knowledge. Desire is the ruling force in the astral world. Knowledge is the ruling principle in the spiritual world. Beings inhabit the astral world as animals inhabit the physical world. They are moved and guided by desire. Other beings inhabit the spiritual world and they are moved by knowledge. While one is confused and uncertain about a thing he need not consider that he is "spiritually minded," though it is quite likely that he may be psychic. One who may enter the spiritual world of knowledge is in no uncertain state of mind about it. He does not merely desire to be, nor does he guess, or believe, or think that he knows. If he knows the spiritual world it is knowledge with him and not guesswork. The difference between the astral world and the spiritual world is the difference which there is between desire and knowledge.

෨෩

*Is each organ of the body an intelligent entity or does it do its work automatically?*

No organ in the body is intelligent though every organ is conscious. Each organic structure in the world must be conscious if it has any functional activity. If it were not conscious of its function it could not perform it. But an organ is not intelligent if by intelligence is meant an entity with mind. By an intelligence we mean a being who may be higher, but who is not lower, than the state of man. The organs of the body are not intelligent, but they act under a guiding intelligence. Each organ in the body is governed by an entity who is conscious of the organ's particular function. By this conscious function the organ causes the cells and molecules and atoms which compose it, to contribute in work to the function of the organ. Each atom entering into the makeup of a molecule is ruled by the conscious entity of the molecule. Each molecule entering into the composition of a cell is controlled by the dominant influence of the cell. Each cell making up the structure of an organ is directed by the organic conscious entity of the organ, and each organ as a component part of the bodily organization is governed by a conscious co-ordinating formative principle which governs the organization of the body as a whole. Atom, molecule, cell, organ are each conscious in their particular sphere of action. But none of these can be said to be intelligent though they perform their work in their different fields of action with mechanical exactness.

❧

*If each organ or part of the physical body is represented in the mind, then why does an insane person not lose the use of his body when he loses the use of his mind?*

The mind has seven functions, but the body has a greater number of organs. Therefore, not each organ can represent or be represented by a particular function of the mind. The organs of the body may be divided into many classes. The first division could be made by distinguishing the organs which have, as their first duty the care and preservation of the body. Among these come first the organs which are engaged in digestion and assimilation. These organs, such as the stomach, liver, kidneys and spleen are in the abdominal section of the body. Next are those in the thoracic cavity, the heart and lungs, which have to do with the oxygenation and purification of the blood. These organs act involuntarily and without control of the mind. Among the organs connected with the mind primarily are the pituitary body and pineal gland and certain other interior organs of the brain. A person who has lost the use of his mind will, as a matter of fact, appear upon examination to have some of these organs affected. Insanity may be due to one or many causes. Sometimes the immediate cause is physical only, or it may be due to some psychically abnormal condition, or insanity may be due to the mind having entirely left and departed from a person. Insanity may be brought about by some physical cause, such as a disease of one of the internal organs of the brain, or by an abnormal condition or loss of the thyroid gland. If any of the organs which are connected with the mind, or through which the mind operates the physical body, are lost or their action interfered with, then the mind cannot act directly upon and through the physical body, though it may be connected with it. The mind is then like a bicyclist whose machine has lost its pedals, and though upon it, he cannot make it go. Or the mind may be likened to a rider strapped to his horse, but whose arms and legs are tied and his mouth gagged so that he is unable to direct the animal. Owing to some affection or loss of an organ of the body by which the mind operates or controls the body, the mind may be in contact with the body but unable to guide it.

A FRIEND

# NOVEMBER 1909

[From *The Word*, Vol. 10 No. 2]

*It does not seem reasonable that two or more contradictory opinions can be right concerning any truth. Why are there so many opinions concerning some problems or things? How then shall we be able to tell which opinion is right and what the truth is?*

The abstract One Truth cannot be proven or demonstrated to the human mind, nor could the human mind understand such proof or demonstration were it possible to give it, any more than the laws, organization, and work of a universe can be proven to a bumble bee, or than a tadpole can understand the building and operation of a locomotive. But although the human mind cannot understand the One Truth in the abstract, it is possible to understand something of a truth concerning any thing or problem in the manifested universe. A truth is a thing as it is. It is possible for the human mind to be so trained and developed that it may know any thing as it is. There are three stages or degrees which the human mind must pass through, before it can know any thing as it is. The first state is ignorance, or darkness; the second is opinion, or belief; the third is knowledge, or a truth as it is.

Ignorance is the state of mental darkness in which the mind may dimly perceive a thing, but is quite unable to understand it. When in ignorance the mind moves in and is controlled by the senses. The senses so cloud, color and confuse the mind that the mind is unable to distinguish between the cloud of ignorance and the thing as it is. The mind remains ignorant while it is controlled, directed and guided by the senses. To get out of the darkness of ignorance, the mind must concern itself with the understanding of things as distinguished from the sensing of things. When the mind tries to understand a thing, as distinguished from sensing the thing, it must think. Thinking causes the mind to pass out of the state of dark ignorance into the state of opinion. The state of opinion is that in which the mind senses a thing and tries to find out what it is. When the mind concerns itself with any thing or problem it begins to separate itself as a thinker from the thing about which it concerns itself. Then it begins to have opinions about things. These opinions did not concern it while it was satisfied with the state of ignorance, any more than the mentally lazy or sensuous minded will busy themselves with opinions concerning things which do not apply to the senses. But they will have opinions concerning things of a sensuous nature. Opinion is the state in which the mind cannot clearly see a truth, or the thing as it is, as distinct from the senses, or objects as they appear to be. One's opinions form his beliefs. His beliefs are the results of his opinions. Opinion is the middle world between darkness and light. It is the world in which the senses and changing objects commingle with the light and shadows and reflections of the objects are seen. In this state of opinion the mind cannot or does not distinguish the shadow from the object which casts it, and is not able to see the light as distinct from shadow or object. To get out of the state of opinion, the mind must try to understand the difference between the light, the object, and its reflection or shadow. When the mind so tries it begins to distinguish between right opinions and wrong opinions. Right opinion is the ability of the mind to decide as to difference between the thing and its reflection and shadow, or to see the thing as it is. Wrong opinion is the mistaking of the reflection or shadow of a thing for the thing itself. While in the state of opinion the mind cannot see the light as distinct from right and wrong opinions, nor the objects as different from their reflections and shadows. To be able to have right opinions, one must free the mind from prejudice and the influence of the senses. The senses so color or influence the mind as to produce prejudice, and where prejudice is there is no right opinion. Thought and the training of the mind to think are necessary to form right opinions. When the mind has formed a right opinion and refuses to allow the senses to influence or prejudice the mind against the right opinion, and holds that right opinion, no matter if it may be against one's position or the interest of one's self or friends, and clings to the right opinion before and in preference to all else, then the mind will for the time being pass into the state of knowledge. The mind will then not have an opinion about a thing nor be confused by contradictory other opinions, but will know that the thing is as it is. One passes out of the state of opinions or beliefs, and into the state of knowledge or light, by holding to what he knows to be true in preference to all else. He learns to live by knowledge instead of living as theretofore, by ignorance and opinion.

The mind learns to know the truth of any thing by concerning itself with that thing. In the state of knowledge, after it has learned to think and has been able to arrive at right opinions by freedom from prejudice and by continued thinking, the mind sees any thing as it is and knows that it is as it is by a light, which is the light of knowledge. While in the state of ignorance it was impossible to see, and while in the state of opinions it did not see the light, but now in the state of knowledge the mind does see the light, as distinguished from a thing and its reflections and shadows. This light of knowledge means that the truth of a thing is known, that any thing is known to be as it is truly and not as it appears to be when clouded by ignorance or confused by opinions. This light of true knowledge will not be mistaken for any other lights or light which is known to the mind in ignorance or opinion. The light of knowledge is in itself proof beyond question. When this is seen, it is because thinking is done away with by knowledge, as when one knows a thing he no longer goes through the laborious process of reasoning about that which he has already reasoned about and now knows.

If one enters a dark room, he feels his way about the room and may stumble over objects in it, and bruise himself against the furniture and walls, or collide with others who are moving as aimlessly as himself in the room. This is the state of ignorance in which the ignorant live. After he has moved about the room his eyes become accustomed to the darkness, and by trying he is able to distinguish the dim outline of the object and the moving figures in the room. This is like the passing from the state of ignorance into the state of opinion where man is able to distinguish one thing dimly from another thing and to understand how not to collide with other moving figures. Let us suppose that the one in this state now bethinks himself of a light hitherto carried and concealed about his person, and let us suppose that he now takes out the light and flashes it around the room. By flashing it around the room he confuses not only himself but also confuses and annoys other moving figures in the room. This is like the man who is trying to see the objects as they are as distinguished from what they have appeared to him to be. As he flashes his light the objects appear different than they were and the light dazzles or confuses his vision, as man's vision is confused by conflicting opinions of himself and others. But as he examines carefully the object on which his light rests and is not disturbed or confused by other lights of other figures which may now be flashing, he learns to see any object as it is, and he learns by continuing to examine the objects, how to see any object in the room. Let us now suppose that he is able by examining the objects and the plan of the room to discover the openings of the room which have been closed. By continued efforts he is able to remove that which obstructs the opening and when he does the light floods into the room and makes visible all objects. If he is not blinded by the flood of bright light and does not again close the opening because of the light which streams in and dazzles his eyes, unaccustomed to the light, he will gradually see all objects in the room without the slow process of going over each separately with his search light. The light which floods the room is like the light of knowledge. The light of knowledge makes known all things as they are and it is by that light that each thing is known to be as it is.

A FRIEND

# DECEMBER 1909

[From *The Word*, Vol. 10 No. 3]

*Why are precious stones assigned to certain months of the year? Is this caused by anything else than the fancy of people?*

The same stones are said by different people to belong to different months, and certain virtues are said to come from certain stones when worn in the month or during the season that these people say they should be worn in. All of these different opinions cannot be true, and most of them are most likely due to fancy. But fancy is an abnormal working of the mind or a distorted reflection of the imagination; whereas, imagination is the image making or building faculty of the mind. In the same way that the cause of a distorted reflection of an object is the object itself, so may the many fancies about the virtues of stones be due to the virtues in the stones themselves and to the knowledge which once existed concerning the virtues of stones, but of which lost knowledge remain the fancies only, or abnormal working of the mind, as the reflection of past knowledge preserved in the traditions of men. All objects are centers through which forces of nature act. Some objects offer less powerful centers for forces to act through than other objects. This is due to the arrangement of the particles of different elements in certain proportion. Copper which is prepared and wrought into a wire will offer a line along which electricity may be conducted to a given point. Electricity will not run along a silken thread, though it will run along a copper wire. In the same manner as copper is a medium or conductor of electricity, so stones may be the centers through which certain forces act, and as copper is a better conductor of electricity than other metals, such as zinc or lead, so certain stones are better centers for their respective forces than other stones. The purer the stone the better it is as a center of force.

Each month brings a certain influence to bear on the earth and all things on the earth, and, if stones have their respective values as centers of force, it would be reasonable to suppose that certain stones would be more powerful as such centers of force, during the time when the influence of the month was most powerful. It is not unreasonable to suppose that there was a knowledge of the seasons when stones possessed certain virtues and that because of this those of the ancients who did know assigned the stones to their respective months. To attach any particular value to stones is useless for this or that person who may derive his information from an almanac or fortune-telling book or some person with as little information as himself. If one feels a particular liking for a stone for itself, aside from its commercial value, the stone may have some power from or for him. But it is useless and may be harmful to attach fanciful virtues to stones or fancy that stones belong to certain months, because this creates a tendency in that person to depend on some extraneous thing to assist him in what he should be able to do for himself. To fancy and not to have some good reason for belief is injurious to a person rather than helpful, because it distracts the mind, places it on sensuous things, causes it to fear that from which it seeks protection, and makes it depend on extraneous things rather than on itself for all emergencies.

❧

*Has a diamond or other precious stone a value other than that which is represented by the standard of money? and, if so, on what does the value of a diamond or other such stone depend?*

Every stone has a value other than its commercial value, but in the same way that not everyone knows its commercial value so not everyone knows the value of a stone other than its money value. A person ignorant of the value of an uncut diamond may pass it by as he would a common pebble. But the connoisseur knowing its value will preserve it, have it cut in such a way as to show its beauty, then give it a proper setting.

The value of a stone in itself depends on its being a good center for the attraction of certain elements or forces and the distributing of these. Different stones attract different forces. Not all forces are beneficial to the same people. Some forces help some and injure others. A stone which will attract a certain force may help one and injure another. One must know what is good for himself, as well as know the value of one stone as distinguished from others before he may decide intelligently which stone is good for him. It is no more unreasonable to suppose that stones have certain values aside from their money value than it is to suppose that the so-called lode stone has another value than what it is worth in money. Some stones are negative in themselves, others have forces or elements acting actively through them. So the magnet has the force of magnetism acting actively in it, but soft iron is negative and no such force is acting through it. Stones which are the centers of active forces cannot well be changed in value; but negative stones can be charged by individuals and made centers for forces to act through, in the same manner that soft iron can be magnetized by a magnet and in turn become a magnet. The stones which, like magnets, are centers through which one or more forces act are either those which are so arranged by nature or which are charged with force or connected with forces by individuals. Those who wear stones which are powerful centers may attract to them their particular forces, as a lightning rod may attract lightning. Without knowledge of such stones and their respective values, the attempt to use stones for this purpose will only lead to confusion of thought and superstitious ignorance. There is little reason in acting fancifully with stones or with anything else for occult purposes, unless one knows the laws governing the thing which is to be used and the nature of the person or forces in connection with which it is to be used or applied. The best way concerning any unknown thing is to keep an open eye and mind and be ready to accept anything which seems reasonable concerning that thing, but to refuse to receive anything else.

A FRIEND

# JANUARY 1910

[From *The Word,* Vol. 10 No. 4]

*Does the spirit act with man and what are spiritual beings?*

We must question the question before we can answer it. Few people stop to think what they mean when they use such terms as spirit and spiritual. If definitions were demanded of these people there are few who would not feel their ignorance of what the terms mean. There is as much confusion in the church as there is out of it. People speak of good spirits and evil spirits, wise spirits and foolish spirits. There is said to be a spirit of God, a spirit of man, a spirit of the devil. Then there are numerous spirits of nature, such as the spirit of the wind, of the water, of the earth, of the fire, and spirit is attributed to alcohol. Each animal is created with a certain spirit and some scriptures speak of other spirits taking possession of the animals. The cult known as Spiritualism, or Spiritism, speaks of guardian spirits, spirit controls and a spirit land. The materialist denies that there is any spirit. The cult known as Christian Science, making liberal use of the term, adds to the confusion and uses it with interchangeable convenience. There is no agreement as to what spirit is or what state or quality the word spiritual applies to. When the word spiritual is used, generally speaking, it is intended to cover qualities, attributes and conditions that are supposed to be not physical, not material, not earthly. Thus we hear of spiritual darkness, spiritual light, spiritual joy, and spiritual sorrow. One is told that people have seen spiritual pictures; one hears of spiritual persons, spiritual expressions, spiritual sentiments and even of spiritual emotions. There is no limit to the indulgence in the use of the words spirit and spiritual. Such confusion will continue so long as people refuse to think definitely of what they mean or what they express in their language. We must use definite terms to represent definite thoughts, so that thereby definite ideas may be known. Only by a definite terminology may we hope to exchange views with each other and find our way through the mental confusion of words. Spirit is the primary and also the ultimate state, quality, or condition, of all things manifested. This first and last state is far removed from physical analysis. It cannot be demonstrated by chemical analysis, but it may be proved to the mind. It cannot be detected by the physicist, nor by the chemist, because their instruments and tests will not respond, and because these are not on the same plane. But it may be proven to the mind because the mind is of that plane and may go to that state. The mind is akin to spirit and may know it. Spirit is that which begins to move and act apart from a parent substance. The parent substance of spirit is actionless, motionless, passive, quiescent and homogenous, save when a portion of itself departs from itself to pass through a period of manifestation called involution and evolution, and save when that portion which has departed returns again into its parent substance. Between the departure and the return the parent substance is not as above described. At all other times it is inactive and the same throughout itself.

The substance when it is thus put forth is no longer substance, but is matter and is as one great fiery, aethereal sea or globe in rhythmic movement, the whole being made up of particles. Each particle, as is the whole, is dual in its nature and indivisible. It is spirit-matter. Although each particle may and must later pass through all states and conditions, yet it cannot in any way or by any means be cut, separated or divided in itself. This first state is called spiritual and although of a dual, yet inseparable nature, the spirit-matter may be called spirit while in this first or spiritual state, because spirit entirely predominates.

Following the general plan toward involution or manifestation in this universal, spiritual or mind matter, the matter passes into a second and lower state. In this second state the matter is different than in the first. The duality in the matter is now shown plainly. Each particle no longer appears to move without resistance. Each particle is self-moved, but meets with resistance in itself. Each particle in its duality is made up of that which moves and that which is moved, and though dual in its nature, the two aspects are united as one. Each serves a purpose to the other. The stuff may now properly be called spirit-matter, and the state in which the spirit-matter is may be called the life state of spirit-matter. Each particle in this state though called spirit-matter is dominated and controlled by that in itself, which is spirit, and the spirit in each particle of spirit-matter dominates the other part or nature of itself which is matter. In the life state of spirit-matter, spirit is still the preponderating factor. As the particles of spirit-matter continue toward manifestation or involution they become heavier and denser and slower in their movement until they pass into the form state. In the form state the particles which were free, self-moving, and perpetually active are now retarded in their movements. This retardation is because the matter nature of the particle is dominating the spirit nature of the particle and because particle coalesces with particle and through all, the matter nature of the particles dominate their spirit-nature. As particle coalesces and combines with particle, becoming denser and denser, they finally come to the borderland of the physical world and the matter is then within the reach of science. As the chemist discovers the different characters or methods of the matter they give it the name of element; and so we get the elements, all of which are matter. Each element combining with others under certain laws, condenses, precipitates and is crystallized or centralized as the solid matter around us.

There are physical beings, element beings, life beings, and spiritual beings. The structure of physical beings is of cells; element beings are composed of molecules; life beings are atomic; spiritual beings are of spirit. The chemist may examine physical and experiment with molecular matter, but he has not yet entered the realm of spirit-matter except by hypothesis. Man cannot see nor sense a life being or a spiritual being. Man sees or senses that to which he is attuned. Physical things are contacted through the senses. The elements are sensed through the senses attuned to them. To perceive spirit-matter or beings of spirit-matter, the mind must be able to move freely in itself apart from its senses. When the mind can move freely without the use of its senses it will perceive spirit-matter and life-beings. When the mind is thus able to perceive it will then be able to know spiritual beings. But the spiritual beings or the life beings thus known are not and cannot be those creatures of the senses without physical bodies, which are carelessly and negligently called spirits or spiritual beings, and which long and lust for flesh. The spirit acts with man in proportion as man attunes his mind to the state of spirit. This he does by his thought. Man is in his highest part a spiritual being. In his mental part he is a thinking being. Then in his desire nature he is an animal being. We know him as a physical being of flesh, through whom we often see the animal, frequently come in contact with the thinker, and at rare moments we catch glimpses of him as a spiritual being.

As a spiritual being man is the apex of evolution, the primary and the ultimate manifestation and result of an evolution. Spirit at the beginning of involution or manifestation is indivisible.

As the primary spirit-matter involved gradually, stage by stage, from state to state, and finally that which was spiritual matter is held in bondage and imprisoned by the other side of the nature of itself which is matter, so the spirit gradually, step by step, reasserts its supremacy over the matter of itself, and, overcoming the resistance of the matter of itself, finally redeems that matter step by step from the gross physical, through the world of desire, by long stages at last reaching the world of thought; from this stage it ascends by aspiration toward its final achievement and attainment the world of spirit, the world of knowledge, where it rebecomes itself and knows itself after its long sojourn in the underworld of matter and the senses.

A FRIEND

# FEBRUARY 1910

[From *The Word*, Vol. 10 No. 5]

*Is there not a belief that the Atlanteans could fly? If so, where is such belief stated?*

Plato was perhaps the first to acquaint the western world with the lost continent of Atlantis. Others following him have taken up the subject and commented upon the bit of history which he gave as coming from his ancestor, Solon, who claimed to have had it transmitted to him from the old priests of ancient Egypt. Many legends have come down in various forms, of the island or continent of Atlantis. Bacon wrote about it, but the most notable book is that of Ignatius Donnelly: "Atlantis; the Antediluvian World." We do not think that any of those who have written about Atlantis, have mentioned anything about aerial navigation, or the ability of the Atlanteans to fly.

Not until Madame Blavatsky published her "Secret Doctrine" in 1888 was anything definitely said about the Atlanteans and flying. In the "Secret Doctrine" Madame Blavatsky states that, with the Atlanteans, aerial navigation was a fact and she gives a bit of history concerning the cause of the downfall of Atlantis and how navigation of the air played an important part in the fall. Madame Blavatsky does not claim the honor of this discovery for herself. She says in the "Secret Doctrine" that that which she states was given to her from the actual history of Atlantis, taken from the records of those wise men who have become immortal and who keep and pass on the history of the rise and fall of continents and the geological and other changes of the earth, in connection with the racial development of humanity and the rise and fall of its civilizations throughout time. The writer of the question and others to whom the "Secret Doctrine" may not be accessible will be interested in the following quotation from the work:

"It is from the Fourth Race that the early Aryans got their knowledge of 'the bundle of wonderful things,' the Sabha and Mayasabha, mentioned in the Mahabharata, the gift of Mayasura to the

Pandavas. It is from them that they learnt aeronautics, Viwan, Vidya, the 'knowledge of flying in air-vehicles,' and, therefore, their great arts of Meteorography and Meteorology. It is from them, again, that the Aryans inherited their most valuable Science of the hidden virtues of precious and other stones, of Chemistry, or rather Alchemy, of Mineralogy, Geology, Physics and Astronomy." (3d Ed. vol. II., p. 444.)

. . . . .

"Here is a fragment of the earlier story from the Commentary:

"'. . . And the 'Great King of the Dazzling Face,' the chief of all the Yellow-faced, was sad, seeing the sins of the Black-faced.

"'He sent his air-vehicles (Vimanas) to all his brother-chiefs (chiefs of other nations and tribes) with pious men within, saying: Prepare. Arise, ye men of the Good Law, and cross the land while (yet) dry.

"'The Lords of the storm are approaching. Their chariots are nearing the land. One night and two days only shall the Lords of the Dark Face (the Sorcerers) live on this patient land. She is doomed, and they have to descend with her. The nether Lords of the Fires (the Gnomes and Fire Elementals) are preparing their magic Agnyastra (fire-weapons worked by Magic). But the Lords of the Dark Eye ("Evil Eye") are stronger than they (the Elementals) and they are the slaves of the mighty ones. They are versed in Astra (Vidya, the highest magical knowledge). Come and use yours (i. e., your magic powers, in order to counteract those of the Sorcerers). Let every Lord of the Dazzling Face (an Adept of the White Magic) cause the Vimana of every Lord of the Dark Face to come into his hands (or possession), lest any (of the Sorcerers) should by its means escape from the waters, avoid the rod of the Four (Karmic Deities), and save his wicked (followers, or people).'". (ibid., p. 445.)

. . . . .

"'(But) the nations had now crossed the dry lands. They were beyond the watermark. Their Kings reached them in their Vimanas, and led them on to the lands of Fire and Metal (East and North).'"

. . . . .

"'The waters arose, and covered the valleys from one end of the Earth to the other. High lands remained, the bottom of the Earth (the lands of the antipodes) remained dry. There dwelt those who escaped; the men of the Yellow Faces and of the straight eye (the frank and sincere people).

" 'When the Lords of the Dark Faces awoke and bethought themselves of their Viwans in order to escape from the rising waters, they found them gone. ' " (ibid. p. 446).

ॐ

*Are the individuals who are trying to solve the problem of aerial navigation, reincarnated Atlanteans?*

In all probability many of the minds which worked through Atlantean bodies are again appearing in the civilization which is now being built up, this civilization having its center in the United States with its branches and ramifications extending to all quarters of the globe. In all probability the inventors of this age are those minds who worked out or were instructed in the sciences of Atlantis and who are causing to reappear similar inventions in our age with which they have been familiar in Atlantis. Among the inventions is that of flying. The possibility of man's flying, or the navigation of the air, was scoffed at and ridiculed up to very recent times, and even the most "scientific" minds sneered at the suggestion or spoke of it as an ignis fatuus or a childish superstition. The invention of the aeroplane and dirigible balloon have demonstrated that navigation of the air is possible, and what has been done indicates that at a time not far distant man will be able to steer his way through the air as effectively as he now steers his way through the water. The mind of man is fast overcoming the difficulties of aerial navigation. But he has not yet discovered the means nor is he able to contact the means by which easy flight is attained. Man may fly as easily as birds now fly, but only when he has learned to contact and use the force which birds use in their flight. Birds do not depend only on physical force to fly. They call into operation a force which is not physical and which they contact with their bodies and which moves their bodies. Birds do not depend on their wings for the power of flight. They use their wings and tail more as a balance or lever by which the body is balanced and directed through the currents of the air. Man may do with his body what the birds now do with theirs, or, man may build machines with which he may navigate the air. He will navigate the air, most successfully only when he has learned to adjust and relate the force which is in himself to the flying machines which he may build. if man may do this in this age it is quite likely and highly probable that man has done the same in times past. It is quite probable that the Atlanteans did have a knowledge of the power which causes flight and were capable of causing this power to act through their bodies, thereby enabling them to fly, and of adjusting the same power to aerial machines, thereby regulating the flight of such machines according to their will. The mind reincarnates from age to age, from one physical race to another. The mind of man is not educated and perfected in one race or civilization. It is necessary for the mind to pass through many or all races and civilizations in its gradual development. It is logical to suppose that the minds which are engaged with the question or practice of aerial navigation are the same minds which have been concerned with the problem in Atlantis.

෧෧

*If the Atlanteans had solved the problem of aerial navigation, and if those who are now concerned with the same problem were Atlanteans, then why have these individuals not reincarnated since the sinking of Atlantis and before the present time, and if they have reincarnated before the present age, why have they not been able to master the air or to fly before the present time?*

That the Atlanteans did solve the problem of aerial navigation is not yet proven, nor is it proven that Atlantis existed. At least it is not proven by any of those proofs which are required by modern science. Much evidence has been given that Atlantis did exist, such as those mentioned or that furnished by the Sargasso Sea. But if present humanity can solve the problem of navigation of the air, it is not unreasonable to suppose that the humanity in Atlantis could also have solved it. If reincarnation be a fact, it is quite probable, indeed it is almost certain, that if those who live today and construct machines with which they navigate the air were acquainted with the aerial problem in Atlantis, and that they have reincarnated many times and possibly in many lands since the submersion of Atlantis. Yet, what was possible at one period in a great civilization may not be possible at every other time in every other civilization. It does not follow that because an individual mind had solved the aerial problem in Atlantis he should be able to fly or build flying machines in other bodies in other lands and at unpropitious times.

Aerial navigation is a science, however, it is only one of the sciences. It depends on and cannot do without other sciences. Until certain of the sciences had been developed the physical side of aerial navigation could not have been achieved. A knowledge of such sciences as mechanics, of steam, chemistry, electricity, are necessary to the successful navigation of the air. Whatever fundamental knowledge the mind may have in itself as to its knowledge and its power and ability to fly, yet until physical devices have been contrived and until the mind has become acquainted with the laws which govern physical bodies, no aerial ships or machines could be successfully constructed or used. Only in modern times have these sciences been rejuvenated or rediscovered. Only when the information which they furnish was or is applied to flight through the air, is it reasonable to suppose that aerial navigation is possible. It is quite likely that the ancients did have a knowledge of the sciences, but they have left us no records such as are required as proof to show that they had a working knowledge of all of the sciences together, as is now being gradually developed.

An individual mind reincarnating in any of the countries of Europe or Asia within the past five thousand years could not have found the necessary conditions to build airships and fly in them. If for no other reason, then because religious prejudices of the country would have prevented him from using the knowledge which he may have applied in Atlantis. For example: if all of the text books of modern science were removed from the world and some of our great inventors and scientists were to die and reincarnate in some part of the world not in touch with modern civilization, the greatest of these scientists and inventors would be unable in that life to provide the conditions which the civilizations they had left had afforded. The most they could do even with a knowledge that they had lived and had known and done what is now known to be done would not enable them to do the same thing under changed conditions. The most that they could do would be to act as pioneers. They would be obliged to educate the people among whom they reincarnated up to an appreciation of future possibilities, to acquaint the people with certain facts, and educate them to an understanding of the rudiments of the sciences. One life would not allow them the time necessary to build up the conditions and educate the people up to the desire for modern advantages. Only as other advanced minds incarnated among the people, and advanced minds continued to incarnate and "discover" certain laws and improve the industries and customs of the country, would it be possible to have the working basis for a civilization. It has taken ages for humanity to be educated and developed to its present condition, after it sank into the darkness following the downfall of previous civilizations. As humanity emerges from the darkness and ignorance and prejudices and as the incarnated minds become freer, then what existed in past civilizations may again, will again, be introduced and perfected. We are evidently approaching the time for the reappearance of what have been considered as wonders, but which are gradually becoming necessities and parts of our life. Though the individuals who lived in Atlantean bodies and who there navigated the air, must have many times reincarnated since the sinking of Atlantis, and though the season and time prevented their using the knowledge of aerial flight, the time is at hand when these individuals may call to the present their knowledge of the past, because the conditions are ready and they will be able to master the air and fly in the future as they were masters of the air in forgotten Atlantis.

A FRIEND

# MARCH 1910

[From *The Word*, Vol. 10 No. 6]

*Are we or are we not in union with atma-buddhi?*

We are not. The question is general and vague, and takes for granted that we know all the factors on which it is based. The factors are atma and buddhi with which "we" are or are not "in union." The question is evidently asked from the theosophical standpoint. Atma is said to be the universal conscious spirit pervading all things. Buddhi is said to be the spiritual soul, the vehicle of atma, and that through which atma acts. "We" are said to be individual self-conscious minds. "Union" is a state in which one or more are joined to or blended with each other. Atma the universally conscious spirit and buddhi its vehicle, are in union always; because they act co-ordinately at all times and buddhi is conscious of atma and the two are united. They may thus be said to be a united One which is universally conscious. For the singular of we to be in union with atma-buddhi, the I must be conscious as I and must know who it is as I; it must be aware of its own individuality and identity and must also be conscious of buddhi and atma, and must be conscious that as an individual it is joined to, united with, the universal buddhi and atma. When an individual I is conscious of its identity and is conscious that it is at one with the universally conscious atma and buddhi then that individual can rightly say that it is "in union with atma and buddhi." There would then be no speculation by that individual as to what atma and buddhi and we are, and what union is, because that individual would know and the knowledge would end speculation. In the present condition of man, "we" do not know who we are. If we do not know who "we" are, we do not know who or what buddhi and atma are; and if we do not know who we are and are not universally conscious, we are not as self conscious beings in union with the universally conscious principles of atma and buddhi. Union is a close, and on that plane conscious contact with the thing united. A self conscious being cannot truly say that he is united to or in union with anything of which he is not fully conscious, even though that other thing may be present with him. Atma and buddhi are present with man at all times but man even as a self conscious being is not aware or conscious of atma and buddhi as universal and spiritual principles. Because he is not universally conscious and because he is not even conscious of his own individual identity, therefore, he, man, as a thinking being is not in union with atma-buddhi.

ॐ

*Is it not true that all that we can become is already in us and that all we have to do is to become conscious of it?*

Generally speaking, that is quite true, and, all that we at first have to do is to become conscious of all there is in us. This is enough for the present. Then, perhaps, we shall have to become conscious of everything there is outside of us and then see the difference between that and all there is in us.

The question as a statement is as soothing and easy as a gentle breeze in summer—and as indefinite. If one will content himself with such a question and the answer "yes" or an answer as indefinite as the question, there will be as little benefit derived as would come to an agriculturist who contents himself with the thought that he has stored somewhere in his barn all the seeds of all the things that grow. One who knows or believes that he has in his make up all that it is possible to become or to know about, and who does not become something of what he knows, is worse off and more to be pitied than the one who does not dabble with abstract propositions but who tries only to better his present physical conditions. In Eastern countries it is common to hear devotees repeating in their respective languages: "I am God"! "I am God"! "I am God"! with easy and most confident assurance. But are they? Usually these would-be gods are beggars on the streets and they know little more than enough to make the assertion; or they may be very learned and able to enter into long arguments in support of their claim. But few of those who make the claim give evidence in their life and work that they understand and have a right to it. We have imported these affirmations together with different kinds of these devotees and are still receiving new shipments into the United States. But if they are gods, who wants to be a god?

It is good for man to believe that all things are possible for him; but it is hypocrisy in him to try to make himself believe that he has already attained to that state which may be remotely possible. The chemist in his laboratory, the painter at his easel, the sculptor at his marble, or the farmer in his fields, are more god-like than those who walk about and blandly and loquaciously affirm that they are god, because the divine is within them. It is said: "I am the microcosm of the macrocosm." True and good. But it is better to act than to say it.

To know or to believe a thing is the first step to the attainment of it. But to believe a thing is not having or being the thing believed. When we believe that all that we can become is within us, we have only become conscious of our belief. That is not being conscious of the things in us. We shall become conscious of the things about which we believe by trying to understand them and by working toward them. Guided by our motive and according to our work we shall become conscious of the things within us and come to the attainment of our ideals. By his work the chemist brings into being that which he is working for according to formulae. The painter makes visible the ideal in his mind. The sculptor causes the image in his mind to stand out from the marble. The farmer causes to grow those things which were potential only in seeds. That man has all things within him is a divine thought. This thought is the potential seed of divinity. This divine thought is abused, ridiculed and debased when it is banded about lightly. When it is blown lightly about by unthinking mouths it, like a seed blown over frozen ground, will not take root. One who knows the value of and desires to cultivate a seed will not expose it, but will place it in suitable soil and will nurture and care for that which grows out of the seed. One who constantly says that he is divine, that he is the microcosm of the macrocosm, that he is Mithra, Brahm, or another formal Deity, is exposing and blowing away the seed which he has and is not likely to be one in whom the seed of divinity will take root and grow. He who feels that he is a veritable Noah's Ark and feels the divine within, holds sacred and nurtures the thought. By cultivating and improving his thoughts and by acting in accordance with his belief, he furnishes the conditions in and through which intelligence and divinity grow up naturally. Then he will become gradually conscious that all things are within him and that he is gradually becoming conscious of all things.

A FRIEND

# APRIL 1910

[From *The Word*, Vol. 11 No. 1]

*Is darkness the absence of light, or is it something separate in itself and which takes the place of light. If they are distinct and separate, what is darkness and what is light?*

Darkness is not "the absence of light." Light is not darkness. Darkness is something in itself, not light. Darkness may for a while take the place of light and obscure light, but light will dispel darkness. Light will eventually overcome darkness by the raising of and causing darkness to become light. The light and darkness which we perceive through the senses are not light and darkness in themselves, though that which we perceive as light and dark have their origin in the true light and in darkness. As a thing, darkness is homogeneous substance, which is the root, basis or background of all manifestation as matter. In its original state, it is quiet and is the same throughout itself. It is unconscious, unintelligent and undisturbed. Light is the power which comes from the intelligences who have passed through the evolutions and are above or beyond manifestation. When intelligences direct their light power on unconditioned and homogeneous substance, which is darkness, that portion of substance or darkness, and on which light is directed, springs into activity. With the beginning of activity, the substance which was one becomes dual. In action darkness or substance is no longer substance, but is dual. This duality of substance or darkness is known as spirit-matter. Spirit and matter are the two opposites of the one thing, which is substance in origin, but spirit-matter in action. The units into which substance is thus divided as spirit-matter, as well as the manifesting spirit-matter as a whole, have impressed upon them and it the origin of their root parent and also the cause of their action or manifestation. Substance is the root and parent of every indivisible unit particle of the manifesting mass as well as of the mass as a whole. Light is the cause of the manifestation and of the action in each unit as well as of the manifesting mass as a whole. So that in each indivisible unit, as well as throughout the manifesting mass as a whole is represented: the root parent as substance and the acting power as light. In each unit called spirit-matter there is potentially the parent, substance, and the power, light. Substance is represented by that portion of the indivisible unit which is called matter, and light is represented by the other side or portion of the same indivisible unit called spirit. All universes or manifestations are called out of the unfathomed substance or darkness into manifestation by the light power of intelligences, and this light keeps the spirit-matter thus called into action continuously in action throughout its period of manifestation. During the period of the manifestation the light which is present in manifestation with darkness is the cause of that which we call light. The matter which is manifesting is the cause of what we call darkness. Light and darkness seem ever in conflict and seem to give place to each other throughout manifestation. Day and night, waking and sleeping, life and death, are the opposites or reverse sides of the same thing. These opposites act alternately in short or long periods, until darkness is turned into light. Each seems to the other as the undesirable though each is to the other a necessity. Man has in him darkness and the light power. To man the senses are his darkness and his mind is his light. But this is not usually so considered. To the senses the mind seems as darkness. To the mind the senses are darkness. That which to the senses seems to come from the sun, we call sunlight. To the mind the senses and that which they call light is as darkness when it, the mind, is illuminated by the light power of its parent intelligence. The sunlight and the intelligent perception of it may come to us even while the mind is immersed in and in conflict with the darkness; then we shall see the sunlight as a reflection or symbol of the real light. Darkness gives place to and is changed into permanent light as it is overcome by perceptions and by actions of the mind. When our minds have won in the conflict with darkness we shall perceive the true light which shines in the darkness even though darkness now knows it not.

ॐ

*What is radium and how is it possible for it to throw off continuously a great energy without any apparent waste and loss of its own power and body, and what is the source of its great radioactivity?*

It is supposed that the writer of the question is familiar with the scientific statements concerning the recent discovery of radium, such as its being extracted from pitchblende, its discovery by Madame Curie, its light power, the effect of its action on other bodies, its scarcity and the difficulties attending its production.

Radium is a physical state of matter through which force and matter finer than physical are manifested to the senses. Radium is physical matter in contact with other matter and forces usually speculated about as being hypothetical. Ether and these forces are states of matter finer than the physical and they act on or through what is called physical matter, whether the physical matter is a diamond or a molecule of hydrogen. Were it not for ethereal or hypothetical matter acting through the physical matter there would be no change or decomposition of physical matter. The action of finer through gross matter causes the "chemical" combinations and changes of the matter in ordinary use and as dealt with by chemists.

Radium is physical matter which is acted directly upon or through by astral matter without a third factor and without being perceptibly changed by the action of astral matter. Other physical matter is acted on by astral matter, but in lesser degree than radium. Generally, the results of the action of the astral on other physical matter are not perceptible because physical matter cannot offer the contact and resistance to astral matter which is offered by radium, and most other matter is not so directly in contact with astral matter as is radium. Infinitesimal and imperceptible particles of radium are present in all matter. But thus far pitchblende seems to be the source from which they may be collected in the greatest amount, little though it is. When the particles called radium are compacted into one mass, astral matter acts directly on and through it in a quality and power apparent to the senses.

The radio-activity of radium is not, as is now supposed, due to its generating or throwing off from itself particles of its own body. The

physical matter of which radium is composed does not furnish the radio-activity or other power which manifests through it. Radium is not a force, but a medium of force. (Matter is twofold and exists on different planes. On each plane it is matter when it is passive and force when it is active. So physical matter is passive matter and force is active matter. Astral matter is passive astral matter and force on the astral plane is active astral matter.) Radium is the body through which astral matter manifests. Radium is matter of the physical world; radio-activity is astral matter from the astral world which becomes visible by means of physical radium. The astral world is around and through the physical world, and, as its matter is finer, it is in and through gross physical matter, as science says that ether is in and through a crowbar, or as it is known that electricity acts in and through water. Like a candle which gives light, radium emits light or energy. But unlike the candle, it is not burnt out in giving the light. Like a generator or an electric wire which seems to generate heat or light or power, radium seems to generate or throw off energy; and so it does, perhaps. But the light or other power which seems to be generated is not furnished by the wire. It is known that the power of electricity does not originate in a dynamo or in an electric wire. It is also known that the electricity which manifests as heat or light or power is directed along the wire. In a similar manner, that quality or force known as radio-activity manifests through radium from a source which is at present unknown to science. But the source is not radium any more than the source of electricity is a dynamo or a wire. The particles of its body are thrown off and burnt out or used up in a less degree than the particles of a dynamo or electric wire by the action of electrical energy. The source of that which is manifested through radium is the same as the source of the manifestations of electricity. Both come from the same source. The difference between the manifestation of electricity as heat, light or power and that which is manifested through physical radium is in the medium of manifestation and not in electricity or radio-activity. The particles of which are composed the dynamo, generator or wire, are not of the same quality as the particles of which radium is made up. Astral matter and the forces which act in astral matter act directly on radium without any other factor or mediation. The current which plays through an electric wire is made manifest by other factors, such as batteries, magnets, generators, dynamos, steam and fuel. None of these factors are required by radium because it is directly in contact with and itself allows astral matter to manifest through or about it, the radium.

It is known that the electric current does not go through the wire, but around the wire. It will also be found that in a similar manner the radio-activity is not in the radium, but around or about the radium. Electricians have tried and are still trying to devise some means by which electric energy can be made to manifest and directed without the use of steam or fuel or galvanic action. Radium suggests and illustrates how this may be done.

A FRIEND

[From *The Word*, Vol. 11 No. 2]

*Is it possible to develop a new species of vegetable, fruit or plant, totally different and distinct from any other known species? If so, how is it done?*

It is possible. One who has achieved in that line a most remarkable and widely known success is Luther Burbank of Santa Rosa, in California. Mr. Burbank has not yet, as far as we know, developed a wholly different and new species, but there is nothing to prevent him from so doing if he continues with his work. Up to the present time, so far as we are aware, his efforts have been directed to the crossing of certain varieties of fruits and plants, producing not a totally different species, but one having the characteristics of both or of one of the two or more varieties used in developing the new growth. Many accounts have been published of Mr. Burbank's work, though it is quite likely that he has not told all he knows and all he does, to achieve the success which is his. He has rendered inestimable service to man: he has taken some hitherto useless and objectionable growths and developed them into useful shrubs, wholesome foods or beautiful flowers.

It is possible to develop any vegetable, plant, fruit, or flower, of which the mind can conceive. The first thing necessary to develop a new species is: to conceive it. If a mind cannot conceive a new species, that mind cannot develop one, though he may by observation and application produce new varieties of old species. One who desires to invent a new species must ponder well on the genus of the species which he would have and then must brood intently and confidently over it. If he has confidence and will use his mind industriously and will not let his thought wander on other types nor indulge in idle fancies, but will think and brood on the species which he would have, then, in the course of time, he will conceive the thought which will show him the type he has so desired. This is the first proof of his success, but it is not enough. He must continue to brood over the thought which he has conceived and think patiently of that particular thought without wandering to others.

As he continues to think, the thought will become clearer and the means by which the new species may be brought into the world will be made plain. In the meantime, he should set himself to work with those species which are nearest the one which he has in mind; to feel in them; to know the different movements and to be in sympathy with and impress the sap of the plant running through its arteries and veins, to feel its likes and to supply them, to cross the plants which he has selected and then to think his species into the crossing, to feel it develop from the two varieties he has chosen, and to give it physical form. He should not, and he will not, if he has gone thus far, be discouraged if he does not see at once his new species as the product. He should try and try again and as he continues to try he will in time rejoice to see the new species coming into being, as it will surely do if he does his part.

One who would bring a new species into being need know little of botany when he first begins, but he should acquaint himself with all he can learn of this work. All growing things have feeling and man must feel with them and love them, if he would know their ways. If he would have the best there is in them, he must give the best that he has to them. This rule holds good through all kingdoms.

A FRIEND

# JUNE 1910

[From *The Word,* Vol. 11 No. 3]

*Is it possible and is it right to look into the future and predict future events?*

It is possible but seldom right to look into the future. That it is possible is attested on many pages of history. As to its being right that must be determined by one's own fitness and good judgment. A Friend would not advise another to try to look into the future. One who looks into the future does not wait to be advised. He looks. But of those who look into the future, few know what they are looking at. If they look and do see, it is only when the future has become the past that they know what they saw when they looked. If one sees into the future naturally, there is no particular harm in his continuing to look, though few are able to derive any benefit from the operation. Harm comes almost invariably from predicting what the looker thinks he sees.

If one looks or sees into the future he does so with his senses, that is, his astral senses; or with his faculties, that is, the faculties of the mind; and there is no particular danger in doing so, providing he does not attempt to mix the world in which he sees with this physical world. When he attempts to predict future events in this world from what is seen in another world, he becomes confused; he cannot relate what he has seen and fit it into its place in the future in this physical world; and that is so even though he did see truly. His predictions cannot be relied on when applied to future events in this physical world, because these do not occur as predicted in time, nor in manner, nor in place. He who sees or who tries to see into the future is like an infant seeing or trying to see objects about it. When the child is able to see, it is quite pleased, but it makes many mistakes in its understanding and judging of what it sees. It cannot appreciate relation nor distance between objects. Distance does not exist for the infant. It will try to grasp the chandelier with as much confidence as it lays hold of its mother's nose and does not understand why it does not reach the chandelier. One who looks into the future sees events and fancies that they are about to occur, because he has no judgment as to the relation between what he sees in the world in which he sees it, and the physical world, and because he is unable to estimate the time of the physical world in which it may occur in relation to the event at which he is looking. Many predictions do come true, though not always as predicted. It is unwise, therefore, for people to depend on the predictions of those who try to look into the future by use of clairvoyance or other of the inner senses, because they cannot tell which of the predictions will be correct.

Those who depend on predictions coming from what are usually called "inner planes" or "astral light," lose one of their most valuable rights, that is, their own judgment. For, however many mistakes one may make in attempting to judge things and conditions for himself, he will judge correctly only by learning, and he learns by his mistakes; whereas, if he learns to depend on others predictions, he will never have sound judgment. One who predicts future events has no certainty of their coming true as predicted, because the sense or faculty by which the prediction is made is unrelated to the other senses or faculties. So one who sees only or hears only, and that imperfectly, and who attempts to predict what he saw or heard, is likely to be correct in some respects, but to confuse those who rely on his prediction. The only sure way of predicting future events is for the one who predicts to have his senses or his faculties intelligently trained; in that case each sense or faculty will be related to the others and all will be so perfected that they can be used with as much accuracy as that with which a man is able to use his senses in his action and relation to this physical world.

The much more important part of the question is: Is it right? In man's present condition it is not right, because if one be able to use the inner senses and relate them to events and conditions of the physical world, it would give him an unfair advantage over the people among whom he lives. The use of the inner senses would enable a man to see what has been done by others; the seeing of which would as surely bring about certain results as the tossing of a ball in the air would result in its fall. If one saw the ball tossed and was able to follow the curve of its flight, and had experience, he could estimate accurately where it would fall. So, if one could use the inner senses to see what had already been done in the stock market or in social circles or in matters of state, he would know how to take unfair advantage of what was intended to be private, and could so shape his actions as to benefit himself or those in whom he was interested. By this means he would become the director or ruler of affairs and could take advantage of and control others who were not possessed of powers such as his. Therefore, before it can be right for a man to look into the future and predict future events correctly, he must have overcome covetousness, anger, hatred and selfishness, the lust of the senses, and must be unaffected by what he sees and predicts. He must be free from all desire of possession or gain of worldly things.

A FRIEND

# JULY 1910

[From *The Word*, Vol. 11 No. 4]

*Is it possible to put a thought out of the mind? If so, how is this done; how can one prevent its recurrence and keep it out of the mind?*

It is possible to keep a thought out of the mind, but it is not possible to put a thought out of the mind as we would put a tramp out of the house. The reason why so many are not able to keep away undesirable thoughts, and are not able to think on definite lines, is because they believe in the prevalent notion that they must put thoughts out of their minds. It is impossible to put a thought out of one's mind because in putting it out attention must be given the thought, and while the mind gives the thought attention it is impossible to get rid of that thought. The one who says: Go away you bad thought, or, I will not think of this or that, keeps that thing in his mind as securely as though it were riveted there. If one says to himself that he must not think of this or that thing, he will be like the ascetics and hermits and fanatics who make a list of things they are not to think about and then proceed to go over this list mentally and to put those thoughts out of their mind and fail. The old story of "The Great Green Bear" illustrates this very well. A mediaeval alchemist was pestered by one of his pupils who wanted to be told how to transmute lead into gold. His master told the pupil that he could not do it, even though he were told, because he was not qualified. On the continued pleading of the pupil, the alchemist decided to teach the pupil a lesson and told him that as he was going on a journey the following day he would leave him the formula by which he might succeed if he were able to follow all instructions, but that it would be necessary to pay the closest attention to the formula and to be accurate in every detail. The pupil was delighted and eagerly began the work at the time appointed. He followed the instructions carefully and was accurate in the preparation of his materials and instruments. He saw that metals of the right quality and quantity were in their proper crucibles, and the temperature required was produced. He was careful that the vapors were all conserved and passed through the alembics and retorts, and found that the deposits from these were exactly as stated in the formula. All this caused him much satisfaction and as he went on with the experiment he gained confidence in its ultimate success. One of the rules was that he should not read through the formula but should follow it only as he proceeded with his work. As he proceeded, he came to the statement: Now that the experiment has proceeded thus far and that the metal is at white heat, take a little of the red powder between the forefinger and thumb of the right hand, a little of the white powder between the forefinger and thumb of the left hand, stand over the glowing mass which you now have before you and be ready to drop these powders after you have obeyed the next order. The young man did as ordered and read on: You have now reached the crucial test, and success will follow only if you are able to obey the following: Do not think of the great green bear and be sure that you do not think of the great green bear. The young man paused breathless. "The great green bear. I am not to think of the great green bear," said he. "The great green bear! What is the great green bear? No, I will not think about the great green bear, but, confound it, I *am, thinking* about the great green bear." As he continued to think that he should not think about the great green bear he could think about nothing else, until finally it occurred to him that he should go on with his experiment and although the thought of a great green bear was still in his mind he turned to the formula to see what the next order was and he read: You have failed in the trial. You have failed at the crucial moment because you have allowed your attention to be taken from the work to think about a great green bear. The heat in the furnace has not been kept up, the proper amount of vapor has failed to pass through this and that retort, and it is useless now to drop the red and white powders.

A thought remains in the mind as long as attention is given to it. When the mind ceases to give attention to one thought and places it on another thought, the thought which has attention remains in the mind, and that which has no attention gets out. The way to get rid of a thought is to hold the mind definitely and persistently on one definite and particular subject or thought. It will be found that if this is done, no thoughts which do not relate to the subject can intrude themselves upon the mind. While the mind desires a thing its thought will revolve around that thing of desire because the desire is like a center of gravity and attracts the mind. The mind can free itself from that desire, if it wills. The process by which it is freed is that it sees and understands that the desire is not the best for it and then decides on something that is better. After the mind decides on the best subject, it should direct its thought to that subject and attention should be given to that subject only. By this process, the center of gravity is changed from the old desire to the new subject of thought. Mind decides where its center of gravity will be. To whatever subject or object the mind goes there will its thought be. So the mind continues to change its subject of thought, its center of gravity, until it learns to place the center of gravity in itself. When this is done, the mind withdraws into itself its ramifications and functions, through the avenues of sense and the sense organs. The mind, not functioning through its senses into the physical world, and learning to turn its energies into itself, finally awakens to its own reality as distinct from its fleshly and other bodies. By so doing, the mind not only discovers its real self but it may discover the real self of all others and the real world which penetrates and upholds all others.

Such realization may not be attained at once, but it will be realized as the final result of the keeping undesirable thoughts out of the mind by attending to and thinking of others which are desirable. No one is at once able to think only of the thought which he wishes to think of and thus to exclude or prevent other thoughts from entering the mind; but he will be able to do so if he tries and keeps on trying.

A FRIEND

# AUGUST 1910

[From *The Word*, Vol. 11 No. 5]

*Does the belonging to Secret Societies have the effect of retarding or advancing the mind in its evolution?*

Membership in a secret society will prevent the mind from or assist it in its development according to the nature and development of that particular mind and the kind of Secret Society of which that one is a member. All secret societies may be classed under two heads: those whose object is to train the mind and body for psychic and for spiritual purposes, and those whose object is physical and material benefit. People sometimes form themselves into what may be said to be a third class, which is made up of the societies which teach psychic development and claim communication with spiritual-beings. It is said that strange phenomena are produced in their circles and sittings. They also claim to have and to be able to confer on whom they see fit, physical advantages over others. All these should come under the second class, because their object will be found to be sensual and physical.

The secret societies of the first class are few as compared to the second class; of these few only a small percentage really help the mind in its spiritual development. Under this first class are included societies of religious bodies who try to assist their members in spiritual awakening and unfolding—who have no such objects as political training or military instruction or instruction in business methods—and also organizations of a philosophical and religious basis. Those who are of particular religious faiths may be benefited by belonging to a secret society within that faith if the objects of the society do not allow the mind to be kept in darkness and do not prevent it from acquiring knowledge. Before one of any faith joins a secret society of his faith he should inquire well into their objects and methods. There are many secret societies within each of the large religions. Some of these secret societies keep their members in ignorance concerning the knowledge of life, and they prejudice their members against other faiths. Such secret societies can do great harm to the minds of their individual members. Such prejudicial training and enforced ignorance may so warp, stultify and cloud the mind that it will require many lives of pain and sorrow to rectify the wrongs which it may have been lead into committing. Those who have religious convictions of their own regarding a religion, may be benefited by belonging to a secret society of that religion if the objects and methods of that society meet with the approval of that mind, and as long as that particular mind belongs to or is being educated in that particular religion. The religions of the world represent the different schools in which some minds are trained or educated for spiritual development. When one feels that a religion satisfies the spiritual longings of his mind, he belongs in the class of spiritual life which that religion represents. When a religion no longer supplies what is generally called the spiritual food of the mind, or when one begins to question "the truths" of his religion, it is a sign that he no longer belongs to it or that he is being separated from it. If one doubts, if he is dissatisfied with and denounces the teachings of his religion without having other reasons than dumb and ignorant discontent, this is a sign that his mind is being closed to spiritual light and growth and that he is falling below his class in spiritual life. On the other hand, if the mind feels that his particular religion or the religion in which he was born is narrow and cramped and if it does not satisfy or answer the questions of life that his mind yearns to know, this is a sign that his mind is unfolding and growing out of that class which is represented by that particular religion and it shows that his mind demands something which will supply the mental or spiritual food which it needs for continued growth. All secret societies under the first class, which have as their object the development of psychic tendencies, will retard the mind because all things of the psychic nature have to do with the senses and bring the mind under the dominion of the senses.

The secret societies of the second class are made up of those organizations whose objects are the attainment of political, social, financial and mercenary advantages. Under this class come the fraternal and the benevolent societies, those who are secretly organized to overthrow a government, or those who band themselves together for purposes of blackmail, murder or sensual and vicious indulgences. One may easily tell whether or not any of these will assist or retard the development of his mind if he knows its aims and objects.

The idea of secrecy is the knowing or the having of something which others have not, or in sharing knowledge with a few. The desire of this knowledge is strong and is attractive to the undeveloped, the youthful and the growing mind. This is shown by the desire which people have to belong to something which is exclusive and hard to enter and which will excite the admiration or envy or awe of those who do not belong. Even children like to have secrets. A little girl will wear a ribbon in her hair or on her waist to show that she has a secret. She is the object of envy and the admiration of all the other little girls until the secret is known, then the ribbon and secret loses its value. Then another little girl with another ribbon and a new secret is the center of attraction. Excepting the political, financial and the vicious or criminal societies, most of the secrets of the secret societies in the world, have as little worth or are of as little importance as the secrets of the little girl. Yet those who belong to them may be furnished with "play," which is as beneficial to them as the girl's secret is to her. As the mind matures it no longer wishes secrecy; it finds that those who wish secrecy are immature, or that their thoughts and deeds seek darkness to avoid the light. The maturing mind wishes to spread knowledge broadcast, though he knows that knowledge cannot be given alike to all. As the race advances in knowledge, the demand for secret societies for the development of the mind should decrease. Secret societies are not necessary for advancement of minds beyond the school girl age. From business and social and literary sides, ordinary life has all the secrets necessary for the mind to solve and by which the mind will be advanced through its youthful stages. No secret society can advance the mind beyond its natural development nor enable it to see through the secrets of nature and to solve the problems of life. A few secret organizations in the world may benefit the mind if the mind will not stop on the surface, but will penetrate the real meaning of their teachings. Such an organization is the Masonic Order. Comparatively few minds of this organization derive other than business or social benefit. The real worth of symbolism and the moral and spiritual teaching is almost entirely lost to them.

A truly secret organization which is of benefit to the mind in its development is not known as a secret society, nor is not known to the world. It must be as simple and plain as natural life. Entrance into such a secret society is not by ritual. It is by growth, through self effort of the mind. It must be grown into, not entered. No person can keep a mind out of such an organization if by self effort that mind continues to grow. When a mind grows into the knowledge of life that mind endeavors to dispel ignorance by removing the clouds, uncovering secrets and by throwing light on all problems of life and to help other minds in their natural unfoldment and development. Belonging to a secret society will not help the mind who wills to grow into its own.

2

*Is it possible to get something for nothing? Why do people try to get something for nothing? How do people who appear to get something for nothing, have to pay for what they get?*

Everyone inherently feels that no one can get something for nothing and that the proposition is wrong and the attempt unworthy; yet, when he thinks of it in connection with some object of *his* desire, good judgment is ignored and he with willing ears listens to the suggestion and deludes himself into believing that it is possible and that *he* may get something for nothing. Life requires that a just return or account be made for everything received. This requirement is based on the law of necessity, which provides for the circulation of life, the maintenance of forms and the transformation of bodies. He who tries to get for nothing something which would not otherwise come to him, interferes with the circulation of life and the distribution of forms according to natural law, and he thereby makes of himself an obstruction in the body of nature. He pays the penalty, which nature as well as all law-governed bodies exacts and is made to return that which he took or else is he altogether suppressed or removed. If he objected to this by arguing that what he got was only what would have come to him anyway, his argument fails because if what he got for nothing, apparently, would have come to him without his effort, then he need not have made the effort which he did to get it. When things come to one without apparent effort, such as what is called accident and chance or by inheritance, they come because of and according to the natural working out of law, and in this way it is legitimate and according to law. In all other cases, such as receiving physical and sensual benefits by wishing only, or by thinking only, or by making demands according to phrases known as the law of abundance or the law of opulence, it is impossible to get something for nothing even though one does appear to get something for nothing. One of the reasons why people do try to get something for nothing, is because although they feel that this cannot inherently be true, they see that others have obtained what those others do not seem to have worked for, and because it is said by other people that they do get things by simply wishing for them or demanding them and claiming them until they have them. Another reason is because the one's mind is not sufficiently matured and experienced enough to know that it cannot get something for nothing notwithstanding all allurements, inducements or pretences that it can. Another reason is because the one who thinks that he can get something for nothing is not truly honest. In ordinary business life the biggest rogues are those who believe they can outwit the law and can get something for nothing, but this is because they intend to make the people less crafty than themselves supply their wants. So they provide a get-rich-quick-scheme or some other scheme and induce others as dishonest but with less experience than themselves to come into it. Most of those who are taken into the scheme are often shown by the schemer how he is going to get the best of some other people and which explains how they also can get rich quick. If these were honest they would not be taken into the scheme but, by appealing to the avarice and covetousness in his dupes and through his own dishonest methods, the schemer gets what his victims provide. When one is truly honest he will know that he cannot get something for nothing and he will not try, though he may accept that which lawfully comes to him when it comes by natural means.

People who get something have to pay for what they get. If people get things which seem to come out of the air and to fall in their laps as the result of a call on the law of abundance or the universal storehouse or on the law of opulence, or what not, they are like the short-sighted ones without means who make lavish purchases on credit, unthinking of the time of settlement. Like those without resources who buy on credit, these sanguine temperaments often get what they do not really need; like these thoughtless purchasers, the demanders of "the law of abundance" dream and fancy they will do much with what they get—but they find themselves near bankruptcy when the time of settlement comes. A debt may not be acknowledged, but the law exacts its payment nevertheless. One who asks physical health and physical wealth by claiming and demanding these from "the law of abundance," or from "the absolute," or from anything else, and who obtains something of what he demands, instead of getting it legitimately in the realm where it belongs, must return what he has obtained plus the interest demanded for the use.

One may correct nervous disorders and restore the body to health by an attitude of mind; but it will be found that nervous disorders are in most cases brought on and continued by a troubled mind. When the right attitude is taken by the mind the nervous trouble is corrected and the body resumes its natural functions. This is a legitimate cure, or rather a removal of a cause of sickness, because the cure is effected by treating the trouble at its source. But not all diseases and poor health is due to a troubled mind. Ill health and disease is usually brought about by the eating of improper foods and the gratifying of morbid appetites and unlawful desires. Physical conditions and possessions are provided by seeing that they are necessary to one's work, and then by working for them according to the recognized legitimate physical means.

It is possible to cause diseases brought on by improper feeding to disappear, and it is possible to obtain money and other physical advantages by claiming and demanding these from whatever phrase the mind is pleased to invent or adopt. This is possible because the mind has power to act on other minds and cause them to bring about the conditions which it desires and because the mind has power and may be able to act on the state of matter of its own plane, and this matter in turn may act upon or bring about the conditions demanded by the mind; it is possible because the mind may exert its power over the body and cause a physical disease to disappear for a time. But in every case where the mind goes against natural law to bring about physical results the law demands a readjustment, and the reaction is often more severe than the original trouble. So when health is claimed and when the physical requirements for physical health are not provided, the mind may compel the disappearance of an unhealthy growth, such as a tumor. But for such apparent cure payment is demanded by nature for trying to prevent the exactment of her laws. By forcing the dispersion of the tumor the matter of the tumor may be—as when lawless people are compelled to leave their haunts by meddlesome and foolish reformers—driven to seek residence in another part of the community, where it will do more harm and be more difficult to locate and treat. When dispersed by mental compulsion the tumor may disappear from one part of the body as a tumor and reappear in another part of the body as a loathsome sore or a cancer.

When one insists on and is provided with physical possessions by demanding them from "the absolute" or "the storehouse of the absolute," he will enjoy them for a time as a gambler enjoys his ill-gotten gains. But the law demands that not only shall he restore what he did not get honestly, but that he shall pay for the use of that which he had. This payment is called for when the demander has actually worked for a desired object—and which is lost when just within his reach; or the payment may be made after he has earned certain possessions and loses them in some unforeseen way; or he may have them taken from him when he feels most sure of them. Nature requires payment in the coin or its equivalent of the debt contracted.

When a mind attempts to make itself a servant to the body by illegitimate means, and prostitutes its powers from its own plane to the physical, the laws of the mental world require that mind to be deprived of power. So the mind loses its power and one or many of its faculties are obscured. The payment required by law is made when the mind has suffered the deprivation of power, the suffering and trouble which it has caused others in obtaining the objects of its desires, and when it has struggled through the mental darkness in which it is, in its efforts to correct its wrongs and restore itself as a mind to its own plane of action. Most of the people who appear to get something for nothing do not have to wait for another life to be compelled to pay. Payment is usually called for and exacted in their present life. This will be found true if one will look into the history of people who have tried to get something for nothing and who have appeared to succeed. They are mental criminals who are self-imprisoned in jails of their own building.

A FRIEND

[From *The Word,* Vol. 11 No. 6]

*What are the essential differences between Theosophy and New Thought?*

Motives, methods and definiteness.

These differences are not based upon the talk and actions of so called theosophists nor of new thoughters, but upon the books of the theosophists and those of the new thought. Most members of present day theosophical societies make claims and act as unreasonably as most of the people of the New Thought. Each set of people shows the side of human nature which is working out at that particular time. The doctrines of Theosophy are: karma, the law of justice; reincarnation, the development of the mind and of the matter of the physical and other bodies by means of the mind's return from life to life in human bodies into this physical world; the sevenfold constitution of man, the principles and their interaction which enter into the makeup of man; the perfectibility of man, that all men are potentially gods and that it is in the power of every man to attain to the state of highest perfection and become consciously and intelligently one with God, the Universal Mind; brotherhood, that all men come from one and the same divine source and that all men are related and the same in essence though differing in degree of development, and that spiritually all have duties to and are related to each other as members of one family, and that it is the duty of each member of it to help and assist the others according to his powers and capacities.

The motives advocated or suggested in the books of theosophists and of new thoughters differ widely. The motives as urged by theosophical doctrines are: to comply with the requirements of Karma by fulfilling one's obligations, that is, duty, because it is demanded by the law of justice; or because by so doing, one will make good karma; or because it is right—in which case duty will be done without fear and without hope of reward. Immortality or perfection is looked forward to not because by its attainment one shall escape responsibilities and enjoy its fruits, but because by reaching it one is the better able to assist others in their overcoming of ignorance, sorrow and misery and attaining the same goal. The motives which prompt the new thoughter to action are first his own betterment, generally for physical benefits, and the enjoyment of that, and then to tell others that they too can have their desires along these lines satisfied.

The methods which Theosophy advises for the attainment of its objects are by doing one's duty wherever placed, by acting, unselfishly for the good of others, by controlling the desires through the intellect, by becoming illumined and by devoting a reasonable amount of one's time, money and work to the spreading of the doctrines. This is done, without money or charges of any kind. The methods of the New Thought are to promise physical benefits and mental satisfaction, and money is charged for courses in instruction in the thought and for practical application.

Another difference is that the doctrines of Theosophy are definite, as to principle and statement; whereas, in the New Thought societies vague claims are made, and a lack of definiteness in terms and philosophy is shown in the teachings. New Thought teachings speak mildly, if at all, of karma and reincarnation. Some of their writers speak of the seven principles or of some of them; they hold that man is divine in origin and fact, and believe that men are brothers. But there is a lack of definiteness in all these New Thought teachings which is a marked difference from the direct and insistent statements made in theosophical books.

The distinguishing features then are: that the motive which prompts the follower of Theosophy is unselfishness and service for the purpose of realizing the God within, whereas, the motive which prompts the new thoughter is to apply such information as he has for personal, material gain and advantage. The methods of work of one who follows Theosophy is to spread the doctrines without pay; whereas, the new thoughter says that the laborer is worthy of his hire and he charges money for benefits, or alleged benefits, conferred. The follower of

Theosophy has definite objects and doctrines which are distinct in themselves, whereas the adherent of the New Thought is not particular as to doctrine, but has a hopeful and cheerful disposition and is confident that he will get all he desires. These are differences according to doctrine and books, but the so called theosophist is human and frail as well as the new thoughter; each acts according to his nature notwithstanding his particular conviction or beliefs.

Where Theosophy begins New Thought ends. Theosophy begins with one's duty in life, and aims to reach perfection in the physical world; and through that perfection, perfection in the spiritual world. New thought begins with a cheerful and confident belief in one's divinity, and seems to end with physical, wealth, prosperity and happiness— sometimes and for the time being.

ॐ

*What is the cause of cancer? Is there any known cure for it or will some method of treatment have to be discovered before its cure can be effected?*

There are immediate and remote causes of cancer. The immediate causes are those engendered in the present life. The remote causes originate in and come over from the action of the mind in previous human births. The immediate causes for the appearance of cancer are such as a bruise or continued irritation, which cause an obstruction to the blood circulation, tissue proliferation and which furnish soil favorable to the development of, what is believed to be a cancer germ, or they may be due to improper foods which the body is unable to assimilate or excrete and by reason of which the cancer germ develops, or that disease may be due to the restraining, suppressing and killing, but retaining in the body of the vital fluid during sexual practices. The killing, retaining and accumulation in the body of the life germs of the vital fluid is fertile soil which calls the cancer germ into existence; by continuing the practice the body abounds with cancerous growth. Again similar conditions may be furnished by the inability of the body to bring the vital germs to maturity, failing to do which the life germs die and decay and remain within the body which is unable to assimilate or excrete them.

The remote causes are brought over by the mind from its actions in previous incarnations in which the mind took part in excess and indulgence, but in which incarnation it did not reap the harvest which it then sowed, in the same way that those who are addicted to morbid and wrong sexual practices in the present life may not now reap, but are sowing, the causes for future harvest—unless they set up contrary causes by present thought and action. Unless cancer is physically transferred or transplanted, all cases of cancer are due to karmic causes; that is to say, they are caused by the action and interaction between the mind and desire in the field of one's physical body. This action between mind and desire must have taken place in the present life or in a preceding life. If it has taken place in the present life, it will be recognized as the immediate cause of the cancer when the attention is directed to it. If none of these or similar causes have been set up in the present life, in which cancer appears, then the disease is due to a remote cause which may be recognized. One may act against the law for a time, only, but he is checked in time. The cancer cell and its development may be destroyed, but the cancer germ is not physical and it cannot be destroyed by any physical means. The cancer germ is astral and is the form in which the cell grows and develops, although the cancer cell shows the form of the cancer germ. The cancer cell and germ can be treated and transformed by physical means.

There is a treatment for the cure of cancer, and cures have been effected. Cures have been made by the Salisbury treatment. This treatment has been known for over forty years, but comparatively few physicians have tried it. The Salisbury treatment of diseases has not found favor with the medical profession. A few who have tried it fairly, have had remarkable results in the treatment of most of the so called incurable diseases. The basis of the Salisbury treatment is the eating of well broiled lean beef from which all fat and fiber and connective tissue have been removed, and which eating is accompanied by the drinking of hot water not less than an hour and a half before and after meals. This treatment is too simple and inexpensive for most physicians. Nevertheless this treatment, when it is consciously applied, strikes at the roots, and effects cures of nearly every known disease. Well cooked lean beef, from which tissue and fat has been removed, and water furnish the simplest and most important material for the maintenance of healthy human animal bodies. The eating of lean beef and the drinking of pure water affects the physical body and its astral counterpart, the form body. Lean meat will not supply the material favorable to the growth and development of any germs which may bring disease to the body into which the lean meat is taken. When the supply of food is withheld from a disease and such food is taken in the body as cannot be used by the disease, but is wholesome to the body, the disease dies away. So when lean beef is taken into the body, it will not supply food favorable to the cancer or other disease germs, and if other food is withheld, the unhealthy growths in the body gradually die and disappear by a process of starvation. This may take years and the body may appear emaciated and feel weak and physically exhausted. This condition is due to the sloughing off of the diseased portions of the body, but if the treatment is persisted in the body will regain health. What takes place during the process is that the old diseased physical body is gradually being allowed to die off and is eliminated, and in its place there is being grown and developed gradually, another physical body built up on the lean beef. The drinking of the boiled water taken hot an hour and a half before and after meals is as important as the eating of the meat, and the meat should not be eaten to cure disease without drinking hot water and at the times stated. The drinking of a quantity of hot water neutralizes the acids and injurious matter and passes them off from the body, and in that water this matter is passed off from the body. The meat is the food of the body; the water irrigates and cleanses the body. The lean beef builds healthy cells of the body, but the meat cannot touch or directly affect the invisible cancer germ. Hot water does this. Hot water affects and transforms the cancer germ and other germs in the body and adjusts these to the needs of the body. The meat builds up the physical body; the water supplies the needs of the astral body.

A body built up on this basis is clean and wholesome and is a good working instrument for the mind. By such a treatment not only is one's physical and astral body changed and made healthy, but the desires will also have been affected, curbed and trained. Only the Salisbury treatment of diseases deals directly with the physical body which is the field of the cancer cell and with the astral body which is the seat of the cancer germ. By the Salisbury treatment the mind also is trained, indirectly, because considerable determination and will must be exercised by the mind in order to hold the body and desires strictly to the treatment. Many fail in the treatment because they will not hold to it and because of mental discontent and rebellion which often appear in those who try it and which they do not overcome. If the rebellion is quelled and discontent replaced by a patient and confident attitude of mind, a cure will inevitably result. By training one's body according to reasonable methods, the mind is self-instructed by the operation and learns mastery not only of the body but also of its own disquietude and restlessness. When there is a harmonious relation between the body and the mind disease can find no home in that body. The cancer germ and cell will not cause disease unless the constitution of the body is unable to use them. There are many cancer germs and cells in nearly every human body. In fact myriads of germs swarm in the human body. Any of these will cause virulent diseases if the condition of the body is not such as will keep the germs in order and preserve a well organized body. Germs of diseases yet unknown teem in the body, but the body and the mind have not yet provided the conditions which will let these germs become known to the world as special diseases. They may be called into evidence at any time when the mind becomes aware of the possible disease, and the pathological conditions are provided by improper eating and living.

The cancer germ and cell belong to the period in the history and development of the human race when the human body was bi-sexual. At that period it would have been impossible to have the disease now called cancer because that was the normal cell used in the building up of bodies. Our present race has reached a point in its evolution which brings it to the same plane as that which the race passed in its involution, that is, the plane on which took place the involution or development of bi-sexual male—female bodies into the sexual male bodies and female bodies we now know.

The physical body is built up and maintained by a constant creation and destruction of germs. It is a war of the germs. The body is established according to a certain form of government. If it preserves its form of government it maintains order and health. If order is not preserved, opposing factions enter the government and cause disorder, if they do not cause revolution or death. The body cannot remain inactive or passive. The armies of germs which build up the body and other armies of germs which defend it against the attacks and invasion of opposing germs must be able to capture and assimilate the invaders. This is done when the body eats of wholesome food, drinks of pure water, breathes deeply of fresh air, and man entertains healthy thoughts and tries to think of influences and actions according to right motives.

A FRIEND

# OCTOBER 1910

[From *The Word,* Vol. 12 No. 1]

*Why is a snake regarded so differently by different people?. Sometimes a snake is spoken of as the representative of evil, at other times as the symbol of wisdom. Why does man possess such an inherent fear of snakes?*

Education and training has much to do with the manner in which man regards snakes and all other creatures. But there is something in the man himself apart from his education which accounts for the rest. A snake may be properly considered as venomous and evil or as the symbol of wisdom. It depends on the standpoint that is taken. Aside from destruction of the vermin which some snakes feed upon, it is not known that snakes confer any special benefits on man and the world, or that they exhibit any habits more wonderful than other animals, or that they show symptoms of intelligence greater than other animal forms. On the contrary, they are sometimes deaf and blind; they may so glut themselves as to go into a stupor, unable to defend themselves or keep out of danger, and the bite of some snakes is so deadly as to produce death soon after the victim has been bitten. But there are comparatively few snakes which are not harmless, and the movements of a snake are among the most graceful and the quickest of all creatures.

There is nothing which a snake does nor any purpose which it serves which would warrant its being spoken of as the wisest of creatures or as the symbol of wisdom. Yet from the earliest of times sages have spoken of and scriptures mention it as the wisest of all creatures, and used it as a symbol of wisdom.

There are many reasons why the snake may truly be called a symbol of wisdom. Better than any other creature the snake represents, is related to and moved by the electrical power of the universe, which power gives wisdom to man, when man makes himself ready to receive it. In man's present condition he is unfit and unable to have this power act directly through him. The organism of the snake is so constituted as to allow the direct action of this electrical power. But the power does not give wisdom to the snake; it only acts through the snake body. A mind is necessary to be aware and make use of the wisdom. This the snake has not. The snake has the most completely and economically vertebrated animal body. The spinal column runs throughout the snake, and it is the spinal column through which the electrical power acts. The spinal column in man is in the form of a snake, but the spine in man will not allow the electrical power to act directly through it because the current is switched off from the spinal column by the present uses to which the nerve currents of the body branching out from the spinal cord are put. The present arrangement of nerves and the uses of the nerve currents prevent the universal electrical power from acting directly through the body and enlightening the mind of man. In the abdominal and pelvic regions of the body the nerves are coiled, serpent-like. These nerves now supply the generative organs with their power of action. It is said in Eastern books that kundalini, the serpent power, is coiled within the body and asleep; but that when this serpent power is awakened it will enlighten the mind of man. Interpreted, this means that certain nerve currents of the body, now unused or misused, must be called into their proper action; that is, that they will be opened and connected with the spinal cord. The doing of this is like the turning of the key on an electrical switchboard which turns on the current and starts the machinery into operation. When the current is opened and related to the spinal cord in the body of man the electrical power is turned on. This current first acts through the nerves of the body. If the nervous organization of the body is not strong and fit the current burns up the nerves. According to the unfitness, it will make the body diseased, disorganized, produce insanity or cause death. If the nervous organization is fit the power electrifies the astral form body and then clarifies and illuminates the mind, so that almost instantly the mind may know of any subject concerning the physical world or the astral world. This power has the movement of a snake and it acts through the spinal cord within the spinal column, which is in the form of a snake. Like a snake, the power will cause death to the one who arouses and is not able to master it. Like a snake, the power develops a new body and sheds its old one as the snake sheds its skin.

Man has an inherent fear of animals because each animal in the world is a separated and specialized form of the desire in man, and the animal that man fears shows him the specialized form of his own desire which he has not mastered. When he masters and is able to control his desire man will not fear the animal and the animal will have no fear of and do no harm to man. Man has an inherent fear of a snake because he has not mastered and is not able to control the force in him which the snake represents. Yet a snake has an attraction for man, though he fears it. The idea of wisdom is also attractive to man. But he must overcome fear and love truth before he can get wisdom, else, like the serpent-like power, it will destroy him or make him mad.

ॐ

*Is there any truth in the stories that the Rosicrucians had ever burning lamps? If so, how were they made, what purpose did they serve, and can they be made and used now?*

There is no valid reason why the Rosicrucians or other mediaeval bodies should not have made and used ever-burning lamps. The reason why we of to-day think ever-burning lamps are a myth invented by fancy, is chiefly due to our notions that a lamp must be a vessel containing combustible matter, such as wicks and oil, or through which illuminating gas is used, or through which an electric current passes and gives light by incandescence of the filaments. The idea of a lamp is, that it is that through which light is given.

The fabled ever burning lamp of the Rosicrucians is thought to be unreasonable because we think that a lamp cannot give light without fuel or something which is supplied to it. It is thought that an ever-burning lamp is only one of the many supposed impossibilities which abound in traditions concerning Rosicrucian and mediaeval times.

We cannot now say how the Rosicrucian or some men in the middle ages made an ever-burning lamp, but the principle on which such lamp may be made can be explained. Let it first be understood that an ever-burning lamp does not consume oil nor gas nor any other material which it is necessary to supply by mechanical means. The body and form of an ever-burning lamp may be of a material suitable to the uses to which the lamp is to be put by the mind who conceives and makes it. The important part of the lamp is the particular material through which the light is given. The light is induced from the ether or astral light. It is not produced by a burning process. The material which is used to induce light must be carefully prepared and adjusted or attuned to the etheric or astral light. The preparation of this material and the tempering and adjusting of it to the ether or astral light was one of the secrets of the Rosicrucians and Fire Philosophers. That all this could have been, is now demonstrated by the discovery of radium. Radium seems to give light without consuming itself or diminishing in quantity. Radium does not as is supposed give light from itself. The light is induced and focussed by the radium. The light which appears to be shed by radium is from the ether or astral light. The radium serves as a medium only through which the light is brought from the astral world and manifested to the physical senses.

The material through which came the light of the ever-burning lamps of the Rosicrucians was arranged on similar principles though it could have been prepared differently and may have been of different material than radium, as there are forms of matter other than radium through which light from the ether or astral world may be manifested in the physical world.

Ever-burning lamps have most likely been constructed for many and different purposes. A lamp constructed for one purpose could not be put to all uses for which ever-burning lamps were made. Thus for instance, radium gives a light, but radium is not now used for light because not only is the preparation of it too costly for it to be put to such use, but because the light radiated injures near animal bodies.

Here are a few of the purposes for which ever-burning lamps may have been made and used: To give light at secret gatherings; to look into and investigate the astral world and some of its entities; to keep away adverse influences and entities opposed to the work in which one or more may have been engaged; to protect the physical and astral body during sleep or while in trance; as a means for the treatment of metals for transmutation; as a means of preparing certain simples for medicinal purposes or for effecting curses; to adjust the senses of the physical to the astral or inner senses by which the unseen astral world could be entered.

Other ever-burning lamps could be made now, but although they may be made in the future it is not necessary to use them now. They have been used for psychic or astral practices and purposes. The time for such work has passed. The mind of man should be growing out of such practices. What was controlled by astral means may and should be now controlled by the mind and without other means than that furnished by man's own bodies. The mind should be a light unto itself. Its body should be the lamp. Man should so prepare his body and bring it so under control of the mind that the mind will shine through it and enlighten the surrounding world, and make of the man who is seen an ever-burning lamp which will radiate light for all time.

A FRIEND

# MAY 1912

[From *The Word*, Vol. 15 No. 2]

*Why is the eagle used as an emblem of various nations?*

It is likely that various motives have prompted the taking of the eagle as an emblem by the many nations which have adopted it. Yet it may be supposed that it was taken because it best represented the nature and the policy, the ambition, the ideal of the nations who have borne it as their standard.

The eagle is king of birds and of the air, as the lion is said to be king among beasts. It is a bird of prey, but also of victory. It is a bird of great endurance, capable of swift and long flight. It swoops rapidly on its prey, rises quickly, and soars in majesty at great heights.

A nation desires strength, endurance, courage, swiftness, dominion, power. An eagle has all of these to a high degree. It is reasonable to suppose that these are some of the reasons which led nations or tribes or rulers to adopt the eagle as their standard. The fact is that it has been the symbol of many of the conquering nations of our historical period, and particularly of those who conduct war at great distances.

These are the characteristics of the eagle. But the nation who adopts this bird as its symbol, usually qualifies or specializes its particular nature or intent or ideal either by a motto accompanying the eagle or by placing a symbol in the eagle's talons or in his beak, such as a branch, arrows, a flag, a shield, the sceptre, the lightning, each of which alone or in combination with other emblems symbolizes the character of the nation or the characteristics the nation likes and what its aims are.

All this is from a practical and material standpoint. There is another symbolism of the eagle where the same characteristics may be viewed from a more spiritual standpoint.

It is one of the four "Living Beings" mentioned in the Apocalypse who are said to stand around the throne of God. The eagle is assigned to the sign Scorpio of the Zodiac. It symbolizes the spiritual power in man. The eagle is the virile, spiritual power in man which may rise to the greatest heights. The nation or man who takes the eagle as an emblem in the spiritual sense aims to attain in a spiritual way all that is represented by the eagle in its material symbolism. He aims for victory over all that is below him and uses his power to rise to higher realms. By directing this power represented by the eagle, he is the conqueror of his desires, gains dominion in the region of his body through which he ascends and, like the eagle, makes his home in the mountain heights of the body above the cervical vertebrae. So he rises from the sign Scorpio, which is the lowest end of the spine, to the top, which leads into the head.

ॐ

*Does the double headed eagle now used as the national emblem of some countries, and which is found on the monuments of the ancient Hittites of Biblical times, allude to the androgynous condition of man?*

When a double-headed eagle is used as a national emblem it is sometimes intended to signify among other things intended, that two nations or countries are united as one, though there may be two heads to the government. Unless other symbols accompanied the double-headed eagle on the monuments of the ancient Hittites, this symbol would not refer to androgynous man. Androgynous man or dual sexed man, must include two functions, two powers of opposite natures. The double headed eagle is the same in nature, as both heads are of eagles. For androgynous man to be represented by an eagle, the eagle should be accompanied by or be connected with a lion, which, though in a different realm, represents among the animals what the eagle is among the birds. The ancient Rosicrucians spoke of "The Blood of the Red Lion," by which they meant the desires, or animal nature in man. They also spoke of "The Gluten of the White Eagle," by which they meant the psycho-spiritual power in man. These two, the blood of the red lion, and the gluten of the white eagle, they said, should meet and commingle and marry, and from their union would develop a greater power. This sounds like empty ravings of a lunatic unless the symbolism is understood. When it is, it will be realized that they understood more about physiological processes than they were given credit for.

The blood of the red lion is the active desire which lives in the blood of the body. The gluten of the white eagle is in its first aspect the lymph in the body. The lymph enters the heart and so is united with the blood. From this union there is born another power which impels to generation. If this impulse is gratified, the Alchemists said, that the lion would become weak and the eagle would lose the power to rise. If, however, the gluten of the white eagle and the blood of the red lion should continue to mingle together without giving way to the impulse, the lion would become strong and the eagle powerful, and the new-born power from their commingling would give youth to the body and strength to the mind.

These two, the lion and the eagle, symbolize the two principles, the masculine and feminine aspects of man from the psycho-physical standpoint. The androgyne is one who has the masculine and feminine natures and functions. The lion and the eagle, the blood and the lymph, commingling in the same body and performing their functions to generate a new power within that body and without giving way to the impulse for outward expression, create a new bodily power from which is born a new being which, like the eagle, may rise from the earth and soar into higher realms.

A FRIEND

# JUNE 1912

[From *The Word*, Vol. 15 No. 3]

*At the four quarters and half quarters of the circle on the Masonic Keystone of the Royal Arch Chapter are the letters H. T. W. S. S. T. K. S. Have they any relation of the Zodiac, and what do their positions around the circle indicate?*

The letters H. T. W. S. S. T. K. S. are read from left to right, but they must also turn from right to left. As we know the zodiac, the first letter H. is at the place of aries, the first T. at aquarius, W. at capricorn, the first S. at scorpio, the second S. at libra, the second T. at leo, K. at cancer, and the third S. at taurus. The letters may be found in Masonic books, but neither the words for which these letters stand, nor their meanings, are given in any book. It must, therefore, be inferred that their significance is secret and important and not intended for the instruction and illumination of those who have not taken the degree of the Royal Arch Chapter. The writer is not a member of the Masonic Fraternity, has received no instruction from any of that Fraternity concerning Masonry, and does not pretend to any knowledge of the secrets of the Masonic Craft. But symbolism is a universal language. Whoever understands it truly should read the meaning of the keystone by the light of Masonry, which is included in the zodiac, and made clear by the light which the zodiac gives, and according to the degree to which the one who receives it is raised. The four signs of the zodiac, gemini, virgo, sagittary and pisces, are omitted as not being necessary to the work, or else they are included in the signs, taurus, leo, scorpio and aquarius. Taurus, leo scorpio and aquarius are marked by the letters S. T., S. T., which are placed midway between the signs aries, cancer, libra and capricorn. If the signs or letters opposite each other are connected by lines, two crosses will be formed. The cross formed by the vertical line H. S. and the horizontal line K. W. is the stationary cross of the zodiac, aries-libra and cancer-capricorn. The cross formed by the lines S. S. and T. T. is a movable cross of the zodiac, formed by the signs of taurus-scorpio and leo-aquarius. These movable signs and cross are characterized by the four sacred animals: the bull or ox, taurus, indicated by the letter S.; the lion, leo, for which is the letter T.; the eagle or scorpio, in place of which is the letter S.; the man (sometimes angel) or aquarius, in place of which is the letter T. A glance at the relationship and positions of letters and signs of these two crosses: The letter H. and its opposite S., represent the head of the keystone and its base, and correspond to aries and libra. The letters K. and W. represent the two sides of the keystone, which correspond to the signs cancer-capricorn. This is the stationary cross of the zodiac. The upper letter S. and the lower letter S. represent the upper corner and its opposite lower corner of the keystone and correspond to the signs taurus-scorpio of the zodiac. The upper letter T. and the lower letter T. correspond to the other upper corner and its opposite lower corner of the keystone, and to the signs aquarius-leo of the zodiac, which form a movable cross of the zodiac. These letters of the keystone, or the signs of the zodiac, may be used in pairs in many ways. It will be noticed the letters of the head and base and sides of the keystone are different and the opposite letters (S. S. and T. T.) of the corners which correspond to a movable cross of the zodiac, characterized by the four animals mentioned above, are the same. If the letters of the keystone and their positions, and the signs of the zodiac were merely to puzzle the mind and mystify inquisitive people, they would be of little use and should be cast aside. But they have, in fact, a deep significance, a physical and a spiritual value. Too little thought is given them by men who should make such subjects of practical value, and have them as realities in their lives.

The zodiac represents man in the universe and the universe in man; the keystone is representative of man. An explanation of the positions in which man is placed in the world and the cultivation of the virtues by which he overcomes the vices that torture him, before he rises to the crown and glory of his lives, is too lengthy to attempt. Only the briefest outline can be here given. As physical man is placed in the physical world in his zodiac, so man as a spirit is placed in physical man, his physical body. As man who is born of woman should arise from his low state of physical matter, work through his animal nature, and arise to the glory of intellectual manhood in the world, so man as a spirit must subdue and ascend from his base animal nature and rise and complete the man of intellect as his spiritual crown and glory. Like Ixion in the mythology of the Greeks was bound and turned on a cross, to atone for his misdeeds, so is man placed in the world to work out his destiny; and, so is man as a spirit placed in his physical body to undergo the tests of his physical nature, to be tormented by, until he shall overcome it, the animal nature, thereafter to pass through and be purified by all manner of tests and trials, so that he will be fitted and prove himself worthy to fill his proper place in the universe. The signs of the zodiac show the stages and the law according to which the physical and psychic and mental and spiritual men work in their respective zodiacs, within the all-inclusive zodiac. The letters on the keystone should show the way and the means by which man as a spirit works within the physical body in his zodiac in which he is placed, in order that he may become the true keystone which completes the royal arch. The work of the Royal Arch Chapter may give the symbolism of the letters and the keystone; but it can only be the symbolism. Man as a spirit may build his arch, but he does not complete it—does not really fill it in one life. He is overcome; he is slain by his adversaries. As often as he dies he is raised and comes again, and will continue his work until he rises and does fill his place and complete his arch in the temple. The circle of his lives, the arch, will be complete. He will then go out no more.

The physical keystone of every Mason who has taken the Royal Arch Chapter is symbolical of himself when he shall be worthy and ready to complete and fill the arch of his lives—in that temple not built with hands. Man as a Mason, the keystone of the temple, now lies at the lowest part of the structure. He, it, is at the place of sex, libra, of his zodiac. He must arise, must raise himself. After taking the positions indicated by the letters on the keystone, or by the signs of the zodiac, and doing the work required by each letter or sign, he must rise by his own worth and work to the head—which is the crown and glory of man. When the stone is raised from the place of sex to the head, he, man, the keystone, will become immortal. He will then be all that is said of the White Stone on which is a new name, his new name, which he himself makes as his mark on that stone, the stone of immortality.

A FRIEND

---

[From *The Word*, Vol. 15 No. 4]

*What Is Taste in Food?*

Taste is a function of the form body for registering the values and qualities in liquids and solids. There is no taste in food until water has related the food with the tongue. As soon as water, moisture, saliva, has brought the food into relationship with the tongue, the organ of taste, the nerves of the tongue instantly convey to the form body the impressions of the food. Without water to make the connection between food and the nerves of the tongue, the nerves cannot convey the impressions of the food to the form body and the form body cannot perform its function of taste.

There is a subtle relationship between bodies having qualities of taste, the nerves and the form body, and water. The subtle relationship is the bond which causes the two parts of hydrogen and one part of oxygen to become what we call water, which is different from either of the characteristics of hydrogen or oxygen of which water is composed. There is water in every particle of food. The bond which unites the two gases to produce water is the same subtle bond which unites food, the nerves in the tongue, water, and the form body.

Whenever the physical water relates an article of food to the tongue, the subtle element in water is present and acts at once on the form body, if the nerves of the tongue are intact. The subtle element in the water which relates the food to the tongue is the same in the water and in the food and the tongue and the nerve. That subtle element is the real, the occult element water. The water which we know is only the outermost expression and manifestation of the subtle occult element water. This subtle water is the element of which the form body itself is chiefly composed.

Taste is a function in this form body of taking into itself through its own occult element water the essences or qualities contained in food. Taste is a function of the form body, but it is not the only function.

Taste is one of the senses. The form body is the seat of all the senses. The form body registers all sensations. Sensations are experienced by man only through the form body. The form body relates each sense to the other. The purpose of the senses is that each should contribute to the general good of the body, that the body may be a fit instrument for use by and development of the mind. The purpose of taste is that by it the form body might register the sensations produced by the food so that it can distinguish between them and refuse such food as is unnecessary and injurious, and select only such as is most suitable to the uses of the mind in building and maintaining the physical structure and the form body.

Taste would guide men and certain animals as to which foods are the most needed and useful for the body, if men and those animals lived in a normal and natural manner. But men are not normal and natural, and not all animals are, because of the influences which man has brought and brings to bear on them.

The sense of smell is more nearly related to food and to taste than any of the other senses because smell has to do directly with and corresponds to physical matter, and food is made up of the elements which enter into the composition of physical matter.

૨ૡ

*Has taste in food any value as nourishment apart from the food?*

It has. The gross food nourishes the physical body. The subtle occult element, water, just referred to, is nourishment to the form body within the physical. The taste of that occult element is nourishment to a third something which is within and through the form body. In the human, this third something is not yet a form, though it is expressed in specialized forms by types of animals. This third something which receives nourishment in man from the taste in food is desire. Desire reaches into the senses and used them to draw into itself the gratification which all the sensations afford. Each sense thus ministers to the desire. However, the special sense which corresponds to desire, and which desire uses to relate itself to the other senses, is touch or feeling. So desire relates itself through touch to taste, and draws through the sense of taste all the pleasures which it can experience from foods through taste. Were the form body allowed to perform its function of taste without having to obey the demands of desire, it would automatically select only such foods as it needs to maintain its form and the structure of the physical. But the form body is not allowed to select the foods most needed. The desire rules the form body and uses it to experience the gratification of the sensations which it cannot obtain without the form body. The taste which most pleases the desire, desire demands through the form body, and man, deluded into believing that the desire is himself, contrives as best he can to supply it with such foods as it unreasonably demands through taste. So the taste is cultivated to gratify the desire, the unreasoning animal brute, which is a part of the make-up of man. By supplying the demands of desire through taste foods are taken into the body which are injurious to its maintenance, and in the course of time its normal condition is disturbed and ill health results. Hunger should not be confused with taste. Hunger is the natural craving of the animal for the satisfying of its needs. Taste should be the means by which an animal may select the foods needed for its maintenance. This animals in the wild state, and away from the influence of man, will do. The animal in man, man often confuses and then identifies with himself. In the course of time the tastes for food have been cultivated. The desire or animal in man has been nourished by the subtle tastes in food, and the animal breaks down the form body and prevents it from performing its natural functions in the maintenance of the health of the body as a whole and in serving as a reservoir of life on which man may call for use in his work in the world.

Taste has a value apart from the food. Its value is to nourish the desire, but to give it only the nourishment it needs, and not to increase its strength beyond that which the form body is able to bear.

A FRIEND

# OCTOBER 1912

[From *The Word*, Vol. 16 No. 1]

*How can one protect himself against the lies or slander of others?*

By being honest in thought, truthful in speech, and just in action. If a man will think no lie and is truthful in speech, lies or slander cannot prevail against him. In view of the seeming injustice and unmerited slander in the world, this statement would not appear to be borne out by facts. Yet, it is true. No one wishes to be slandered; no one wishes to be lied about; but the majority of people do lie about and slander others. Perhaps the lie is only a little one, a "white lie"; perhaps the slander is only done in the way of gossip, to make conversation. Nevertheless, a lie is a lie, however it may be colored or called. The fact is, it is difficult to find anyone who thinks honestly, speaks truthfully and acts justly. One may admit this statement to be generally true of others, but he is likely to deny it if it is applied to him. His denial, however, proves the statement true in his case, and he is his own victim. The universal habit of crying out against lies and denouncing slander in general, but not decreasing our contributions to the supply, causes and keeps so large a variety and stock of the commodity in active circulation, and causes those who have to do with the supply to be so susceptible to or injured by lies and slander.

A lie is in the moral world what murder is in the physical world. The one who tries to murder would kill the physical body. The one who lies about another injures or attempts to destroy the character of that other. If the would-be murderer can find no entrance for his weapon in his intended victim's physical body, he will not succeed in his attempt at murder, and it is likely that when caught he will suffer the penalty of his act. To prevent the entrance into his body of the murderer's weapon, the intended victim must have protected himself by a coat of armor or some thing which resists the attack. The murderer in the moral world uses a lie, falsehood, slander, as his weapons. With these he attacks the character of his intended victim. To protect himself against the murderer's weapons, the intended victim must have armor about him. Honesty in thought, truthfulness in speech, and justice in act, will build about him an armor invulnerable to attacks. This armor is not seen, but neither is a lie or slander seen, nor is character seen. Though not seen, these things are more real than is a pistol, a knife, or armor of steel. A lie or slander cannot affect the character of one who is guarded by honesty and truthfulness, because truthfulness and honesty are permanent virtues; lies and slander are their opposites, and are vices which are impermanent. A lie cannot prevail against a truth. Slander cannot prevail against honesty. But if instead of being honest in his thought a man thinks lies and speaks falsely, his thinking and speech make his character vulnerable and negative to the positive lies or slander aimed at him. If, however, his character is protected by an armor made of his honesty in thought and truthfulness in speech, then the weapons aimed at him will recoil on the one who hurled them and who will himself suffer the consequences of his own act. Such is the law in the moral world. He who injures another's character by lies and slander will in turn suffer from the falsehoods of others, though the penalty may be deferred. It is better for one's murderous intentions toward another to at once recoil on him and from the armor of honesty and truthfulness of his intended victim, because he is more likely to see and will the sooner see the futility of wrong thought and action, and will the sooner learn not to lie, not to do wrong because he cannot do wrong without injury to himself. After he has learned that he must not do wrong if he would avoid the penalty of wrong, he will soon learn to do right because it is right and best.

Little "white lies" and idle slander are not the little harmless things which they appear to be to unseeing eyes. They are the seeds of murders and other crimes, though much time may intervene between the planting of the seeds and the reaping of the fruit.

When one tells a lie which is undetected, he is sure to tell another, and another, until he is found out; and he becomes a hardened liar, confirmed in the habit. When one lies, he invariably tells another lie to hide his first, and a third to hide the two, and so on until his lies contradict each other and stand out as strong witnesses against him. The more successful he at first is in adding to the number of his lies, the more over-whelmed and crushed will he be when these children of his thought are summoned to bear witness against him. One who protects himself by honesty, truthfulness, justice, in his thought and speech and action, will not merely protect himself from attacks of falsehood and slander; he will teach how not to attack him those who would attack him and how they protect themselves by having an invisible though invulnerable armor. He will be a true philanthropist because of the moral strength which others have been stimulated to develop. He will be a true reformer, by the establishment of honesty, truthfulness and justice in thought and speech. So with the ceasing crime, houses of correction will be done away with and prisons abolished, and with active minds, man will have happiness and will perceive what freedom is.

A FRIEND

# NOVEMBER 1912

[From *The Word*, Vol. 16 No. 2]

*How do the hibernating animals live without food and apparently without air during their long periods of hibernation?*

No animal organism can live without food. The need and functions of the organism determine the kind of food required. Hibernating animals do not live without food nor usually without air, though it is not necessary for them to take food into their digestive organs to keep alive during the period of their hibernation. Hibernating animals with lungs usually breathe, but their respirations are no more than enough to keep their bodies in contact with their life currents which are at so low an ebb that the animals seem not to breathe at all.

Types of animals and their habits are arranged according to certain economic laws of nature for the preservation of creatures of nature. Food is necessary for the maintenance of every bodily structure, and man's civilization has made it necessary that as to him the intervals at which food is taken should be of short duration. Man accustomed to his three or more meals a day does not understand or appreciate how it is that animals can go days or weeks without food, and that some can live through the winter without eating. Animals in their wild state require proportionately less food than man. The food eaten by natural animals is to supply their needs and so must the food man eats supply his bodily needs.

But man's food must also supply the energy required for the activity of his brain and his wants. According to the economy of nature the food man eats would increase his store of energy and add to his power. Usually he drains his energies into excesses of pleasures. What more than enough the animal eats to supply its present needs is stored in its body as so much surplus energy, and on that it draws when the supply of food is not sufficient for its needs.

As winter approaches, the animals which hibernate increase in fat and are ready to begin their winter's sleep. The cold cuts off their food supply, freezes the ground and drives them into their dens. Then they coil or fold themselves into the position which best conserves their heat and protects from cold. Breathing slows down, the number and lengths of respirations are regulated to the amount of fuel necessary to keep active the flame of life. The food used is not now for muscular activities, but to supply the organism with the energy needed to keep it intact, through its long period of dormancy and sleep. This food or fuel is the surplus energy which it had stored up in its body in the form of fat and which is drawn on during its hibernating according to the body's needs.

As the earth inclines to the sun, the sun's rays, instead of glancing off the earth's surface as in winter, now strike more directly into the earth, increase the magnetic currents and start the sap and flow of life in trees. The sun's influence also awakens the hibernating animals from their sleep, each according to its nature, and as its food supply is made ready by the sun.

Circulation of the blood makes respiration necessary on account of the oxygen which the blood needs and which it gets through the lungs. Increased respiration causes increased circulation. The circulation is as active as the respiration is rapid and deep. Bodily activity makes the blood active and the active circulation increases the number of respirations, all of which uses up the energy supplied by food. Inactivity of the animal decreases its circulation. In the hibernating animal the circulation slows down to the minimum and its respiration is hardly if at all perceptible. But there are animals in whom the circulation and respiration stop and in whom the functions of the organs are suspended.

ॐ

*Can an animal with lungs live without breathing? If so, how does it live?*

Some animals with lungs do live without breathing. Such animals keep alive by suspending the functions of the organs requiring a food supply and by keeping in touch the animating principle within with the life principle of nature, the invisible and intangible ocean of life, through the magnetic co-ordinating formative principle of its physical body. Seldom if ever a year goes by that the newspapers do not give some facts connected with the discovery of an animal which has lived for an immense period without the possibility of its breathing. Frequently the writer of the article is one who has for the first time heard of a fact such as that of which he writes, and he is likely to describe it as being the first case of its kind on record. As a matter of fact, there are numerous well authenticated cases on record, in reputable scientific journals. Not many months ago one of the morning papers gave an account of such a remarkable discovery. A party of explorers were in search of certain specimens in the interest of science. They had occasion to cut through a section of rock. In one of their cuts the solid rock opened and disclosed a toad which had been embedded in that solid mass. Immediately the toad became the chief object of interest. While looking at it as it lay flattened into its little stone chamber where it had been entombed for centuries, one of the party poked it to see if it was petrified, and the toad surprised them all by hopping out of his tomb. The member who reported his discovery said that he had heard and read of such cases, but had always doubted their possibility until he had witnessed the phenomenon. At the time of the report the toad was alive and well. On another occasion it was reported by persons of repute that while cutting through certain strata of rock in the side of an old watercourse, as the rock parted a lizard rolled out, and was captured when it began to crawl lazily away.

Animals which are found alive fastened between ledges of rocks, or entombed in solid rock, or which have grown into trees, or been buried in the ground, are animals which hibernate, but which can also suspend all organic functions by cutting off the air supply and at the same time cut off the physical connection with certain nerve centers and put them into etheric contact. This is done by rolling the tongue back into the throat and filling the air passage with the tongue. The tongue so rolled back presses into the larynx and stops the windpipe or trachea at its upper end. The tongue thus serves two purposes. It plugs the windpipe, and so prevents the passage of air into the lungs, and, thus placed, it makes a battery through which the life current flows into the body as long as the circuit is kept closed. When the air supply is shut off from the lungs, the blood cannot be aerated; oxygenation of the blood ceases; without blood supply the organs cannot perform their functions. Ordinarily under these conditions death follows, because the current of the breath is broken, whereas the breath must be kept swinging for the physical machinery of life to keep running. But if when the air supply is cut off from the lungs a more subtle connection than the breath is made between the physical body and the life ocean, the physical body can be kept alive as long as the connection with life is made and the body remains quiet.

As long as the tongue is kept in the position described, the animal will live; but it cannot move, because air breathing is necessary for physical activity, and it cannot breathe while its tongue stops its air passage. When the tongue is removed the connection with the subtle life flow is broken, but the physical life current begins with the swing of the breath.

Aside from the fact that toads and lizards have been found alive in solid stone, much speculation has been indulged in, as to how, unhurt, they got there. As to how a toad or a lizard could have been entombed in stone, the following may suggest two of the several possible ways.

When a creature is found in stone of aqueous formation by a river bank, it is possible that, during a period of its physical inactivity, the water rose and covered it and that there were deposits from the water which settled around the creature's body and so imprisoned it. When an animal is found in stone of igneous origin, it is possible that while in its physically quiescent state, it stood in the way of and was covered over by a cooling stream of molten rock flowing from a volcano. Objections might be made that no toad or lizard would remain in the water long enough and suffer deposits to accumulate into a mass of stone about it, nor could they stand the heat and weight of molten rock. These objections will lose much of their importance to one who has been observant of the habits of toads and lizards, when he recalls the intense heat which they seem to enjoy, and when it is understood that while physically dormant and in contact with the subtler current of life, they are insensible to physical conditions and sensation.

ॐ

*Does science recognize any law by which man can live without food and air; if so, have men so lived, and what is the law?*

According to modern science there is no such law, because no such law is known to modern science. That a man can live for a long period without food and air is not admitted by official science. There cannot, according to science, be any law which allows a man to live without food and air, all evidence notwithstanding, until science has formulated the law and officially approved it. Nevertheless, men have lived for long periods, without food and cut off from air, according to trustworthy witnesses, and as chronicled in public records. In India there are numerous records in modern times, and accounts and legends going back many centuries, of yogis who because of certain practices were able to and did suspend bodily functions and remain without air for long periods of time. Almost any Hindu has either heard of or witnessed such a performance. One such account will serve to illustrate. In order to prove that man could acquire extraordinary powers usually considered impossible, a certain Hindu yogi offered to demonstrate to some English officers that he could live for a long period without food or air. The Englishmen proposed test conditions, which were accepted, it being understood however that no other than the yogi's chelas, disciples, prepare him for the ordeal and care for him after it. At the time appointed a large gathering of people assembled to witness the wonder about to be performed. Surrounded by his large audience, the yogi sat in meditation until his disciples attending him saw a certain change come over him. Then they placed him at length in a coffin which was covered and in turn placed in a leaden casket. The cover of the casket was put on and hermetically sealed and was lowered over six feet into the ground. The earth was then thrown on the casket, and grass seed was sown over it. Soldiers kept constant guard around the spot, which was also a place of attraction to visitors. Months passed, the grass grew into a heavy sod. At the time agreed upon all parties concerned were present, and the audience was large, as the news of the wonder had spread far. The grass was carefully examined with satisfaction. The sod was cut into and removed, the ground opened, the leaden casket raised, the seals broken and cover removed, and the Yogi was seen lying as he had been placed. He was reverently removed. His disciples rubbed his limbs, manipulated his eyes and temples, pulled out and washed his tongue. Soon respiration began, the pulse beat, a sound issued from the Yogi's throat, his eyes rolled and opened and he sat up and spoke. The only difference in the Yogi was that he appeared to be more emaciated than at the time of interment and burial. This case is recorded in one of the government reports.

Those who claim to be acquainted with the practices necessary to go into such trance conditions, state that Yogis prepare themselves by certain breathing exercises and by certain treatment of the tongue and throat. It is said by them and also stated in books dealing with the subject of "Yoga," that by meditation and exercises in the exhalation, inhalation and retention of the breath, the operation of the physical organs may be suspended and the body still kept alive. It is said to be necessary for one who would go into a long trance to be able to roll his tongue back into his throat. To make this physically possible, it is claimed that the connection between the lower jaw and the tongue must be cut or worn away. Then the would be Yogi is supposed to pull—or what is called "milk"—his tongue in order to stretch it to the required length necessary for the operation. His teacher shows him how.

Whether or not those kind of Yogis have learned to imitate hibernating animals and patterned the natural trance conditions of certain animals, nevertheless the conditions and processes are similar, though what the Yogi lacks in the natural endowment he acquires by practice, or artificial means. The tongue of the toad or lizard requires no operation to give it length, nor do these animals require breathing exercises to connect them with an inner flow of life. Season and place will determine when they shall become entranced. What an animal can do by natural endowment, man may also learn to do. The difference is that man has to supply with mind, what he lacks by nature.

For man to keep alive without breathing he must make connection with his psychic breath. When his psychic breath flows his physical breath stops. The psychic breath is sometimes induced unintentionally by a mental attitude or disturbance, or it may be induced by the magnetism or the mind of another, as in deep magnetic or hypnotic trance. When a man, of his own will, passes into a state where he lives without breathing he does so by some such physical and breathing exercise as described or, except for natural breathing, without any physical movement whatever. In the first case he makes contact with his psychic breath from his physical body below. In the second case he relates his psychic breath to his physical from his mind above. The first method is by means of the senses, the second is by means of the mind. The first method requires the development of the inner senses, the second method is accomplished when one learns how to use his mind intelligently, independently of his senses.

Many grades of matter and more than one body enter into the construction of man. Each of his bodies or grade of matter is supplied from the world to which it belongs. But the main life supply is through one of the bodies which transfers life to the others. When the life supply is taken through the physical it is used and transferred to the psychic. When the main supply comes through the psychic it transfers to and keeps alive the physical. The law is that man can keep his body alive by the breath he is able to give it.

A FRIEND

---

# DECEMBER 1912

[From *The Word,* Vol. 16 No. 3]

*Why is time divided as it is?*

In order that man may keep a record of events; that he may estimate the distances of events in the perspective of the past, and anticipate those to come. As defined by some philosophers, time is "a succession of phenomena in the universe." That man might keep track of his life and business, as well as of other peoples', he was obliged to devise means of fixing events in time. It was natural to measure events on earth by the "succession of phenomena in the universe." The measures or divisions of time were furnished him by nature. Man had to be a good observer and to keep account of what he had observed. His powers of observation were keen enough to notice his life was marked off by a succession of periods of light and dark, of day and night. The light period was due to the presence, the dark to the absence, of the sun. He saw the seasons of warmth and cold were due to the sun's position in the heavens. He learned the constellations and noticed their changes, and that the seasons changed as the constellations changed. The sun's path appeared to pass through star clusters, constellations, which the ancients numbered as twelve and called the zodiac, or circle of lives. This was their calendar. The constellations or signs were called by different names among different peoples. With few exceptions the number was counted as twelve. When the sun had passed from any one sign through all the twelve and began at the same sign, that circle or cycle was called a year. As one sign passed down and another came up, the people knew from experience that the season would change. The period from one sign to another sign was called a solar month. The Greeks and the Romans had trouble in dividing the number of days in a month, and even the number of months in the year. But finally they adopted the order as used by the Egyptians. We use the same today. A further division was made by the phases of the moon. It took 29 days and a half for the moon to pass through its four phases from one new moon to the next new moon. The four phases constituted one lunar month, of four weeks and a fraction. The division of the day from sunrise to the highest point in the heavens and to sunset was marked according to the plan suggested in the heavens. The sun dial was later adopted. A marvel of astronomical knowledge is shown by the accuracy with which the stones at Stonehenge at Salisbury Plain in England were set up, in prehistoric times. Instruments were devised, such as the hour glass, and water clock to measure periods. Finally the clock was invented and patterned after the twelve signs of the Zodiac, except that the twelve was, as they thought, for convenience sake, numbered twice. Twelve hours for day and twelve hours for night. The complications of life made by civilization necessitated the division of the hour into minutes and the minutes into seconds, and in order to record the occurrence of certain phenomena the second is too great a period of time, which is therefore divided into fractions running into almost unlimited number.

Without a calendar, to measure and fix the flow of time, man could have no civilization, no culture, no business. The watch which may now be had for a trifle, represents work done by a long line of mechanics and thinkers. The calendar is the result of the sum total of the thought of man to measure the phenomena of the universe, and to regulate his affairs by this measure.

A FRIEND

# JANUARY 1913

[From *The Word*, Vol. 16 No. 4]

*Has time in its divisions into years, months, weeks, days, hours, minutes and seconds any correspondence with the physiological or other processes in the human body? If so, what are the correspondences?*

There is an exact correspondence between the natural measures of time by the cycles of the sun, moon and planets and certain physiological processes in the human body, but the division made by the mechanical contrivances of man is not exact.

The universe as a whole is represented by all that can be seen or understood of the heavens or space; this universe corresponds to the physical body of man; the star clusters, for instance, correspond to the nerves and the ganglia in the body. The sun, moon, the earth, and the stars called planets with their respective satellites or moons, move in their own atmospheres.

Speaking of or supposing time to be a "succession of phenomena in the universe," marked off by the movements of what are called the heavenly bodies in space, and changes and phenomena thereby produced in relation to the earth, there is a correspondence between these phenomena and the normal human body with its physiological processes and the changes and results produced therefrom. But it is not well for our safety that we discover these things; lest we should open Pandora's box.

It is important and enough to know there are two germs in the human body which represent and correspond to the sun and the moon. The generative system in the body corresponds and is related to the solar system. But each of the organs in the solar system has its corresponding organs in the body. The seed and soil in the generative system is the result of the action of the organs in the body corresponding to the sun and the moon. The essence or the extracts resulting from the action of the organs, corresponding and related to the planets, perform their work through the different systems of the body, and all work together in the general economy of the body for the period of its natural life, so that the particular work to which the life of the body is devoted may be accomplished.

There is in the body a principle which is representative of and corresponds to the sun. This passes down and up or around the body, as the sun is said to make one complete circle through the twelve signs of the zodiac. From the sign aries corresponding to the human head, down by way of the sign cancer, corresponding to the breasts or chest, to the sign libra corresponding to the place (not the organs) of sex, and up by way of the sign capricorn, corresponding to the spine in the region of the heart, and back again to aries the head, passes the germ or sun of the body through its signs of the zodiac in the time of one solar journey of a year. There is in the body another germ representative of the moon. The lunar germ should pass through all the signs of its zodiac. However, such is not usually the case. The zodiac of the moon is not the zodiac of the universe. The moon makes a revolution through its zodiac in the body in twenty-nine and a fraction days, corresponding to the lunar month. When the moon is full it is in aries of its zodiac and its correspondent germ in the body should be in the head; the last quarter is the cancer of its zodiac and the breast of the body; the dark of the moon turning to the new moon is the libra of its zodiac and then its germ in the body is in the region of sex. In the first quarter of the moon it is in its capricorn and the bodily germ should be along the spinal cord opposite the heart, and from there the germ of the body should pass upward to the head, when the moon is full in its sign aries. So the solar year and the lunar month are marked in the body by the passing of their representative germs through the body.

The week is perhaps the oldest measure of time in any human calendar. It is recorded in the calendars of the most ancient people. Modern people, necessarily, have borrowed it from them. Each day of the week is related to the sun, moon, and planets, from which the days take their names. The life of the human body corresponds to one manifestation of a solar system. The week in the human body corresponds in smaller measure to the same.

The day, which is the revolution of the earth once around its axis, is one of the seven periods of the week, and in it the larger period is represented again. In the human body, the germ or principle corresponding to the earth makes one complete round through its particular system, which corresponds to the revolution of the earth. These correspondences, the solar year and month, the lunar month, the week, day with the physiological operations of man's body, ends with the day. There are numerous other minor measures of the "succession of phenomena in the universe" which correspond exactly with substances and processes in the human body. But for the hour, minute and second, there can only be claimed a kind of analogy between universal and physiological claimed a kind of analogy between universal and physiological phenomena. The hour, minute and second may be said to be comparatively modern measures. When the measure called a second was adopted it was thought that it being so short a period there would never be need of any attempt to divide it. Physical science made the same mistake when they gave the name of atom to the minute parts of what they considered to be primitive elements. Later they discovered each of those "atoms" to be a little universe in itself, the divisions of which were named electrons, ions, though possibly the ion is not such an ultimate division. The human body is regulated to and should act in accord with the phenomena in the universe, but invariably man interferes with the body's natural processes and normal functions. Then he gets into trouble. Pain, suffering and disease are the result, which are the natural processes of the body in the effort of nature to restore a normal condition. These processes in the human body have their correspondence with conflicts and cataclysms in nature, to maintain an equilibrium. If man in his body will work with and not too much against nature he may learn the exact correspondence between each part of his body and its corresponding part in the universe and their reciprocal processes.

A FRIEND

---

# FEBRUARY 1913

[From *The Word,* Vol. 16 No. 5]

*Can a man live through, finish the tasks of, and die to more than one*
*life during his allotted span of years on this earth?*

Yes; he can. The fact of reincarnation is of course granted in the
question. Reincarnation—as a teaching, that man, considered as a mind,
comes into a physical body of flesh to learn certain things and to do certain work in the world in that life, and then leaves his body which there-
upon dies, and that after a time he takes on another physical body, and
then another and still others until his work is finished, knowledge is
gained in and he graduates from the school of life—reincarnation is
invariably accepted by those who have grasped the teaching and applied
it in explanation of the inequalities in every respect of children of the
same parents, and of the men and women they know who hold different
positions in life and are different in development of character, irrespective of their heredity, environments and opportunities.

Although once known, yet for many centuries the doctrine of reincarnation has been foreign to the civilization and teachings of the West.
As the mind becomes more familiar with the subject it will not only
grasp reincarnation as a proposition, but will understand it as a fact,
which understanding then opens up new views and problems of life.
The question is asked from a different viewpoint than are those usually
put. It is usually understood that when the mind has another physical
body prepared for it, and incarnates, it just takes up that body and goes
on with its work and experiences where the mind left off in the last life,
as a bricklayer adds other bricks to those he had laid on the job of the
day before, or as an accountant carries over his debits and credits on the
set of books with which he is engaged. This applies to the majority,
probably, of those who live. They come into life with their burdens and
drudge through it sullenly, like donkeys with their loads, or they resist
and kick at duties and everything in general, and refuse to accept and

bear responsibilities, like mules which balk at and throw and kick their loads and anything that comes their way.

The minds incarnated in the West are of a different order from those of the East, as is shown by the intensity of civilization, the inventions, improvements, constantly changing methods and activities of the day, in the West. The strain and stress may be greater now than in the past; but because of the very intensity of things more can be done now than could be done in the past.

Times and environments may set limits to man's work, but a man can use times and environments for his work. A man may pass through life automatically, or he may rise from obscurity and be a prominent actor in world history and give long employment to his biographers. The history of a man may be written on his tombstone as: "Here lies the body of Henry Jinks. He was born in this township in 1854. He grew up, got married, was the father of two children, bought and sold merchandise, and died," or the history may be of a different order, such as that of Isaac Newton or Abraham Lincoln. One who is self-moved, and who does not wait for so-called circumstances to move him, will have no limits set him. If a man wills to do so, he may pass out of one phase of life and into another, and work through that phase and into another, as Lincoln did; and if he continues to work, bent on doing something in the world and guided by right motive, he will have some great work entrusted to him, by doing which he will do not only the work of many lives for himself but will perform a work for the world; and in that case the world will in his future lives be an aid instead of a hindrance to him and his work. This applies to every public character who has done the work of and passed from one station of life to another.

But there are men who, irrespective of the place of their birth or station in life, live an interior life. This interior life of a man seldom goes on public record, and is seldom known to intimate acquaintances. As a man may go through many stations in public life, the attainment of any one of which may be the life's work of another man, so the man who lives an interior life may in one physical life learn not only those lessons and do that work which it was intended that he should in that life, but he may learn and do the work which it would have taken him other reincarnations to accomplish, if he had refused or failed to do his first allotted work.

It depends on the man, and what he is willing to do. Usually the man's position or environment changes with the finishing up of one work and with the readiness to begin another, though this is not always the case. Each change of work or character may symbolize a different life, though it may not always be equal to the work of an entire incarnation. One may be born in a family of thieves and be compelled to work with them. Later he may see the wrong of thievery and leave it for an honest trade. He may leave the trade to fight in a war. He may at its conclusion enter business, but aspire to attainments not connected with his business; and he may realize much he aspires to. The changes in his life may appear to have resulted from conditions into which he was thrown, and these to have been brought about by accidental happenings. But they were not. Each change in such a life was made possible by his attitude of mind. His attitude of mind created or opened the way for the desire, and so was brought about the opportunity to make the change. Attitude of mind brings about or allows man's changes of conditions in life. By the attitude of his mind a man can in one life do the work of many lives.

A FRIEND

# MARCH 1913

[From *The Word*, Vol. 16 No. 6]

*Can elementary matter, by magical processes, be brought into concrete form by means of the hands; if so, what particular form can be produced and how is it done?*

It is possible for one who has the necessary mental powers and psychic organization to give physical existence by magical processes to any form he desires; and yet, it may be cheaper in the end for him to get that object as other people get the objects of their desire. With the hands as matrix any mineral deposit or geometrical form can be precipitated from elemental matter. Likewise can elemental matter be by the hands drawn together and moulded into solid form.

The spiritual and mental powers necessary in one who would give a physical form to invisible matter are: faith, will, and imagination. In addition, his astral body must be able to retain and to generate much magnetism. Everybody has faith, will, and imagination; but, in a magician, these must be raised to a higher power. No work is performed without faith. For the work in hand, our magician must have faith, and that is knowledge in action. This faith may not be the result of his works and efforts in the present life. Our magician must have faith in his ability to bring into visibility that which is not visible, to make the inaudible audible, to make tangible that which is not tangible, to produce to the senses that which they are usually unable to sense. If he has not the faith that these things can be done, if he has not the faith that he can do them, then—he cannot. If he believes he can perform magic works because somebody tells him he can, his belief is not faith. It remains belief, a notion. For success in his work his faith must well up within him, and be unshaken by anything that may be said. The faith which thus wells up comes from a forgotten knowledge, acquired in the past. He must not remain satisfied with an unshaken faith, but he must bring the past into present knowledge. He must use his mind. If he is willing to exercise his mind by thoughts, his faith will guide him in his mental operations and will provide the way for the past to become present knowledge.

As to imagination, our magician must be different from those who are called people of imagination, because they have flights of fancy. Imagination is the making of images, or the state in which images are made. The images which our magician makes are mental images and which, when made, are not as easily broken as are those of clay or other physical matter. The images of our magician are harder to make and to break and will last longer than those fashioned of marble or steel. To have imagination necessary for his work, our magician must fix his mind on that to which he would give physical form. He must make an image of it. This he does by keeping his mind on the form until it is to him an image, which he may summon again by thought. When he has faith and can make images at will, he has also will. That is to say, he is able to call on will to aid in his work. The will is everywhere and like electricity is always ready to lend its power to anyone who provides the field for its operations and who can make it contact the field.

All the movements of swimming may be described with mathematical accuracy; yet, if one in the water tries to follow directions but has no faith in his ability to swim and does not imagine himself swimming while making the movements, then he wills not to swim. Doubt and then fear seizes him, and he sinks. In trying to walk a tight rope, one who has not faith that he can walk it and does not imagine himself on the rope and walking the rope wills to fall, and he does. Familiarity with the laws of gravitation and physics will not keep him on that rope. Faith shows him how. Imagination keeps him on the rope. Will gives him the power to walk. As long as he imagines himself on the rope and his confidence continues, he cannot fall. But should his thought change, and should he for a fraction of a second imagine himself falling, the picture which he makes of his falling will unbalance and pull him down.

Equipped with faith, will, and imagination, one can produce by means of his hands physical phenomena by magical processes. To illustrate: To give physical visibility to form, the form must be held or imagined. The fluid matter whirling, invisible, must be held compact until it becomes fixed and in thought solid. This is work for imagination. Passes can now be made with the hands around and about the desired form. By the movements of the hands around the form, elemental matter is drawn and precipitated into that form and, gradually, with continued precipitations, the form becomes visible and physical. This is done by the power of faith, which makes the laws controlling elemental matter known and how to draw it into form. The will lends the power to do all this and is the agent by which all the work is accomplished. The thought is the guide which causes the will to fuse or blend the elemental matter and to bring it into form. If the thought wavers in the operations, the work stops. If the thought is steady, the work of imagination and faith will be completed by the will. The form is made physical, and is of the size and color desired. A small object, such as a stone or crystal or gem, may be formed by placing the right hand over the left, the center of the palms opposite each other. Then the stone or gem or crystal must be imagined and that image must be held in thought and its precipitation willed. The magnetism of the operator's hands is the ground in which the image of the crystal or gem, as a germ or seed, begins to grow. With the magnetic force between the hands, the ray or rays of light are made to precipitate into the matrix in the mind, until the gem of the desired size and color and luster is produced. Forms have been and can be produced by magical processes, but it is easier to procure the desired forms in the usual methods than to go through the necessary training in order to produce them by magical means. But it is well for a man to have faith, to develop his imagination, to learn the uses of the will. The development or acquirement of these three magical powers will make a man of him. Then he can, but it is not likely that he will, be a maker of precious stones or other forms by magical processes.

ॐ

*How should the hands be used in the healing of one's own physical body or any part of the body?*

Directions cannot be given which would be fit for all kinds of diseases, but directions can be given to aid in the cure of constitutional and local ills, and which may apply generally to many others. It is best for those who would heal to understand a few fundamentals about the body and its magnetic nature, before they attempt magnetic treatment, of their own bodies or those of others.

The physical body is a mass of matter organized according to certain laws, each part to perform certain functions and serve certain purposes, for the common welfare of the whole. The physical mass is held together, repaired and maintained, by a fine magnetic body of form within the mass. The natural functions of the physical body, such as absorption, digestion, assimilation, elimination, and all involuntary movements, are carried on by the magnetic body of form within the physical mass. Certain laws govern all functions of the body. If these laws are transgressed, physical ills will inevitably follow. These ills are evidence that some wrong has been done, and that there is an obstruction or that there are many obstructions in the body which prevent the magnetic body from bringing about a harmonious relationship of its parts or functions, or that there is a greater expenditure of energy than its resources can supply. The magnetic form body is a storage battery through which universal life acts. The magnetic body is the medium which connects universal life with physical matter. Without the magnetic body, the physical mass would crumble into dust.

In the cure of ills by means of the hands, the right hand is placed on the forehead and the left hand at the back of the head. After remaining there quietly for a few minutes, the right hand should be placed on the chest and the left hand opposite on the spine. In a few minutes the left hand should be placed in the small of the back and the palm of the right hand on the navel. In a minute or two the right hand should be moved slowly and gently around the entire surface of the abdomen—in the direction in which a watch is wound—forty-nine times and then be brought to its first position and allowed to remain about three minutes.

The left hand should be kept still, with the palm under the spine, during the movements of the right hand. The body should be in a reclining position.

With regard to any local treatment, the left hand should be placed underneath the part affected and the right hand on the other side over the part and there allowed to remain about five minutes or until such time as one feels naturally that it is time to stop. The local treatment should be preceded or followed by the general treatment first described. The parts of the body may be rubbed, but the rubbing should be gentle. Harsh treatment is usually injurious according to these methods.

The physical hands do not produce the cure; the magnetic form within the hands does not produce the cure. The cure is produced by the universal life, which is conducted to the magnetic form within the physical body by means of the hands. The object of placing the hands on the body is to conduct universal life to the magnetic form and to strengthen the magnetic form so that it may receive and store and be in direct contact with universal life. In treating one's own body or the body of another, it must be well understood that the mind does not effect the cure, and that the mind must not try to direct the current or interfere with its flow in any way. If one cannot keep his mind in a calm and restful attitude, so as not to interfere with the cure, it is much better not to follow the practices here suggested. An attempt of the mind to direct the current of the cure does harm to the large part of the body to satisfy a small part. But in reality all parts are damaged by the pull. This is not mind or mental healing. This magnetic treatment as described will stimulate the magnetic body to renewed action and universal life will replenish it. In order to effect a cure and keep the body well, the body should be given the foods which one finds that it needs to repair and maintain its structure, and all wastes or drains on the body must be stopped.

A FRIEND

# APRIL 1913

[From *The Word*, Vol. 17 No. 1]

*What is necessary for growth in devotion?*

Thinking of how best to serve that to which one is devoted, and working for it.

Devotion is a state or frame of mind toward a principle, cause, being or person, and a readiness to act in some capacity for that to which one is devoted. Growth in devotion depends on the capacity of one to do, to serve, and the capacity is increased by acting with intelligence. The devotional nature impels one to show his devotion by doing something expressive of his devotion. This impulse of devotion does not always produce the best results, yet, though the intention be of the best, what is done may be to the detriment of that for which it is done.

Devotional natures act from the heart. This action from the heart, though it is the right beginning, is not enough for real growth. Knowledge is necessary to wise action. A man with a devotional nature does usually not listen to reason before acting, but prefers to follow the dictates or impulses of his heart. Yet, only by the exercise of the mind can knowledge be acquired. The true test of one's devotion is to study, to think, to work the mind regarding the best interests of that to which he is devoted. If one falls back into emotional action and fails to think patiently and persistently, then he has no true devotion. If one with a devotional nature persists in exercising his mind and so acquires the power to think clearly he will add knowledge to his devotion and his capacity to serve that to which he is devoted will increase.

❧

*What is the nature of incense, and how long has it been in use?*

The nature of incense is of the earth. Earth, as one of the four elements, corresponds to the sense of smell. Incense is an aromatic mixture of gums, spices, oils, resins, woods which during burning gives out pleasing odors from its fumes.

Incense was in use before man began to record institutions, customs, and events. Many scriptures speak of incense as necessary in acts of worship. Incense was used in sacrificial rites and as an offering, an evidence of devotion by the devotee and worshipper, to that which was worshipped. In many scriptures the offering of incense as an act of worship is described at great length, and rules given for the kind of incense to be used, its preparation and burning.

❧

*Are any benefits derived from the burning of incense, during meditation?*

Benefits may be derived from the burning of incense during meditation, concerning the physical and astral worlds. Incense burning will not reach beyond the astral or psychic world. Incense burning will not aid meditation on subjects concerning the mental or spiritual worlds.

If one gives allegiance to the great spirit of the earth and lesser earth spirits, or any of the beings of the astral world, then he may derive benefits from the burning of incense. He receives benefits for benefits given. The earth gives food to nourish physical man. Its essences also nourish the creatures of the earth and beings of the astral world. Incense burning serves a double purpose. It attracts and establishes communication with the beings desired, and it repels other beings to which the incense is unsuited. If one desires the presence of certain influences, then the burning of incense may help in attracting these influences and establishing rapport. However, if one does not know the nature of the incense which he would use and does not know the nature of the kind of influence or being he wants, then he may get instead of benefits, what is undesirable and harmful. This applies to meditation concerning the physical and astral or psychic worlds, and to sensuous objects.

For serious meditation on subjects of the mental and spiritual worlds, incense burning is not needed. Alone thought and attitude of mind decide what influences shall be around and what beings attendant in mental and spiritual meditation. Incense burning often holds the mind to sensuous objects and prevents it from entering a state of abstraction necessary to meditation concerning the mental and spiritual worlds.

ᢀᢣ

*Are the effects of incense burning observable on any of the planes?*

They are. Depending on the power of the operator the information he has of his subject, visible and other sensuous effects will be apparent. The fumes and smoke arising from the incense offer the strength and the material body in which the beings desired and invoked may appear. This is one of the reasons why sorcerers and necromancers used incense in their invocations and conjurations. By the burning of incense effects are produced on other planes than the physical, but one must have his psychic senses trained and under the control of his mind in order to see these. Then he will see how and know why influences and beings are attracted or repelled by incense burning, how they affect the one who offers the incense, and other results attending incense burning.

A FRIEND

# MAY 1913

[From *The Word*, Vol. 17 No. 2]

*What colors, metals and stones are attributed to the seven planets?*

There are seven colors to the solar spectrum, red, orange, yellow, green, blue, indigo, violet. This is the division of a ray of sunlight by a prism and as reflected on a surface. These seven colors may be reflected back to a center and again be the ray of light. The colors are said to correspond to the seven planets, mars, sun, mercury, saturn, jupiter, venus, moon. So also are the seven metals, iron, gold, mercury, lead, tin, copper, silver. Colors, metals and planets are said to correspond and be related to each other. The stones, garnet, amethyst, bloodstone, diamond, emerald, agate, ruby, sardonyx, sapphire, opal, topaz, turquoise, are supposed to be connected with the twelve months; each is said to have certain influences when worn on certain days, but more especially during the month to which it belongs. Writers on occult subjects have given different classifications and correspondences to the colors, metals and planets. Whatever classification is adopted, the motive determines what rules and methods should be followed to get benefits by wearing, separately or in combination, colors, metals and stones.

⁂

*Should the wearing of colors, metals and stones be determined by the aspect of that planet under the wearer was born?*

If one believes in the efficacy of faith; if he has faith; if he wills no injury to others by wearing colors, metals and stones—Yes. If he considers it a ridiculous practice, yet tries to see how it works out; if he believes in the potency of colors, metals and stones and would wear them with an object to exert an undue or evil influence over any one—No.

⁂

*Have the colors, metals and stones any special virtues, and how can they be worn without regard to the planets?*

Colors, metals and stones have special values, good or evil. But the strength of each of the colors, metals and stones is determined by the nature of its origin, the manner of its preparation, or by the influence imparted to it. One who is inclined to ridicule the thought that colors have certain values and that they will produce certain effects, will have reason to change his views if he wears a red coat before a bull.

The man who experiments with magnets will not consider as mere fancy or superstition the statement that certain metals have occult properties. No one doubts that there is a peculiar charm which stones have had for individuals in all ages. Aside from economic or decorative purposes colors have particular effects on the emotions of people. It is often observed that when some individuals get into certain psychic or emotional states, they see certain colors which are typical of their condition. For instance: criminals who have confessed guilt say they saw red just before their commission of murder. On the other hand, those who are given to periods of meditation, say they see yellow or golden color when they pass into a state of restful calm or purposeful aspiration.

Metals have occult significance and value, as well as for the common uses to which they are put, and so have stones. But these values must be studied and learned. The senses must become alert to them before their values can be used practically and without danger to body and reason. Study and training are as necessary to the acquirement of a knowledge of the occult values and use of metals as to the science of metallurgy. The one who guesses or has impressions about colors, metals and stones, whose inner senses have not been opened, who will not train his senses and discipline his mind, may act in blind faith and get some results, but he will excite and be subject to ridicule—and he will remain blind.

One can wear colors, metals or stones without regard to the planets when he has that power which is born of knowledge, and which is superior to any influence of colors, metals or stones. The firm and unshaken faith that no extraneous power can harm him, is an antidote for any influence emanating from physical objects. This faith and power comes from right motive, right thought, right attitude of mind. When one has these, colors, metals and stones, with their planetary influences can have no baneful influence on him. But then, perhaps, he need not wear them.

ﻻ

*What letters or numbers are attached or ascribed to the planets?*

Letters, numbers, names, seals, sigels, have been variously ascribed to the planets by writers on astrology, alchemy and magic, and various accounts and applications can be found in books dealing with these subjects. No claim is here made to such knowledge, nor to the right to impart it. No occult knowledge concerning the letters and names of "the planets" can be imparted directly through books or written forms. Books may give much information, but they cannot impart knowledge. Knowledge must be acquired by individual effort. Knowledge is acquired by putting the results of experiences to the best uses. Knowledge of letters, numbers and names will come by examining and analyzing and brooding about the parts and forms of letters and their combinations. For one whose tendency of mind is toward the occult side of letters, numbers, names, it is well to think and theorize about them, but not to attempt to put the theories into practice until theory gives place to certainty. Certainty cannot be gained by theorizing about and practicing with letters, numbers, names, colors, metals or stones. Certainty about these comes only with ability and control of the elements or forces of which they are the outward symbols, and which are represented by desires, passions and emotions within him. Many would-be alchemists and magicians have come to grief because they have attempted to accomplish in the world without, what should be done in the world within.

Visible colors are reflections of psychic states and emotions. Metals are the precipitations or solidifications of the invisible elements with which the spirit of each element is connected and through which it works. The same may be said of stones. Metals and stones are magnetic or electric. Where these go, the element or forces connected with them may be induced and become operative, as the magnetic force operates through iron, or as the electrical force is conducted by a copper wire. The wearing of colors, metals or stones may awaken and excite that within, which corresponds to the element or force without, and may induce such elements or forces to act through their senses on their correspondences within. By a control of the within only that without can be controlled.

A FRIEND

# JUNE 1913

[From *The Word*, Vol. 17 No. 3]

*Is man a microcosm of the macrocosm, the universe in miniature? If so, the planets and the visible stars must be represented within him. Where are they located?*

Thinkers in different times and in various ways, said the universe is epitomized in man. As a metaphor or in fact, this is likely to be true. It does not mean that the universe has fingers and toes and wears eyebrows and hair on a head, nor that the universe is built according to the present dimensions of man's physical body, but it means that the operations of the universe may be characterized and featured in man by his organs and parts. The organs in man's body are not made to fill space, but to perform certain functions in the general economy and welfare of the organism as a whole. The same may be said of bodies in the firmament.

The scintillating rays of light and the steady glowing orbs in the heavens are media through which universal forces act in the body of space, according to universal law and for the general welfare and economy of the whole. The internal organs, such as sex organs, kidneys, spleen, pancreas, liver, heart and lungs, are said to be correspondence of and bearing a direct relation to the seven planets. Such scientists and mystics as Boehme, Paracelsus, Von Helmont, Swedenborg, the fire philosophers and alchemists, have named the organs and planets which correspond to each other. They do not all give the same correspondences, but agree that there is a reciprocal action and relation between the organs and planets. After being aware that there is a correspondence, the student must, if he wishes to know, think out and solve which organs correspond to particular planets, and how they are related and operate. He cannot depend on another's tables in this matter. The table of correspondences may be right for the one who made it; it may not be true for another. A student must find his correspondences.

Without thinking, no one will ever know how universal objects correspond and relate to individual parts of the body, no matter what others may say about them. Thinking must be continued until the subject is known. What corresponds to the constellations, star clusters, nebulae in space, acts in man's body as plexuses, nerve ganglia, nerve crossings. These clusters or crossings in the body emit a light, a nerve aura. This in the heavens is spoken of as light of stars, and by other names. This would seem farfetched and fanciful to the astronomer, but if he thought in his body until he found out the nature of the nerve centers and their currents, he would change his theory about his astronomy. He would know what the stars in the heavens are, and be able to locate them as centers in his body.

એ

*What is meant by health in general? If it is the equilibrium of man's physical, mental and spiritual strength, then how is the balance maintained?*

Health is wholeness and soundness of the body in its structure and function. Health in general is the operation of a body in the work for which it is intended, without impediment of its function or impairment of its parts. Strength is developed and maintained as the result of health. Strength is not a thing apart from health, nor independent of health. Health is maintained by a conservation of the strength or energy developed, and a reciprocal action between the parts of the body and the body as a whole. This applies to the mind and spiritual nature of man, in combination with his human body, as well as to ordinary animal man. There is mental and spiritual health as there is physical health. The health of the whole is maintained when each part of the combination does its work in relation to and for the good of the whole. The rule is easily understood but hard to follow. Health is gained and maintained in the degree that one does what he knows best to gain health, and does what he knows best to preserve it.

A FRIEND

# JULY 1913

[From *The Word*, Vol. 17 No. 4]

*Is it best for a man to leave his physical body unconsciously, that the soul may enter its dream state?*

It is best for a man of responsibility to be conscious of everything he does in the physical and every other state of existence. If man—man meaning the conscious thinking principle in the body—decides to leave his physical body, he leaves it not unconsciously; if he leaves his body unconsciously, he has no choice in the matter.

It is not necessary for the soul—taking it that "man" and "soul" are in the question intended to be synonymous—to depart from its physical body to enter its dream state. Man seldom, if ever, leaves his physical body before death.

Man is conscious in his waking state; he is conscious in the dream state; he is not conscious during the passage from the waking to the dream state; that is, between the last moment when he is awake and the beginning of dreaming. The passing from the physical to the dream state corresponds to the process of death; and though by thought and act man determines what and how the transition shall be, he is not conscious of nor does he know the passing when the time has come, even though he may have some impressions of the passing over.

When man learns how to enter and how to leave the dream stage at will, he ceases to be the ordinary man, and is something more than the ordinary man.

༄

*What height do souls reach who leave their physical bodies consciously and who remain conscious after death?*

That depends on what were the thoughts and actions of what the questioner designates as the soul, and on the mental and spiritual attainments in other physical lives and especially in the last one. If man can leave his physical body consciously at death, he wills or sanctions death. Be it that one has gone through the process of death consciously or be it unconsciously, the state of being conscious, which he will enter, corresponds to and is determined by what he has acquired knowledge of during life in his physical body on the earth. Not acquirement and owning of sums of money and worldly possessions, however great, nor social position, nor acquaintance with and mastery of customs and conventions, nor erudition and familiarity with what other men have thought; none of this counts. Attainment after death depends on the degree of intelligence the man has attained to during life; on what he knows life to be; on the control of his own desires; on the training of his mind and the ends to which he has used it, and on his mental attitude toward others.

Each man can form in life some opinion of the state after death by realizing what he "knows" and what he does in this life with himself, and what is his attitude to the outside world. Not what a man says nor what he believes about after death states will be experienced by him after death. The politics of religion fashioned into articles of a creed and belief by theologians hopeful or with a grudge against the world will not cause the people to be conscious of and get after death what they had heard about before, even if they did believe what they heard. The after death state is not found to be the hot place prepared for those who do not believe, nor do mere belief and church membership give title to choice places in heaven. Belief in after death states can effect those states only in so far as they influence his state of mind and his actions. There is no god in heaven to lift man out of the world and to his bosom; there is no devil to catch man on his pitchfork when he passes out of the world, no matter what his beliefs have been during life, or what he has been promised or threatened with by theologians. Fears and hopes before death will not change the facts of after death states. The facts originating and defining man's after death states are: what he knew and what he was before death.

Man can deceive people about himself while in the world; by practice he may learn to deceive himself about himself during his physical life; but he cannot deceive his own High Intelligence, the Self, as it is

# JULY 1913

JULY 1913 235

sometimes called, as to what he has thought and done; for everything he has thought and sanctioned is in detail and in its totality automatically registered in his mind; and according to the inexorable and universal law of justice, from which there is no appeal and no escape, he is that what he has thought and sanctioned.

Death is a separating process, from the time of leaving the physical body to being conscious in the heaven state. Death strips everything from man that is not of the heaven world. There is no place in heaven for his wage-slaves and his banks. If man be lonesome without them he cannot be in heaven. Only that of him can go into heaven which is of the heaven state, and that which is not subject to hell. Wage slaves and land and banks remain in the world. If a man thought he owned them while he lived on earth, he was mistaken. He cannot own them. He can have a lease on things, but he owns only that which he cannot lose. What man cannot lose goes with him into heaven, remains his on earth, and forever he is conscious of it. He may cloud it over and cover it up on earth with things that do not belong to him, but he is still conscious of it. The mental state which man enters and knows during life he will enter and know after death, while in physical life he is disturbed by troubles and world cares. In the "heights," or heaven, what he is conscious of is free from fear and annoyance. Whatever prevents happiness in the world is eliminated from that state.

A FRIEND

# AUGUST 1913

[From *The Word*, Vol. 17 No. 5]

*Please give a definition of immortality and state briefly how immortality can be attained?*

Immortality is the state in which one is conscious of his identity through all states, conditions and changes.

Immortality must be attained intelligently, by the use of intelligence. Immortality cannot be attained by blind belief in some sort of an eternal existence after death, nor can anyone get into the state of immortality by gift, favor, inheritance. Immortality must be earned by hard work, *with intelligence.*

Immortality must be so earned and acquired before death, during one's life in a physical body in this physical world. After death immortality cannot be attained. All incarnated minds are striving to be immortal. If immortality is not attained before death, the body dies and the mind returns to earth in a new physical body, time after time and until immortality is attained.

The way to immortality is for one to cease identifying himself with his physical body, or with his desires and emotions, his personality. He should identify himself with that which has the prescience of knowledge; that is, with himself. When he thinks of this and identifies himself with it, immortality seems near. To be successful in this, one must take an inventory of the parts and elements making up what he has heretofore identified himself with. After this inventory he must examine what is changeable in him, and what permanent. That with him which persists, and is not subject to time and place, is of himself; all else is transitory.

It will be found that money, lands, antiques, possessions, position, fame and whatever else of this kind the world values most, are among transitory things, and of small or no value to one trying to become immortal. The things that are of value are intangible, not of the senses.

*Right* motive and *right* thoughts in daily life, in all phases of daily life, no matter what the walk of life may be, are the things that count. It is not the easiest life that brings quickest results. The life of a hermit, away from cares and temptations, does not provide the means or conditions. One who has difficulties, trials, temptations, but overcomes them and remains in control of them and true to his intelligent purpose of becoming immortal, will sooner and in fewer lives reach his goal.

The attitude of mind which is preeminently useful is that the seeker shall know himself separate from his body, separate from his personality, his desires, emotions, senses, and their pleasures and sufferings. He must know himself separate and independent of all this, though it appears to touch his very self and at times seems to be himself. His attitude should be, that he is of the infinite, living like the infinite, in eternity, without boundaries and divisions of time, or consideration of space. That is the state of immortality. He must get accustomed to look upon this as a reality. Then he can know. To fancy it is insufficient, and to prate about it, useless and childish.

ॐ

*Are man's likes and dislikes reflections of his own soul? If so, how are they reflected? If not, whence come these likes and dislikes?*

The term "the soul of man" is used promiscuously and stands for many phases of the invisible parts of what as to its visible aspect is called a man. Soul may mean his pre-natal condition, or the senseless shadow-form after death, or the undying universal principle which is in him during life. Man's soul is here considered as the mind—the thinking principle, the conscious light in the body. Man's likes and dislikes are not reflections of his mind. Likes and dislikes result from the action of mind with desire.

When the mind considers some of the desires it likes them; other desires the mind dislikes. That nature of the mind which thinks of desire, the desire likes; that nature of the mind which thinks away from desire and the senses, the desire dislikes. In this way are developed likes and dislikes between mind and desire. The likes and dislikes come from the likeness and unlikeness of mind and desire. Man's brood of likes and dislikes are born and bred within him. Then he manifests his likes and dislikes about him. The likes and dislikes created in one man will create more likes and dislikes in the man he meets; and those cause still other likes and dislikes in other men who likewise spread their likes and dislikes; so that the world is full of likes and dislikes. In this way it may be said that the world is a reflection of the likes and dislikes of man.

Do we like the world and the things in the world? Or do we dislike them? It is futile to try to stop liking or disliking. It is well for man to refuse to sanction with his mind what he knows to be not right. So he registers a worthy dislike. It is best for man to like and to think about that which he knows to be right, and to do it. In this way his likes have worth and power. If he treats likes and dislikes this way with himself, others will do it, too, and the world will change with the likes and dislikes.

A FRIEND

# SEPTEMBER 1913

[From *The Word,* Vol. 17 No. 6]

*Is it best that a man should suppress his sexual desires, and should he strive to live a life of celibacy?*

That must depend upon the motive and the nature of the man. It is never best to try to crush or kill out the sexual desire; but it is always best to restrain and control it. If a person has no object or ideal superior to that of sex; if man is ruled by animal nature; and if one lives to get and to enjoy, to linger in thought on the pleasures of sex, it is impossible for him to try to crush or kill out his sexual desires—though he can "live a life of celibacy."

According to the "Standard Dictionary," celibacy means, "the state of an unmarried person or celibate, especially of an unmarried man; abstinence from marriage; as, the celibacy of the priesthood." A celibate is said to be, "one who remains unmarried; especially, a man bound to single life by religious vows."

One who is physically and mentally qualified to marry, but who lives a life of celibacy in order to escape the ties, responsibilities and consequences of marriage, and who has not the will nor the desire to control his sex nature, is usually a scourge on humanity, whether he is or is not free from vows, whether he has or has not taken orders and is under the shelter and protection of the church. Chastity and purity of thought are essential to a life of celibacy in one who would enter the spirit of that life. There are few celibates, the unmarried, who are less addicted to the thoughts and acts of sex than are those who live in the married state.

Persons who feel at home in the world and who are physically, morally, mentally fit to marry, often neglect duties and shirk responsibilities by remaining unmarried. The reason for one's living a life of celibacy should not be: exemption from ties, duties, responsibilities, legal or otherwise; vows, penance, religious orders; to acquire merit; to get reward; to attain ascendancy in temporal or spiritual power. The reason for living a celibate life should be: that one cannot fulfill the duties he has made his own and wishes to perform, and at the same time be faithful to duties incumbent to the married state; that is to say, that married life would unfit him for what is his work. This does not mean that some work of fancy or a fad is reason to keep one unmarried. No occupation or profession is a warrant for celibacy. Marriage is no deterrent to what is usually called a "religious" or "spiritual" life. Religious offices which are moral can be filled as well by the married as by the unmarried; and often with more safety to the confessor and confessed than when the confessor is unmarried. One who is married is usually more competent to give advice than one who has not entered the married state.

Celibacy is necessary to one who is determined to attain to immortality. But his motive in so living should be, that he will thus better serve his human kind. The confessional is not the place for one who is about to enter the road to immortal life; and when he is far along the way he will have more important work. The one who is fit to live a life of celibacy will not be uncertain of what his duty is. One who is fit to live a celibate life is not free from sex desire; but he does not try to crush or kill it. He learns how to restrain and control it, This he learns and does with intelligence and will. One must live a life of celibacy in thought, before he can in fact. Then he lives for all, without injury to himself or others.

A FRIEND

# OCTOBER 1913

[From *The Word*, Vol. 18 No. 1]

*What is the rationale of the doctrine of the atonement, and how can it be reconciled with the law of karma?*

If the atonement is taken literally, and the causes said to have made the atonement necessary are to be considered literally, there is no rational explanation of the doctrine; no explanation can be rational. The doctrine is not rational. Few things in history are so repellent in ugliness, so barbaric in treatment, so outrageous to reason and the ideal of justice, as the doctrine of the atonement. The doctrine is:

The one and only God, self-existent throughout all time, created the heavens and the earth and all things. God created man in innocence and ignorance, and put him in a pleasure garden to be tempted; and God created his tempter; and God told man that if he yielded to temptation he would surely die; and God made a wife for Adam and they ate the fruit which god forbade them to eat, because they believed it was good food and would make them wise. Then God cursed the earth, and cursed Adam and Eve and drove them out of the garden, and cursed the children they should bring forth. And a curse of sorrow and suffering and death was upon all future mankind because of Adam's and Eve's eating of the fruit which God forbade them to eat. God could not or would not revoke his curse until, as said, "he gave his only begotten Son," Jesus, as a blood sacrifice to remove the curse. God accepted Jesus as atonement for the wrong doing of mankind on condition that "whosoever believeth on him should not perish," and with the promise that by such belief they would "have everlasting life." Because of God's curse, each soul that he made for each body that was born into the world was doomed, and each soul that he makes is doomed, to suffer in the world; and, after the death of the body the soul is doomed to hell, where it cannot die, but must suffer torments without end, unless that soul before death believes itself to be a sinner, and believes that Jesus came to save it from its sins; that the blood which Jesus is said to have shed upon the cross is the price God accepts of his only son, as the atonement for sin and ransom of the soul, and then the soul will be admitted after death to heaven.

To people brought up under the good old fashioned influences of their church, and especially if they are not familiar with the natural laws of science, their familiarity with these statements will salve over the unnaturalness of them and prevent them from seeming strange. When examined in the light of reason, they are seen in their naked hideousness, and not all the threatened fires of hell can prevent the one so seeing from denouncing such doctrine. But the one who denounces the doctrine should not denounce God. God is not responsible for the doctrine.

The literal doctrine of the atonement cannot in any sense be reconciled with the law of karma, because then the atonement would have been one of the most unjust and unreasonable events ever recorded, whereas, karma is the operative law of justice. If the atonement was an act of divine justice, then divine justice would be a misnomer and more unjust than any of the lawless acts of a mortal. Where is there a father who would give his only son to be persecuted and crucified, murdered, by a lot of manikins made by himself, and who, because of his not knowing how to make them act in accordance with his pleasure, had pronounced a curse of destruction on them; then had repented himself of his curse and agreed to forgive them if they would believe he had forgiven them, and that the death and shedding of his son's blood had excused them from their acts.

It is impossible to think of such course of action as divine. No one could believe it to be human. Every lover of fair play and justice would have pity for the manikins, feel sympathy and friendship for the son, and demand punishment for the father. A lover of justice would scorn the notion that the manikins should seek forgiveness of their maker. He would demand that the maker should seek forgiveness of them for making them manikins, and would insist that the maker must stop and correct his many blunders and make good all the mistakes he had made; that he must either do away with all the sorrow and suffering he had caused to be brought into the world and of which he claimed to have had a pre-knowledge, or else, that he must furnish his manikins, not merely reasoning power enough to question the justice of his edicts, but with intelligence sufficient to enable them to see some justice in what he had done, so that they may take their places in the world and go on willingly with the work assigned to them, instead of being slaves, some of whom appear to enjoy unearned luxury and the pleasures, positions and advantages which wealth and breeding can give, while others are driven through life by hunger, sorrow, suffering and disease.

On the other hand, no egotism or culture is a sufficient warrant for a man to say: man is the production of evolution; evolution is the action or the result of the action of blind force and blind matter; death ends all; there is no hell; there is no saviour; there is no God; there is no justice in the universe.

It is more reasonable to say: there is justice in the universe; for justice is the right action of the law, and the universe must run by law. If law is required for the running of a machine shop to prevent it going to smash, law is no less necessary for the running of the machinery of the universe. No institution can be conducted without a guiding or a cumulative intelligence. There must be intelligence in the universe great enough to guide its operations.

There must be some truth in a belief in atonement, which has lived and found welcome in the hearts of people for nearly two thousand years, and today numbers millions of supporters. The doctrine of the atonement is based on one of the grand fundamental truths of the evolution of man. This truth was warped and twisted by untrained and undeveloped minds, minds not enough mature to conceive it. It was nursed by selfishness, under influences of cruelty and slaughter, and grew into its present form through the dark ages of ignorance. It is less than fifty years since people began to question the doctrine of the atonement. The doctrine has lived and will live because there is some truth in the idea of man's personal relation to his God, and because of the idea of self-sacrifice for the good of others. People are now beginning to think about these two ideas. Man's personal relation to his God, and self-sacrifice for others, are the two truths in the doctrine of the atonement.

Man is the general term used to designate the human organization with its manifold principles and natures. According to Christian view, man is a threefold being, of spirit, soul and body.

The body was made from the elements of the earth, and is physical. The soul is the form on or into which the physical matter is moulded, and in which are the senses. It is psychical. The spirit is the universal life which enters into and makes alive the soul and body. It is called spiritual. Spirit, soul and body make up the natural man, the man which dies. At death, the spirit or life of man returns to universal life; the physical body, always subject to death and dissolution, returns through disintegration into the physical elements from which it was composed; and, the soul, or form of the physical, shadow-like, fades away with the dissolution of the body and is absorbed by the astral elements and psychic world from which it came.

According to Christian doctrine, God is a trinity in Unity; three persons or essences in one unity of substance. God the Father, God the Son, and God the Holy Ghost. God the Father is the creator; God the Son is the Savior; God the Holy Ghost is the comforter; these three subsisting in one divine being.

God is mind, self-existent, before the world and its beginnings. God, the mind, manifests as nature and as divinity. The mind acting through nature creates the body, form and life of man. This is the natural man subject to death and who must die, unless raised above death by divine intervention into the state of immortality.

The mind ("God the father," "the father in heaven") is the higher mind; who sends a portion of itself, a ray ("the Savior," or, "God the Son"), the lower mind, to enter and live in the human mortal man for a period of time; after which period, the lower mind, or ray from the higher, leaves the mortal to return to its father, but sends in its place another mind ("the Holy Ghost," or, "the Comforter," or "Advocate"), a helper or teacher, to assist the one who had received or accepted the incarnate mind as its savior, to accomplish its mission, the work for which it had incarnated. The incarnation of a portion of divine mind, called truly the son of god, was and is or can be the redeemer of mortal man from sin, and his savior from death. Mortal man, the man of flesh, into which it came or may come, may, by the presence of divinity within him, learn how to change and may change from his natural and mortal condition into the divine and immortal state. If, however, man should not will to carry on the evolution from the mortal to the immortal, he must remain subject to the laws of mortality and must die.

The people of the earth did not spring from one mortal man and one mortal woman. Every mortal being in the world who is human is called into mortal being by many gods. For every human being there is a god, a mind. Each human body in the world is in the world for the first time, but the minds which are acting through, with, or in, the human beings in the world are not so acting now for the first time. The minds have acted similarly with other human bodies of theirs in past times. If not successful in solving and perfecting the mystery of the incarnation and atonement while acting with or in the present human body, that body and form (soul, psyche) will die, and that mind connected with it will have to incarnate again and again until sufficient enlightenment is had, until the atonement or at-one-ment is accomplished.

The mind incarnate in any human being is the son of God, come to save that man from death, if the personal man will have faith in his savior's efficacy to overcome death by following The Word, which the savior, the incarnate mind, makes known; and the teaching is communicated in degree according to the personal man's faith in him. If man accepts the incarnate mind as his savior and follows the instructions which he then receives, he will cleanse his body from impurities, will stop wrong action (sinning) by right action (righteousness) and will keep his mortal body alive until he has redeemed his soul, the psyche, the form of his physical body, from death, and made it immortal. This course of action of the training of the human mortal and the transforming it into the immortal is the crucifixion. The mind is crucified on its cross of flesh; but by that crucifixion the mortal, subject to death, overcomes death and gains immortal life. Then the mortal has put on immortality and is raised to the world of the immortals. The son of god, the incarnate mind has then accomplished his mission; he has done the work which it is his duty to do, so that he may be able to return to his father in heaven, the higher mind, with whom he becomes one. If, however, the man who has accepted the incarnate mind as his savior, but whose faith or knowledge is not great enough to follow the teaching he received, then the incarnate mind still is crucified, but it is a crucifixion by the disbelief and doubt of the mortal. It is a daily crucifixion which the mind endures in or on its cross of flesh. For the human, the course is: The body dies. The descent of the mind into hell, is the separating of that mind from its carnal and fleshly desires during an after death state. The arising from the dead, is the separation from the desires. The ascent into heaven where he "judges the quick and the dead," is followed by the determining what shall be the conditions of the mortal body and psyche, which shall be created for his next descent into the world, with the object of effecting the enlightenment and atonement.

For the man who is saved, whose incarnate mind makes immortal, the entire life of Jesus must be gone through while still living in the physical body in the physical world. Death must be overcome before the body dies; the descent into hell must be before, not after, death of the body; the ascension into heaven must be achieved while the physical body is alive. All this must be done consciously, willingly, and with knowledge. If it is not, and man has merely a belief in his incarnate mind as the savior, and if, although understanding how but not attaining immortal life before death, he dies, then the next time for the descent into the atmosphere of the world and into that of mortal man, the mind will not enter into the human form which he has called into being, but the mind acts as the comforter (the Holy Ghost), who ministers to the human soul and is a substitute for the son of god, or mind, which was incarnate in the preceding life or lives. It acts so because of the previous acceptance of the mind by man as the son of God. It is the comforter around him who inspires, advises, gives instruction, so that, if man so wills, he may carry on the work for immortality which had been left off in the previous life, cut short by death.

Human beings who will not turn to the mind for light, must remain in darkness and abide the laws of mortality. They suffer death, and the mind connected with them must pass through hell during life, and during its separation from its earthly connection after death, and this must continue through the ages, until it is willing and able to see the light, to raise the mortal to immortality and to become at one with its parent source, its father in heaven, who cannot be satisfied until ignorance gives place to knowledge, and darkness is transformed into light. This process has been explained in the Editorials Living Forever, Vol. 16, Nos. 1–2 [*pp. 195 and 201 in* Monthly Editorials From THE WORD Part II], and in Moments with Friends in The Word, Vol. 4, page 189, and Vol. 8, page 190 [*pp. 34 and 109 in this book*].

With this understanding of the doctrine of the atonement one may see what is meant by "and god so loved the world that he gave his only begotten Son, that whosoever believeth in him should not perish, but have everlasting life." With this understanding, the doctrine of the atonement is reconciled with the law of unswerving inexorable constant and eternal justice, the law of karma. This will explain man's personal relation to his god.

The other truth, the idea of self-sacrifice for the good of others, means that after man has found and follows his mind, his light, his savior, and has overcome death and gained immortal life and knows himself to be deathless, he will not accept the joys of heaven which he has earned, for himself alone, but, instead of being satisfied with his victory over death, and enjoying alone the fruits of his labors, determines to give his services to mankind to relieve their sorrows and sufferings, and help them to the point of finding the divinity within, and of achieving the apotheosis which he has reached. This is the sacrifice of the individual self to the universal Self, of the individual mind to the universal Mind. It is the individual god becoming at one with the universal God. He sees and feels and knows himself in every living human soul, and every soul as being in him. It is the I-am-Thou and Thou-art-I principle. In this state is realized the fatherhood of God, the brotherhood of man, the mystery of the incarnation, the unity and oneness of all things, and the wholeness of the One.

A FRIEND

———————————

# NOVEMBER 1913

[From *The Word*, Vol. 18 No. 2]

*What is laughter, and why do people laugh?*

Laughter is the expression of an attitude of the mind and of the emotions through inarticulate vocal sounds. Upon the individual and the circumstance exciting his laughter, depend the variety and nature of laughter; as the giggle, titter, gurgle, of simple and exuberant youth; the mellow, silvery sweet, or hearty laugh of generous good nature; the laugh of derision, scorn, sarcasm, irony, ridicule, contempt. Then there is the abominable laughter of the hypocrite.

Laughter is as sure an indicator of the character and the combination of the body and mind of the one who laughs, as speech is the index of the development of the mind which gives it articulation. A cold in the head, hoarseness, or other bodily ills, may effect the smoothness and roundness of a laugh, but such bodily impediments cannot disguise the spirit and character which enters into that laugh.

The physical vibrations of the laugh are caused by the action of the vocal cords and larynx on the air force over them. But the attitude of mind at the time of the laugh gives the spirit to the laugh, and so acts on the nervous system as to compel such muscular and vocal agitations as will give body and quality to the sound in which the spirit of the laugh is expressed.

Like many of the wonders of life, laughter is so common that it is not seen to be wonderful. It is wonderful.

Without mind there is no laugh. To be able to laugh one must have mind. An idiot can make a noise, but cannot laugh. A monkey can imitate and make grimaces, but it cannot laugh. A parrot can imitate the sounds of laughter, but it cannot laugh. It does not know what it is trying to laugh about; and everyone in the neighborhood knows when a parrot is imitating laughter. Birds may hop and flutter and twitter in the sunshine, but there is no laughter; cats and kittens may purr, roll, pounce or paw, but they cannot laugh. Dogs and puppies can prance and jump and bark in playful sport, but it is not given to them to laugh. Sometimes when a dog looks into a human face with what is called "such intelligence" and with what seems to be a knowing look, it is said that perhaps he understands the fun and is trying to laugh; but he cannot. An animal cannot laugh. Some animals at times can imitate the sounds of the voice, but that is not an understanding of words. It can at most be only an echo. A dog cannot understand the meaning of words nor of laughter. At best he can reflect the desire of his master, and in some degree respond to that desire.

Laughter is a spontaneous expression of quick appreciation by the mind, of a condition which unexpectedly reveals something of unfitness, awkwardness, inappropriateness, incongruousness. This condition is provided by some happening, or action, or by words.

To get the full benefit of laughter and to be able to laugh readily the mind must, in addition to a quickness to understand the awkwardness, incongruousness, unexpectedness of a situation. have its imaginative faculty developed. If there is no imaginativeness, the mind will not see more than one situation, and therefore lack true appreciation. But when there is imaginativeness the mind will quickly picture from that occurrence other laughable occurrences and situations and relate the incongruities with harmony.

Some people are quick to understand a situation and to see the point in a joke. Others may understand the situation, but without imaginativeness they cannot see what that situation would suggest or lead to and to what it is co-related, and they are slow to see the point in a joke or a humorous situation and tardy in finding out why other people are laughing.

Laughter is a necessity in human development, and especially in the development of the mind to meet all conditions of life. There is little laughter in grinding monotonous pressure and hardships. When life requires a constant struggle to get a bare existence, when war and pestilence sweep over the land, when death reaps its harvests by fire and flood and earthquake, then only the terrors and hardships and the difficulties of life are seen. Such conditions bring out and compel endurance and strength of mind and quickness in action. These qualities of mind are developed by coping with and overcoming such conditions. But the mind also needs ease and grace. The mind begins to develop poise, ease, grace, by laughter. Laughter is necessary for ease and grace of mind. As soon as the bare necessaries of life are supplied, and begin to give place to plenty, laughter comes. Laughter makes the mind unbend and takes away its stiffness. Laughter helps the mind to see the light and cheer in life, as well as the dark and cold. Laughter relieves the mind from strain after its struggle with serious, stern and awful things. Laughter fits the mind for new endeavor. By acquiring the power to laugh, the mind can renew its strength and cope with difficulties, prevent melancholy and even insanity, and may often drive away illness or disease. When a man gives too much attention to laughter, then the love of laughter prevents him from appreciating the seriousness, responsibilities, duties and the work of life. Such a man may be easy and hearty and good-natured, may see the funny side of things, and be a rollicking, jolly good fellow. But as he continues to make laughter a pleasure, he becomes softer and unfit to meet the stern realities of life. He may pity and laugh at the man who he thinks takes life too seriously, yet he understands and appreciates life no better than the one who goes through life carrying a heavy heart and burdened by a frown.

More of a man's character can be known in a short time by his laughter than by his words, because he tries less to conceal and can conceal less in his laughter. With words he can and often does mean the opposite of what he says.

There is scarcely anyone who will not welcome the rich, full sounding, generous laughter of appreciation of quick wit and good humor tempered in its volume and tone to suit the occurrence and place, and who will fail to shun the empty gobble or cackle of a person who boisterously persists in his cackle or gobble, whether or not the occasion provokes it. Whether a person is or is not well bred, the fullness or shallowness of mind or emotion may be known by his laugh. Those with tendencies to nervousness, fits or hysteria, will show them by their short jerky, spasmodic gasps, or their long, sharp, piercing screams of laughter.

The noisy, rasping, metallic sounds, the hiss, the squeal, are indicative of character as surely as a well rounded character is revealed by its harmony in laughter. Harmony in laughter shows a well rounded out development in character, no matter what may occasion the laugh. Discords in laughter show lack of development in a character, no matter how one may try to conceal what he lacks. Discords give place to harmony in laughter, as the character is developed. The tone, the pitch and the volume of discord in the laugh, indicate the lack or twist in development of character.

One who has magnetism in his laugh is usually one of a natural and sensuous disposition. The crafty and cunning and miserly and the cruel will repel by their laughter, though they may entice or deceive by their words.

A FRIEND

# APRIL 1915

[From *The Word*, Vol. 21 No. 1]

*What is the relation between magnetism and gravitation, and how do they differ, if at all? And what is the relation between magnetism and animal magnetism, and how do they differ, if at all?*

Positive science does not state what gravitation is, and admits it does not know. The facts, however, which are observed by scientists, and which are called gravitation, are, briefly stated, that there is a pull which every body has on every other body according to its mass, and that the strength of the pull is lessened with the increase of the distance between the bodies and is increased with their nearness. The sequence of facts, called gravitation, exhibits itself without respect to the arrangement of the particles in the bodies. All physical masses, therefore, are said to gravitate toward each other.

Magnetism is a mysterious force concerning the nature of which science has so far given little information, although some of the facts brought about by magnetic force are well known to scientists. Magnetism is the force which shows itself through magnets. A magnet is a body in which all or some particles are of like polarity, and where the axes between the poles in the particles are approximately parallel. The positive poles of the particles with approximately parallel axes point in one direction, the negative poles of these particles point in the opposite direction. A body is a magnet, according to the preponderance of the particles which have parallel or approximately parallel axes with like polarity. A magnet approaches perfection as a magnet, in proportion to the number of its particles which have like polarity and parallel axes, as compared to the number of particles which have not parallel axes and are not of like polarity. Magnetism manifests through a body according to the proportion of particles in the mass of the body which are magnetic, that is, of like polarity and axes parallel. Magnetism is a force present everywhere in the world, but manifesting only through bodies with magnetic arrangement of their particles. This applies to inanimate objects.

The same force is raised to a higher power in animal bodies. Animal magnetism is the operation of a force through animal bodies, when the bodies are of a certain structural nature. The structure to be magnetic has to be such that the particles in the cells and the cells of the animal body are of a structure so that the universal magnetic force will flow through them. To that end the structure has to be similar to that in inanimate magnets. The axis of the animal body is the spine, and animal bodies are magnetic when the particles in the cells are adjusted in alignment to the corresponding portion of the spine and to the marrow in the bones. The action from the poles of the body is by means of the nerves. The magnetic bath or field is the atmosphere around the body. Any animal bodies coming within the influence of this field, experience the effect of the universal magnetic power which flows through the magnetic animal body and is then called animal magnetism.

Animal magnetism is not personal magnetism, though it has a part in producing what is called personal magnetism. Animal magnetism is not hypnotism, though persons having animal magnetism may use it to produce hypnotic effects.

The linga sharira, or invisible form of the physical body, is a storage battery for life. One of the modes in which life operates is magnetism. If the linga sharira in a human body has its physical counterparts constructed as stated, that is, the particles in magnetic alignment, then it can hold and store life and can transmit the life under the aspect of what is called animal magnetism.

The answer to the question is that there is no direct relation between gravitation and animal magnetism as described. They differ in that, as far as gravitation, every mass pulls every other mass, and the force called gravitation is active at all times; but the force called animal magnetism does not act at all times, but is active in those instances only when there is an animal structure, the features of which are a like polarization of the particles and a true or approximate parallelism of axes.

৽

*How are cures effected by animal magnetism?*

Animal magnetism is a universal force acting through a human body, in which the cells are polarized and arranged in a certain way, which polarization and arrangement induce the universal life into the body and permit the transfer of the life directly to another animal body.

A diseased physical body is one which lacks the proper arrangement of its particles, or is one in which there are obstructions to the life flow, or in which changes have taken place due to the absence of the usual breath and life circulation. One who has much animal magnetism, and one through whom animal magnetism is readily transmitted, may heal diseases in others. He may heal by his presence alone without bodily contact, or he may heal by contacting bodily the one to be healed. When the healing is done by the presence of the healing one it is done by the enclosing of the sick in the atmosphere surrounding the healing one. The atmosphere is a magnetic bath, charged with the universal life acting as animal magnetism. Animal magnetism is a poor name for the great force of the universal life, but we use it here to remain within the familiar usage of the time. The bath acts on the atmosphere of the ailing person and tends to restore in it the circulation of the universal life force, by removing the obstructions, reestablishing the circulation, and by the rearrangement of the molecules in the cells, so that the life force may flow uninterruptedly and the organs in the body be allowed to perform their natural functions.

Healing through animal magnetism, when done by direct contact of the body of the healing one, is best done when the hands of the healing one, acting as the positive and the negative poles, are placed on the body or the part affected. The magnetism may emanate from any part of the body, such as the eyes, breasts, but the most natural means of applying it is by means of the hands. The important feature in effecting a cure is that the mind of the healer should not interfere with the transmission of the magnetism. Usually the mind does affect and interfere with the healing influence, because the healer often fancies that he must direct the flow of magnetism with his mind. In every case where the healer acts with his mind in connection with the magnetism, while he attempts to heal, he will do harm, because the mind does not effect the cure, though it may direct and color the magnetism. The mind interferes with and impedes the natural action of the magnetism. The magnetism will act naturally if not interfered with by the mind. Nature, and not the mind, effects the cure. Man's mind does not know nature, and does not know itself when in the body. If it knew itself in the body then the mind would not interfere with nature.

A FRIEND

# MAY 1915

[From *The Word*, Vol. 21 No. 2]

*Are animal magnetism, mesmerism, and hypnotism related, and if so, how are they related?*

Animal magnetism is a force related to the magnetism which is apparent in inanimate bodies, such as the lodestones and iron magnets. The same force is raised to a higher power in animal bodies. Animal magnetism is the operation of the force through animal bodies which are of a certain structural nature, relating to polarization, so that the structure can induce and then serve as a channel conducting the magnetic force to other physical bodies.

Mesmerism is a name given to an application of animal magnetism, after Mesmer (1733–1815), who rediscovered and then taught and wrote about the force here called animal magnetism.

Mesmer, at times, used animal magnetism naturally; at times he used his mind in connection with the magnetism. His method is called mesmerism. He directed the magnetism as a fluidic force through the tips of his fingers into the body of the patient, thereby causing sometimes sleep, called after him mesmeric sleep, and often effected a subsequent cure. He often put the patient, when the patient was under mesmeric influence, into different states, to which states Mesmer gave different names. His methods and variations are mentioned by numerous writers on that subject.

Hypnotism is, as the name indicates, the causing of a kind of sleep. Self-hypnotism is the causing of sleep through the action of one's own mind when one wholly or partly switches his conscious principle off from the connection with the conscious center in his brain. Hypnotism generally is the operation of one mind upon another, with or without the aid of animal magnetism, so that a sleep of the hypnotic subject is caused by the action of the operator when he interferes wholly or partly with the connection of the conscious principle and center through which it acts consciously in the brain of the subject. The hypnotic sleep, resulting from the interference with the connection of the conscious principle and the center through which it acts consciously, differs from normal sleep.

In normal sleep the intelligence or conscious principle moves away from the conscious center in the brain, so that nature may repair the body and restore the equilibrium between the cells. The conscious principle may hover around the centers of the sense nerves in the brain, or it may recede beyond these centers. When the conscious principle remains around one or more of the centers connecting with seeing, hearing, smelling, tasting, then the sleeper dreams, and his dreams are of sensuous perceptions, either of the physical or of an inner world connected with the physical. In dreamless sleep the conscious principle remains conscious, but inasmuch as it is removed from the senses, man does not know how to interpret what it is conscious of.

Producing hypnotic sleep is an interference with the conscious principle of another, who cannot or will not resist the interference. When the conscious principle of the subject is driven away from its conscious center, with which it is connected during waking, the subject falls into the hypnotic sleep, which is a partially or wholly unconscious sleep, according to the greater or lesser distance to which the hypnotizer has succeeded in driving the conscious principle of the subject. During the hypnotic sleep the hypnotist may cause the subject to see or hear or taste or smell or feel any sensations which can be experienced in waking, or he may cause the subject to do or say what the hypnotizer wants him to do or say, with the single exception, however, that he cannot force a subject to do an immoral act which would be repugnant to the moral sense of the subject in the waking state.

The operator's mind takes the place of the conscious principle of his subject, and the subject will respond to and obey the thought and direction of the hypnotizer, according to the clarity and power of thought of the hypnotizer and the degree to which he is in touch with the brain organism of the subject.

The answer to the question as to the relations of animal magnetism, mesmerism, and hypnotism is that animal magnetism, being a natural force operating from body to body, has to do with human bodies; mesmerism is a method of applying animal magnetism; hypnosis is the result of the use of the power of one mind exerted over another mind. It is possible for a mind to produce magnetic effects by directing the flow of animal magnetism. A hypnotist can predispose a subject to the hypnotic subjection by first working with animal magnetism on the subject; but in their nature magnetism and the hypnotic force are distinct from each other.

ॐ

*How can animal magnetism be activated, and to what use can it be put?*

Animal magnetism of a man can be cultivated by making his body a good magnet and a center to which the universal life force, operating as magnetism is attracted. A man can make his body a good magnet for the universal life by causing the organs in his body to perform their functions naturally and normally and by preventing excesses in eating, drinking, sleeping, and by control of the sensual nature. These excesses result in a breaking down of the storage battery, which the invisible form of the physical body, sometimes called the astral body, is. Absence of excesses allows the form body to become strong and causes that gradual polarization and adjustment of the molecules which has been before mentioned. When so built up the form body becomes a reservoir of magnetic force.

Some of the uses to which animal magnetism can be put are to build up a personal magnetism, to make the body physically strong and healthy, to cure disease in others, to produce magnetic sleep—which is not to be mistaken for hypnotic sleep—and thereby clairaudience and clairvoyance, and prophetic utterances, and to produce magical effects, such as charging talismans and amulets with magnetic powers. One of the most important of the uses to which animal magnetism can be put is to continue the strengthening and polarization of the invisible form body so that it will be rebuilt and regenerated and possibly immortalized.

A FRIEND

———————————

# JUNE 1915

[From *The Word,* Vol. 21 No. 3]

*What is the sense of smell; how does it act; do physical particles engage in the production of the sensation, and what part does smelling play in living?*

What is called smelling, is a perception of certain properties of objects. These properties act on man through his organ of smelling, whence they reach the olfactory nerve. The nerve communicates the subtle element, which is in the physical object, to an entity in the human body. This entity is the being which perceives the nature of the object through the information which it receives through the nerve of smelling. The entity is an elemental, a nature ghost of the class of earth ghosts. The smelling elemental is connected with and is one of the beings which enter into the constitution and structure of the human elemental. The smelling elemental is of the element of earth, and for that reason can perceive properties of the nature of earth, which are exhibited by physical objects. So the answer to the questions "What is the sense of smell and how does it act?" is that it is a being, an earth elemental within the human elemental in the physical body, which smelling elemental perceives the nature of certain attributes in physical bodies, which are called odors or smells.

These attributes are perceived by smelling only. Smelling is all this elemental does. Smelling is its food, which nourishes and sustains it. It perceives certain attributes and conditions of the earth element outside. Smell is the invisible, subtle earth element, which enters into the constitution of the smelling elemental and so into the human elemental.

Physical particles of the object which is perceived by its smell enter into the production of the sensation of smelling. Not alone particles which belonged to the physical object but also such particles of the earth element as had flowed through the object, cause the sensation of smell. The earth element is like a tide, flowing back and forth through the object. The flow is made up by infinitesimal, invisible particles which seem to be a compact mass; but if the inner sense of sight is keen enough and the mind can analyze the flow, that flow will be perceived as being made up of particles.

When the physical atmosphere of the individual contacts the physical atmosphere of the object smelled—that atmosphere being made up of the particles mentioned—the particles are perceived in the atmosphere of the smeller, when they contact the nerve of smell. Smelling is the distinctly physical characteristic of objects perceived. Every physical object has its own distinctive physical atmosphere, in which particles are suspended and circulating. But few objects can be smelled. The reason is that the perception by the sense of smell is not trained and not fine enough. When the sense of smell is trained, as in case of the blind, many objects can be smelled which are now generally regarded as being without odor.

There is yet a keener sense of smell, an inner sense, which may be developed and which some people have already developed, through which an odor of objects which is not physical can be perceived. Beings of another world may make themselves known by an odor, but this is not a physical odor.

The part which smelling plays in living is that smelling aids in the maintenance of life. The smell of food causes the gastric juices to flow and stimulates them, as does the sight of a well-prepared table. Animals detect by their sense of smell places where they can find food. They detect the presence of enemies and dangers by smell.

Whereas man is at present nourished through the absorption of a subtle essence which his system takes out of gross material food which he consumes, it will in the future, when man has better control of his physical body, be possible for him to extract by the sense of smell the essence he now has to get by digestion out of the transformation of physical food. His smelling elemental will then be charged with nourishing the physical body. The two senses of taste and smell will, however, have to be greatly changed from the conditions they are in at present before nourishment by smelling alone is possible. Then the subtle physical particles which will be absorbed by the smelling elemental will be the means of nourishing the physical body.

ॐ

*What is the imagination? How can it be cultivated and used?*

Imagination is that state of the mind in which the image faculty of the mind works consciously to give form to the subject of thought which the motive faculty has conceived and which the focus faculty has brought into and holds within range. These three faculties of the mind have directly to do with imagination. The other four faculties are indirectly concerned. The dark faculty interferes with imagination, as it does with every other work of the mind, and therefore the dark faculty must be in a state where it is controlled sufficiently to allow of the work of imagination. The time faculty furnishes the material used in the work of imagination. The light faculty shows how the work of imagination should be done. The I-am faculty gives identity and individuality to the work of imagination. Imagination is a state of the mind, and is in itself not of the senses. The work of imagination is carried on in the mind before it is related to the senses by the mind and before the senses are called upon to give expression in the physical world to that which has first been done in imagination. This is the case with imagination. However, it is to be borne in mind that that which is usually called imagination is really not imagination at all. What is broadly and without understanding of the meaning of the term called imagination is the play of the mind in the senses, or, in a higher degree, the working of the mind when it is compelled by the senses to reproduce or furnish the things which give pleasure to the senses and to provide new enjoyments or troubles which the senses have indicated and led the mind into. In the case of this condition, which is falsely termed imagination, all of the seven faculties of the mind are agitated through the focus faculty; but these agitations are merely excitations of the other faculties through the focus faculty and are not the work of the faculties. The focus faculty is the only faculty of the mind which is directly in contact with the brain of the average man. The other six faculties are not in contact. Their action is induced through the focus faculty.

To understand better what imagination—that is, the real imagination—is, it should be seen what the false imagination—that is, the mere agitation which is falsely called imagination—is. False imagination is not a conscious action of the faculties of the mind, but the action of one faculty, the focus faculty only, which is agitated by the senses and which when agitated causes an induced agitation of the other six faculties or some of them.

Fancies, day dreams, mooning, are not imagination. Reproductions of the forms and aspects of nature are not imagination. Copying any work, be it of nature or of man, is not imagination, however skillfully it may be performed. Imagination is creation. Every work of imagination is a new creation. Imagination does not copy nature. Nature does not show the mind how to do the work of imagination. Imagination furnishes nature with all her forms and colors and sounds and varied aspects. These are furnished to nature by mind and not by nature.

To cultivate imagination—that is, the state of mind in which the image faculty, the motive faculty, and the focus faculty are co-ordinated and perform their work in harmony, while the dark faculty is limited or suppressed, and the three other faculties, the time faculty, the light faculty, and the I-am faculty contribute to this work—it is necessary to understand the system here mentioned, which is the only system that gives an insight into the operations of the mind.

The second step is to be able to conceive a subject of thought, and the next step is to exercise the image faculty in harmony with the motive faculty and focus faculty. The questioner is referred to the two articles on imagination which appeared in the May and June issues of THE WORD, in 1913 [*p. 242 and 246 in* Monthly Editorials From THE WORD Part II]. As to the faculties of the mind, information can be obtained in the article, "Adepts, Masters, and Mahatmas," printed in THE

WORD in April, May, June, July, and August, 1910 [*pp. 620, 630, 640, 648, 675 in* Monthly Editorials From THE WORD Part I].

A FRIEND

———————————————

# JULY 1915

[From *The Word*, Vol. 21 No. 4]

*What is disease and what connection have bacteria with it?*

Disease of the body is a condition in which the constitution of the tissues of one or more organs of the body is abnormal to such a degree that the function of the organ or organs is impaired or the function of one organ is thrown out of the normal relation to another or other organs. The result is that the elements in nature are no longer in harmonious connection with the human elemental—that is, with the coordinative, formative principle of the body.

Disease is caused by improper eating, drinking, breathing, acting and improper thinking. A disease is an obstruction to the normal working of elementals which compose and work the organs of the physical body.

Bacteria are fungi, microscopic plants, mostly of rod-like, lance-like, rope-like shapes. Bacteria are said to be the cause of many infectious diseases and of non-contagious, constitutional diseases as well.

While bacteria have much to do with diseases, bacteria are not the causes of disease. Bacteria develop as soon as conditions for their multiplication are provided, and these conditions are brought about by improper thinking, acting, breathing, eating and drinking. Bacteria in quantities sufficient to produce disease cannot exist where man has not furnished them a fertile ground for their propagation in his body. Generally, almost uniformly, putrefaction and fermentation in the digestive and excretory systems are primary producing causes of conditions under which bacteria find favorable lodgment and development.

જ

*What is cancer and can it be cured, and if it can be cured, what is the cure?*

Cancer is the name given to a set of malignant new growths in the human body, which develop at the expense of the surrounding normal tissue, and usually prove fatal. Cancer is one of the diseases which are on the increase with the progress of civilization. Civilization breeds diseases, notwithstanding preventative measures and curative treatments which subjugate forms of disease which were prevalent in the past. The nearer the life of human beings is to the animal and natural mode of living the fewer will be the diseases; but the higher bred the body and the farther removed from its simple conditions, the more susceptible will it be to diseases. With the advance of time, forms of disease develop which were before unknown, and diseases which occurred occasionally become more frequent. The higher the development of mind the more susceptible to disease will the body be under the same or like physical conditions. In the nineties of the last century a new disease, known then as la grippe, made its appearance and spread rapidly over large portions of the civilized part of the world. In a similar manner cases of cancer are said to be on the increase.

There is a cancer cell that is physical. There are many of these in every human, but usually they are later developed, and so they remain unnoticed. There is further a cancer germ, and that is not physical, but is astral. The germ is usually present in the astral body, but it is latent; that is, it does not cause the development of the cancer cell. Certain conditions are required for the activity and multiplication of the cancer germ. Two of these conditions which are frequently in evidence are the condition of the matured physical body, which is characteristic of the age of forty years and upward, and a mental state best illustrated by fear. Therefore, fear and the age of about forty favor the production of cancer germs and so development and multiplication of the cancer cells.

Cancer can be cured and has been cured. An answer to this question and a treatment of cancer was outlined in "Moments with Friends" in the issue of THE WORD, September, 1910, Vol. XI., No.6 [*p. 179 in this book*].

A FRIEND

———————————————

# AUGUST 1915

[From *The Word,* Vol. 21 No. 5]

*What is a good way to connect the states of waking and dreaming so that there is no interval during which the sleeper is unconscious?*

The subject of this inquiry is one which is usually not considered. Those who have considered it have generally thought it to be not worthwhile. But the subject is important. Although the unconscious interval between waking and dreaming cannot be done away with as long as man is nothing more than man, it can be shortened considerably. In the waking state a man is conscious of the things about him, and in a certain way he is conscious of himself. In the dreaming state he is conscious in a different way.

The real man is a conscious principle, the conscious light within the body. He, as that conscious principle, contacts in the waking state the pituitary body, which is a gland embedded in the skull. At the pituitary body nature communicates to him information concerning the involuntary operations which are carried on in the body, such as breathing, digesting, secreting, and the results of these operations as pleasurable or paining the nerves. The senses, by means of the nerves, make the conscious principle aware of the things in the world. Nature acts on this conscious principle from within and from without. During the waking state, from within as to the condition of the man's body; from without as to the objects of sense perception in the world. Nature acts on him through the sympathetic nervous system, the recording station of which, in the brain, is the pituitary body. A human has his hold on his body through the central nervous system, the governing center of which is also the pituitary body. So the conscious principle is in contact with nature through the pituitary body, and reacts on nature and has its hold on the body through the same pituitary body.

The pituitary body is the seat and center from which the conscious principle receives impressions from nature and from which the conscious principle controls, acts with or acts against nature by means of the central nervous system. The flashes of contact in the waking state on the pituitary body interfere with and restrain the involuntary and natural functions of the body. That flashing light on the pituitary body places a strain on the natural operations of the body, and prevents the life forces from repairing the tissues and organs and machinery of the body, and so keeping it in vigor. The light flashes keep the whole body in tension, and if the tension were continued long enough death would follow, as no life forces can enter while the body is in tension under the influence of these flashes. To keep the body going it is therefore necessary that the body has periods when it is not interfered with, and when it can rest and recuperate. For this reason a period of what is called sleep is provided for the body. Sleep furnishes a condition to the body where the life forces can enter, repair, and nourish it. Sleep is possible when the light of the conscious principle ceases to flash on the pituitary body.

The conscious principle is a part of the mind; it is that portion of the mind which contacts the body. The contact is made through the central nervous system and is governed through the pituitary body. Waking is the state resulting from the connection existing between the central nervous system and the sympathetic nervous system by means of the common center, the pituitary body. As long as the conscious principle flashes its light on the pituitary body a man is awake—that is, aware of the world. As long as impressions are given to the conscious principle through the sympathetic nervous system, the conscious principle keeps its light flashing on the pituitary body and so grips the whole physical body. When the body is too weary from exhaustion and is depleted of its vital force it cannot receive impressions from nature and can therefore not transmit them to the pituitary body, even though the mind would there receive them. That is the case where the body is tired but the mind wants to be awake. Another phase is that where the mind itself is indifferent to impressions it may receive from nature and is itself ready to withdraw. In both cases sleep will result.

Sleep sets in when the switch connecting the two sets of nerves in the pituitary body is turned so that the connection is broken.

After the connection is broken the conscious principle is in a state of dreaming, or in a state concerning which no memory is retained. Dreams occur when the conscious principle flashes, as it often does, upon the nerves of the senses, which are connected with the brain. If the conscious principle does not flash upon these nerves there are no dreams.

During the waking hours the conscious principle is in intermittent, flash-like contact with the pituitary body. This flash-like contact is what man calls consciousness, but in fact that is not consciousness. However, as far as it goes, and inasmuch as it is all that man in his present condition can know of himself, let it, for the sake of brevity, be called consciousness. That is the basis on which he stands in his waking state. He would hardly be conscious or aware of anything if the exterior world did not act on him and stir him up. While he is stirred up by nature he is conscious in various ways, and the total of all the pleasurable or painful sensations is what he calls himself. The residuum of the total of the impressions furnished by nature he identifies as himself. But that is not himself. This totality of impressions prevents him from knowing what or who he is. As he does not know who he is, this mere statement will not give much information to the average man, still it will be of value if its meaning is realized.

There is, as a man goes to sleep, a dark period between being conscious in the waking state and being conscious in the dreaming state. This dark period, during which man is unconscious, is caused by the break in the connection when the switch is turned off and the light of the conscious principle no longer flashes on the pituitary body.

A man who is not conscious of anything apart from the impressions received through the senses in the waking state or the dreaming state, is, of course, not conscious of himself, as it is called, when no sense impressions are received, either in waking or in dreaming. The conscious light has to be aware of itself apart from the senses in waking or dreaming, in order that a man may be conscious. If the light is not conscious of itself and of a state entirely different from what it is known as in the waking and dreaming states, then it cannot have an unbroken conscious period between the two states. Although man cannot be continuously conscious, he may shorten the interval during which he is not conscious, so that it may seem to him that there is no break.

Before the answer to the question can be understood the existence of these facts has to be understood, even though the facts themselves may not be realized. When these facts are understood, one who wants to be conscious during the dark period between the waking and the dreaming state will understand that that conscious condition is not to be lived in merely at the time in view, unless that conscious condition exists during the waking and the dreaming states; in other words, that a man has to be more than a man who is conscious of what he calls himself, but who is in reality only the residuum of the sum total of the impressions which the senses make on the conscious light of the mind. He should be conscious that he is the conscious light of the mind, as distinct from the perception of the things on which the light is turned.

A FRIEND

# SEPTEMBER 1915

[From *The Word,* Vol. 21 No. 6]

*What urges us to proselytize for our opinions. To what extent are we allowed to oppose our opinions to those of others?*

An opinion is a result of thinking. An opinion is view held between mere belief and knowledge concerning subjects or things. One who has an opinion about a thing, is distinguishable from those who have either knowledge of or a mere belief concerning the subject matter. One has an opinion because he has thought about the subject. His opinion may be correct or incorrect. Whether it is correct or not will depend upon his premises and method of reasoning, If his reasoning is without prejudice, his opinions will usually be correct, and, even though he start with wrong premises, he will prove them to be wrong in the course of his reasonings. If, however, he allows prejudice to interfere with his reasoning, or bases his premises on prejudices, the opinion which he forms will usually be incorrect.

The opinions a man has formed represent to him the truth. He may be wrong, yet he believes them to be right. In the absence of knowledge, a man will stand or fall by his opinions. When his opinions concern religion or some ideal, he believes that he should stand up for them and feels an impulse to get others to adopt his opinions. Thence comes his proselytizing.

That which urges us to proselytize for our opinions is the faith or knowledge on which our opinions rest. We may also be urged by the desire that others should benefit from that which we consider good. If to one's underlying knowledge and the desire to do good are added personal considerations, the efforts to convert others to one's own opinions may develop fanaticism, and, instead of good, harm will be done. Reason and goodwill should be our guides in proselytizing for our opinions. Reason and good-will allows us to present our opinions in argument, but forbid us to try to compel others to accept them. Reason and good-will forbid us from insisting that others should accept and be converted to our opinions, and they make us strong and honest in the support of what we think we know.

A FRIEND

———————————

# OCTOBER 1915

[From *The Word*, Vol. 22 No. 1]

*How is it that problems which have baffled all efforts and seem impossible of solution during waking hours should be solved during sleep or immediately on waking?*

To solve a problem, the thought chambers of the brain should be unobstructed. When there are disturbances or obstructions in the thought chambers of the brain, the process of solving any problem under consideration is hindered or stopped. As soon as the disturbances and obstructions disappear, the problem is solved.

The mind and the brain are factors in working out a problem, and the work is a mental process. The problem may be concerned with a physical result, as what materials should be used and what method of construction be followed in building a bridge so that it may have the least weight and greatest strength; or the problem may be of an abstract subject, such as, how is thought distinguished from and how related to knowledge?

The physical problem is worked out by the mind; but in considering size, color, weight, the senses are called into play and help the mind in solving the problem. The solution of a problem or a part of a problem which is not physical is a mental process in which the senses are not concerned and where the action of the senses will interfere with or prevent the mind from solving the problem. The brain is the meeting-place of the mind and the senses, and on problems concerning physical or sensuous results the mind and the senses work well together in the brain. But when the mind is at work on problems of abstract subjects, the senses are not concerned; however, objects of the outside world are reflected through the senses into the thought chambers of the brain and there disturb or obstruct the mind in its work. As soon as the mind can bring its faculties to bear sufficiently on the problem under consideration, outside disturbances or thoughts which are not concerned are excluded from the thought chambers of the brain, and the solution to the problem is at once seen.

In waking hours the senses are open, and irrelevant sights and sounds and impressions from the outside world rush unceasingly in to the thought chambers in the brain and interfere with the work of the mind. When the senses are closed to the outside world, as they are during sleep, the mind is less hindered in its work. But then sleep usually cuts off the mind from the senses and usually prevents the mind from bringing back knowledge of what it has done while out of touch with the senses. When the mind does not let go of a problem, that problem is carried with it if it leaves the senses during sleep, and its solution is brought back and related to the senses on waking.

That one in sleep has had solved a problem which he could not solve in the waking state means his mind has done in sleep what he was unable to do while awake. If he dreamed the answer, the subject would, of course, be concerning sensuous objects. In that case, the mind, not having let go of the problem, had carried on in dream the process of thought with which it had been concerned while awake; the reasoning process was merely transferred from the outer waking senses to the inner dreaming senses. If the subject is not concerned with sensuous objects, the answer will not be dreamed, though in sleep the answer may come instantly. However, it is not usual for answers to problems to be dreamed or to come while in sleep. Answers to problems may seem to come during sleep, but the answers usually come during the moments while the mind is again making contact with the waking senses, or immediately after waking.

Answers to problems of an abstract nature cannot be dreamed, because the senses are used in dream and the senses would interfere with or prevent abstract thinking. If the mind in sleep and not dreaming solves a problem, and the answer is known when the man is awake, then the mind seems to wake instantly as soon as the answer has been reached by it.

The mind is not at rest in sleep, even though there is no dream or remembrance of mental activity. But the activities of the mind in sleep, and while not dreaming, cannot usually be made known in the waking state, because no bridge has been built between the states of the mind and the states of the waking or the dreaming senses; yet one may get the results of these activities in the form of impetus to action in the waking state. A temporary bridge between mental and sensuous states is formed by one who holds in sleep firmly the problem on which his mind was focussed while awake. If he has exercised his mind sufficiently in his efforts to focus on the solution of the problem while awake, his efforts will continue in sleep, and the sleep will be bridged and he will awake and be conscious of the solution, if he had reached it during sleep.

A FRIEND

# NOVEMBER 1915

[From *The Word*, Vol. 22 No. 2]

*What is Memory?*

Memory is the reproduction of impressions by qualities, attributes, or faculties inherent in *that* on which impressions were made. Memory does not produce a subject or thing or event. Memory reproduces the impressions which were made by the subject or thing or event. All processes necessary to the reproduction of impressions are included in the term memory.

There are four kinds of memory: sense memory, mind memory, cosmic memory, infinite memory. Infinite memory is the being conscious of all states and occurrences throughout eternities and time. Cosmic memory is the reproducing of all happenings of the universe in its eternity. Mind memory is the reproducing or reviewing by the mind of the changes through which it has passed since its origin. There is no practical advantage derived from inquiring into the nature of the infinite and cosmic mind memory. They are here mentioned for the sake of completeness. Sense memory is the reproducing by the senses of impressions made upon them.

The memory which is used by man is the sense memory. He has not learned to use and does not know of the other three—mind memory, cosmic memory, and infinite memory—because his mind is trained to the use of sense memory only. Sense memory is had by the animals and plants and minerals. As compared with man, the number of senses working to produce memory decreases in the animal and plant and mineral. The sense memory of man may be called personality memory. There are seven orders of memories which make up the complete personality memory. There are seven senses in the complete personality of man. These seven sense memories or orders of personality memories are: sight memory, sound memory, taste memory, smell memory, touch memory, moral memory, "I" or identity memory. These seven senses make up the one kind of memory that man has in his present state. Thus personality memory is limited to the time from which the one who re-members reproduces to himself his first impressions of this world, to the reproduction of the impressions made in the moments preceding the present moment. The manner of registering the impressions and the re-producing of the impressions registered through the sight, sound, taste, smell, touch, moral and "I" senses, and the intricate processes and inter-minglings of these to show the detailed work necessary to "a memory," would be too long and tiresome. But a survey can be taken which may be interesting and give an understanding of personality memory.

The art of photography illustrates sight memory—how impressions from objects are received and recorded and how the impressions are afterward reproduced from the record. A photographic instrument is a mechanical application of the sense of sight and the action of seeing. Seeing is the operation of the mechanism of the eye and its connections, for recording and reproducing impressions revealed and made by light. In photographing an object, the lens is uncovered, and turned toward the object, the aperture of the diaphragm is set for the admission of the right amount of light, the focus is determined by the distance of the lens from the object to be photographed; the limit of time for exposure—of the sensitized film or plate ready to receive the impression of the object before it—is given, and the impression, the picture, is taken. Opening the eyelids uncovers the lens of the eye; the iris, or diaphragm of the eye, automatically adjusts itself to the intensity or absence of light; the pupil of the eye expands or contracts to focus the line of vision of the near or distant object; and the object is seen, the picture is taken by the sense of sight, while the focus is held.

The processes of sight and photographing are alike. If the object moves or if the lens moves or the focus changes, there will be a blurred picture. The sense of sight is not one of the mechanical apparatus of the eye. The sense of sight is a distinct thing, a being distinct from the mere mechanism of the eye as the plate or film is distant from the camera. It is this sense of sight, distinct from though connected with the mecha-nism of the eye, which records the impressions or pictures of objects received through the mechanical apparatus of the eye.

Seeing is the taking of the records which may be reproduced by sight memory. Sight memory consists in throwing or printing upon the screen of vision the picture or impression which was recorded and fixed by the sense of sight at the time of seeing the object reproduced. This process of sight memory is illustrated by the printing of pictures from the film or plate after it has been developed. Each time a person or thing is remembered a new print is made, so to say. If one has not a clear picture memory it is because that in him which is sight, the sense of sight, is undeveloped and untrained. When one's sight sense is developed and trained, it may reproduce any scene or object by which it was impressed with all the vividness and realism present at the time it was seen.

Photographic prints even, if taken in color, would be poor copies or illustrations of sight memory when it is well trained. A little experiment may convince one of the possibilities of his sight memory or of the other sense memories which make up his personality memory.

Let one close his eyes and turn them toward a wall or table on which are many objects. Now let him open his eyes for a fraction of a second and close them, he having in that moment tried to see everything on which his eyes were turned. The number of things he sees and the distinctness with which he sees them will serve to show how undeveloped is his sight memory. A little practice will show how it is possible for him to develop his sight memory. He may give a long time or short exposure, to see what he can see. When he draws the curtains over his eyes some of the objects which he saw with his eyes open will be dimly seen with his eyes shut. But these objects will get dimmer and finally disappear and then he cannot see the objects and at best has only a bare impression in his mind of what he had seen with his sight memory. The fading out of the picture is due to the inability of the sight sense to hold the impression made by the object. With exercise of the sight or picture memory to reproduce present objects with the eyes closed or to reproduce past scenes or persons, picture memory will be developed, and may be so strengthened and trained as to produce astonishing feats.

This brief outline of sight memory will serve to indicate what the other sense memories are and how they work. As photography illustrates the sight memory, the phonograph is illustrative of the recording of sounds and the reproduction of the records as sound memories. The sound sense is as distinct from the auditory nerve and the ear apparatus as the sight sense is distinct from the optic nerve and the eye apparatus.

Mechanical contrivances may be produced to copy the taste sense and smell sense and touch sense as the camera and phonograph are counterparts, even though poor copies and copies unknowingly—of the human organs connected with the sight and sound senses.

The moral sense memory and the "I" sense memory are the two distinctively human senses, and are due to and made possible by the presence of the undying mind which uses the personality. By the moral sense the personality learns the laws of its life, and to reproduce these as moral memory where the question of right and wrong is concerned. The "I" sense memory enables the personality to identify itself in connection with any event in the scenes or environments in which it has lived. At present the incarnated mind has no memory beyond the personality memory, and the memories of which it is capable are those only which have been named and which make up the personality as a whole, which is limited to what can be seen, or heard, or smelled, or tasted, or touched, and which feels right or wrong as concerned with itself as a separate existence.

A FRIEND

In the December Word [*p. 282 in this book*] will be answered the question, "What causes loss of memory," and "What causes one to forget his own name or where he lives, though his memory may not be impaired in other respects."

# DECEMBER 1915

[From *The Word,* Vol. 22 No. 3]

*What causes loss of memory?*

Loss of memory is the result of a physical or of a psychic or of a mental cause. The immediate physical cause of the loss of memory is a disorder in the nerve centers in the brain, preventing the senses from functioning through their respective nerves. To illustrate: If there are certain defects of the optic nerve and visual center and optic thalami, so as to cause these to be thrown out of touch with the distinct "sense of sight" or the being which is sight, then this being cannot grasp nor use its physical channels so as to reproduce for the mind the physical object which had been impressed upon the sense. If the ramifications of the auditory nerve and nerve-center have been affected, then the "sound sense" is unable to operate these, and therefore cannot reproduce to the mind the physical sound or name of the object or scene which the sight sense had failed to reproduce, and so there would be loss of sight memory, and sound memory due to physical causes. This will illustrate the loss of taste memory and smell memory, due to physical causes. A pressure on the nerve-centers, a blow on the head, a sudden concussion due to a fall, impaired circulation, nervous shocks from unexpected happenings, may be immediate causes of physical loss of memory.

If the physical obstacle or defect of the nerves in their centers has been removed or repaired, there was only temporary loss of physical memory. If removal or repair is impossible, then the loss is permanent.

Memory is kept not by any part of the physical organism, nor by the physical organism as a whole. The seven orders of memory: sight-memory, sound-memory, taste-memory, smell-memory, touch or feeling-memory, moral-memory, "I" or identity-memory—mentioned in "Moments with Friends," in the November, 1915, issue [*p. 278 in this book*]—make up sense-memory as a whole and which is here named personality-memory. Each one of the sense-memories and all the seven memories co-ordinated and working together make up the personality-memory. Personality-memory has two sides or aspects: the physical side and the psychic side. The physical side of personality-memory has to do with the physical body and the physical world, but the sensing and the memory of these are in the psychic senses and not in the physical body nor in the organs of sense. Personality-memory begins when the human elemental, the human being, manages to adjust and co-ordinate two or more of its senses with their respective sense-organs of its physical body and to focus these on to some physical object. Of course, the "I" sense must be one of the senses co-ordinated and focussed with one or more senses focussed and functioning through their particular organs of sense. The first memory that one has of his existence in the physical world is when his "I" sense of his personality awoke and was co-ordinated with one or more of his other senses, while they were focussed on some physical object or happening. The infant or child can see objects and hear noises before the "I" sense awakes and becomes co-ordinated with seeing and hearing. During that time it is merely animal. Not until the infant is able to think or feel or say "I" in connection with the seeing or hearing or other sensing, does human existence or personality-memory begin. The physical side of personality-memory ends with the death of the physical body, at which time the human elemental with its senses withdraws from its shell, the physical body, and is cut off from the organs and nerve-centers.

The psychic side of personality-memory should begin coincident with or prior to the beginning of personality-memory. Then the "I" sense would be awake and would connect itself as a form with one or more of the psychic senses, such as clairvoyance or clairaudience, and these would be linked with and so related to the physical organs of sense that the psychic world and the physical world would be adjusted and related to the physical body and its organs. But this adjustment of the psychic with the physical side of personality-memory is not made, and the psychic senses are not usually opened up naturally in man. The psychic sense-memories are usually so closely linked with the physical organs and physical objects of sense that man usually is not able to distinguish or have memory of existence apart from his physical body.

If the psychic side of personality-memory is turned toward physical things, the psychic personality will end soon after the death of the physical body, and the life and doings of the personality will be ended and blotted out. Such event will be like a blank or blot or scar made on the mind connected with that personality. When the senses are turned toward ideal subjects of thought, such as the betterment of mankind, the education and improvement of the senses by occupying them with ideal subjects in poetry, or music, or painting, or sculpture, or an ideal pursuit of the professions, then the senses impress themselves accordingly on the mind, and the mind carries over, beyond death, memory of those ideal sensuous perceptions which were impressed upon it. The personality is broken up after death, and the particular memories of the personality connected with physical objects and things in that life is destroyed by the breaking up of the senses which made that personality. Where, however, the psychic senses of that personality were concerned with ideal subjects connected with the mind, there the mind carries with it the impressions. When the mind has built for it the new personality made up of its new senses, the memories of the past personality carried by the mind as impressions will, in turn, impress the senses and aid their development along the particular subjects with which they had in the past been concerned.

Loss of memory of the past life and prior lives is caused by the loss of the last and prior personalities. As mankind has no other memory than the seven orders of personality-memory, a man cannot know or remember himself apart from the senses of his personality, nor apart from objects connected with that personality. He loses memory of a past life because the senses of one personality are disarranged and broken up by death, and there is nothing left to reproduce as sense-memories in the next life, the things with which that personality was concerned.

The partial or total loss of memory of things connected with this life is due to the impairment or permanent loss of the instrument through which that memory works, or to the injury or loss of the elemental beings which produce memory. The loss of sight or hearing may be due to a physical cause, such as an injury inflicted on the eye or ear. But if the being which is called sight or the being which is called sound remains uninjured, and the injury to the organ is repaired, then sight and hearing will be restored. But if these beings were themselves injured, then there would be not only loss of sight or hearing, in proportion to the injury, but these beings would be unable to reproduce as memories the sights and sounds with which they had been familiar.

The loss of memory, when not due to physical causes, is produced by the abuse of the senses or by lack of control and education of the senses, or by wearing out of the sense elementals, resulting in old age, or by the mind's being concerned with subjects of thought without regard to present conditions.

The over indulgence of the sex function inflicts injury on the being called sight; and the degree of the injury sustained determines the degree of partial loss or the total loss of sight-memory. Disregard of the uses of words and the relation of sounds prevents the growth and development of the being known as sound-sense and makes it unable to reproduce as sound-memories the vibrations it had received. The abuse of the palate or the neglect to cultivate the palate, dulls the being called taste and makes it unable to differentiate between tastes and to reproduce taste-memory. The palate is abused by alcohol and other harsh stimulants, and by excessive feeding without attention to the particular niceties of taste in food. Loss of sense-memory may result from irregularities in the actions of the sight and sound and taste senses, by glutting the stomach and intestines with more than they can digest, or by putting into them what they cannot digest. What is called smell is in the personality an elemental being, a magnetically polarized being of sex. Irregularities of action, detrimental to the other senses, can depolarize and throw out of focus the smell-sense, or demagnetize it and make it unable to register or reproduce the emanations characteristic of an object; and, indigestion or improper feeding can stagnate or disorganize and cause the loss of smell memory.

Such are the causes of the loss of the particular sense-memories. There are defects of memory which are not actually loss of memory, though they are often so called. A person goes to purchase certain articles, but on his arrival at the store he cannot remember what he went to buy. Another person cannot remember parts of a message, or what he was going to do, or what he is searching for, or where he puts things. Another forgets the names of persons, places, or things. Some forget the number on the houses or the streets on which they live. Some are unable to remember what they said or did yesterday or the week before, though they may be able to describe with accuracy happenings in their early childhood. Often such defects of memory are signs of the dulling or wearing away of the senses by advancing age; but even such advance of old age is due to the lack of control of the senses by control of the mind, and by not having trained the senses to be true ministers to the mind. "Bad memory," "forgetfulness," "absent-mindedness," are results of one's failure to so control the mind that the mind may control the senses. Other causes of defects of memory are business, pleasure, and trifles, which engage the mind and are allowed to crowd out or efface what it had intended to do. Again, when the mind is engaged with subjects of thought not related to present conditions or to the senses, the senses wander toward their natural objects, while the mind is engaged with itself. Then follows absent-mindedness, forgetfulness.

Failure to remember is due chiefly to not giving the necessary attention to what it is desired to be remembered, and to not making the order clear, and to not charging with sufficient force the order which should be remembered.

ॐ

*What causes one to forget his own name or where he lives, though his memory may not be impaired in other respects?*

The not remembering of one's name and where one lives, is due to the throwing the "I" sense and the sight and sound senses out of touch or out of focus. When the "I" sense is switched off or cut off from the other senses in personality-memory, and the other senses are properly related, the personality will act without having identity—that is, providing it is not obsessed or taken possession of by some other entity. The one having such an experience might recognize places and converse about ordinary things which did not need identification in relation to himself. But he would feel empty, vacant, lost, as though he were searching for something which he had known and forgotten. In this connection one would not have the usual sense of responsibility. He would act, but not from the sense of duty. He would eat when hungry, drink when thirsty, and sleep when fatigued, somewhat as animals do, when prompted by natural instinct. This condition might be caused by an obstruction of the brain, in one of the ventricles, or an interference with the pituitary body. If so, the sense of "I" would be restored when the obstacle was removed. Then the "I" sense would come again into touch and focus with the other senses, and that person would at once remember his name, and recognize his whereabouts and his home.

A FRIEND

# JANUARY 1916

[From *The Word*, Vol. 22 No. 4]

*What is usually meant by the term "Soul" and how should the term Soul be used?*

The term is used in many different ways. Those who use it have as a rule vague notions of what they intend to designate thereby. All they have in mind is that it is something not material; that it is something not of gross physical matter. Further, the term is used indiscriminately, as is natural where there are so many degrees in the development of matter, and no accepted system to designate these degrees. The Egyptians spoke of seven souls; Plato of a threefold soul; the Christians speak of soul as something different from spirit and physical body. Hindu philosophy speaks of various kinds of souls, but it is difficult to pin the statements down to a system. Some theosophical writers distinguish between three souls—the divine soul (buddhi), the human soul (manas), and kama, the animal soul. Theosophical writers do not agree to what the term soul should be applied. So there is no clearness, no conciseness, beyond this that the term soul covers in theosophical literature various aspects of invisible nature. Therefore, it is impossible to say what is usually meant by the term soul.

In common speech phrases like "loves with heart and soul," "I'd give my soul for it," "open my soul to him," "feast of soul and flow of reason," "soulful eyes," "animals have souls," "souls of the dead," add to the confusion.

It seems that the one feature in common is that soul means something invisible and intangible, and therefore not of earthly matter, and that each writer uses the term to cover such part or parts of the invisible as he feels pleased.

In the following are given some views as to how the term soul should be used.

Substance manifests at each period of outbreathing, substance is breathed out. When substance breathes itself out, it breathes itself out as entities; that is, independent entities, individual units. Each individual unit has the potentiality, though not the immediate possibility, of becoming the greatest being conceivable. Each individual unit when breathed out has a dual aspect, namely, one side is changing, the other unchanging. The changing side is the manifested part, the unchanging is the unmanifested or substance part. The manifested part is spirit and soul, force and matter.

This duality of spirit and soul is found through the whole set of changes which succeed each other in a manifestation period.

An individual unit enters into combination with other individual units, yet never loses its individualness, though it has no identity in the beginning.

In the materializing down from the first stages of spirituality into the later stages of concretion, that is, into physical matter, spirit gradually loses its predominance, and matter gains ascendency in similar degrees. The term force is used in place of spirit, to which it corresponds, while matter is used in place of soul.

One who uses the term matter should not think he has dispensed with the term soul and that he knows what matter is. In point of fact, it may be that he knows as little what matter is as he knows what soul is. He knows of the appearance to the senses of certain qualities and properties of matter, but as to what matter is, aside from these, he does not know, at least not as long as his sensuous perceptions are the channel through which information reaches him.

Spirit and soul and mind should not be used interchangeably as synonyms. In the worlds there are seven orders or classes of souls on four planes. The seven orders of souls are of two kinds: the descending souls and the ascending souls, the involutionary and the evolutionary. The descending souls are energized, urged, inspired to action by spirit. The ascending souls are, or if they are not they should be, raised and guided by mind. Four of the seven orders are Nature souls, each order having many degrees in the world to which it belongs. The spirit impels a descending soul along the path of involution from the abstract spiritual into the concrete physical through varieties of lives and forms and phases of nature, until it develops or is brought into the human physical form. The spirit or nature presses the soul onward as long as it involves, but it must by the mind be raised as an ascending soul on the path of evolution, through the various degrees of each of the three orders from the human mortal to the divine immortal. The soul is the expression, essence and entity of the spirit, and life and being of the mind.

To distinguish between the seven orders we may call the descending souls breath-souls, life-souls, form-souls, sex-souls; and the ascending orders animal-souls, human-souls, and immortal-souls. Concerning the fourth, or order of sex, let it be understood that the soul is not sex. Sex is a characteristic of physical matter, in which all souls must be tempered before they can be raised on the evolutionary path by the mind. Each of the orders develops a new sense in the soul.

The four orders of nature souls are not and cannot become immortal without the aid of the mind. They exist as breaths or lives or forms for long periods, and then they exist in the physical body for a long time. After a while they cease to exist as souls in a body and must pass through a period of change incidental to death. Then from the change there comes a new entity, a new being, in which the education or experience in that order is continued.

When mind connects with the soul to raise it, the mind can not at first succeed. The animal soul is too strong for the mind and refuses to be raised. So it dies; it loses its form; but from its essential being which cannot be lost the mind calls forth another form. The mind succeeds in raising the soul from the animal to the human state. There the soul must choose whether it wants to revert to the animal or to go on to the immortal. It gains its immortality when it knows its identity apart and independently from the mind which helped it. Then that which was soul becomes a mind, and the mind which raised the soul to become a mind may pass beyond the four manifested worlds into the unmanifested, and becomes one with the Divine Soul of all. What that soul is was outlined in the editorial "Soul," February, 1906, Vol. II, THE WORD [p. 71 in Monthly Editorials From THE WORD Part I].

There is a soul or soul connected with every particle of matter or nature, visible and invisible; with every body, whether the body be mineral, vegetable, animal or celestial being, or a political, industrial or educational organization. That which changes is the body; that which does not change, while it holds together the changing body connected with it, is the soul.

What man wants to know is not so much about the number and kinds of souls; he wants to know what the human soul is. The human soul is not the mind. The mind is immortal. The human soul is not immortal, though it may become immortal. A portion of the mind connects with the human soul or descends into a human body; and this is called an incarnation or a reincarnation, though the term is not accurate. If the human soul does not offer too much resistance to the mind, and if the mind succeeds in the purpose of its incarnation, it raises the human soul from the state of a mortal soul to the state of immortal. Then that which was a mortal human soul becomes an immortal—a mind. Christianity, and especially the doctrine of vicarious atonement, is founded on this fact.

In a particular and limited sense the human soul is the ethereal and intangible form, the wraith or ghost of the physical body, which holds the shape and features of the constantly changing physical body together and preserves them intact. But the human soul is more than this; it is the personality. The human soul or personality is a wonderful being, a vast organization, in which are combined for definite purposes, representatives from all the orders of descending souls. The personality or human soul holds together and includes the outer and the inner senses and their organs, and regulates and harmonizes their physical and psychic functions, and preserves experience and memory throughout the term of its existence. But if the mortal human soul has not been raised from its mortal human state—if it has not become a mind—then that soul or personality dies. The raising of a soul to be a mind must be done before death. This becoming a mind means that one is conscious of identity independently of and apart from the physical body and the outer and inner senses. With the death of the personality or human soul the representative souls composing it are loosed. They return to their respective orders of descending souls, to enter again into combination of a human soul. When the human soul dies it is not necessarily and not usually lost. There is that in it which does not die when its physical body and its ghostly form are destroyed. That of the human soul which does not die is an invisible intangible germ, the personality germ, from which is called forth a new personality or human soul and around which is built a new physical body. That which calls forth the germ of personality or soul is the mind, when that mind is ready or is preparing to incarnate. The rebuilding of personality of the human soul is the basis on which is founded the resurrection doctrine.

To know of all the varieties of souls one needs an analytical and a comprehensive knowledge of the sciences, among them chemistry, biology and physiology. Then it is necessary to abandon the twistings which we like to call metaphysics. That term should stand for a system of thought as accurate and as dependable as mathematics is. Equipped with such a system and with the facts of science, we would then have a true psychology, a soul science. When man wants it he will get it.

A FRIEND

# JUNE 1916

[From *The Word,* Vol. 23 No. 3]

*Is not the Theosophical doctrine of our suffering on earth as karmic retribution, on a par with the Theological statement of our suffering as a retribution in hell, in that both assertions have to be accepted on faith merely; and, further, one is about as good as the other to produce moral goodness?*

Both doctrines are on a par, and have to be taken on faith only while the mind is in an unreasoning or child state. The doctrines are accepted, similarly as the alphabet and the multiplication table are taken by a child—on faith.

When the reasoning mind examines the doctrines, it finds that suffering on earth is based on law and justice and evidenced by experience in life, and that the hell doctrine is an arbitrary edict framed by theological policy. The mind can find no reason for eternal suffering in hell as retribution for wrongs done largely through ignorance in one short life on earth, especially when the wrongs seem to be compelled often by force of circumstances and environment, which was not caused by the sufferer.

Reincarnation, and suffering on earth as karmic retribution, when applied to explain the facts of life, are found to work according to law, similarly as the multiplication table and arithmetic. Suffering is seen as the result of having acted against the law, and is not punishment, but the experience necessary to the learning not to so act. It is more creditable to intelligence that the world and man's place in it are the result of law rather than the result of the whim of a despot.

The theological doctrine of hell cannot truly be said to be about as good as the theosophical doctrine of karmic retribution, to produce moral goodness, for never can moral strength be born of servile fear. The hell doctrine is to compel goodness through fear of punishment. Instead it breeds moral cowardice and suggests unjust action.

The doctrine of karmic retribution through reincarnation, helps the mind to find its own place and work in the world, and shows it the true way through life. Moral goodness is the result.

There is no proof of the theological hell. The sense of justice rebels against and dispels the fear of it as the mind grows in strength and understanding. The proof of karma is the sense of justice inherent in man. The ability to see and understand it, depends on his willingness to see his wrongdoing and to right it by just action.

A FRIEND

# FACSIMILE OF THE FIRST
## "MOMENTS WITH FRIENDS"

On the following two pages is a photographic reproduction of the first installment of Harold W. Percival's column "Moments With Friends" in the March 1906 issue of his magazine *The Word*.

# MOMENTS WITH FRIENDS

"How can we tell what we have been in our last incarnation?" asked a visitor the other night after a lecture.

The only way to tell is to know positively as who we lived before. The faculty by which this knowledge comes is memory, of a higher order. In the absence of that, each may form estimates of what he was before by what he really likes now. It is only reasonable to suppose that, if we have any choice in the matter, we would not select as the condition or environments into which we were to come, such as were unsuited to our tastes or development and, on the other hand, if we have no choice, then, the law which governs reincarnation would not put us into conditions unsuited for development.

We feel in sympathy with or are opposed to certain ideals, characters, classes of people, types of people, crafts, professions, arts and occupations, and this would indicate whether we had worked for or against these before. If we feel at home or ill-at-ease in good or bad society, that would indicate to what we had been accustomed before. A tramp, accustomed to sunning himself idly on an old wharf or along a dusty country road, would not feel comfortable in polite society, a chemist's laboratory, or on the rostrum. Nor would one who had been an active industrious man, mechanically or philosophically inclined, feel comfortable and at ease sunning himself, unwashed, in ragged clothes.

We may with fair accuracy infer what we were in the past life not by wealth or position in the present, but to what our impulses, ambitions, likes, dislikes, controlling passions, draw us in the present.

---

"Can we tell how many times we were born before?"

The body is born and the body dies. The soul is neither born nor dies, but incarnates into the body which is born and leaves the body at the body's death.

To know how many lives a soul has spent in this world, take a glance at the different races now in the world. Consider the moral, mental and spiritual development of an African, or South Sea Islander; and then that of a Newton, Shakespeare, Plato, Buddha, or Christ. Between these extremes think of the different grades of development which humanity presents. After this ask where do "I" stand between these extremes.

After averaging the position see how much "I" have learned from the experiences of the present life—the ordinary man learns but little—and how do "I" act what "I" have learned. After this interesting question, we may perhaps form some idea of the number of times it must have been necessary to have lived in order to have reached even the present state.

There is no way for any one person to tell how many times he has lived before except by actual knowledge and a continued consciousness from the past. If he were told he lived twice or fifty thousand times the information would not benefit him, and he would not be able to verify it except by knowledge which comes from his own soul. But by the illustration given we may perhaps form some idea of the millions of years through which we must have come to have reached the present state.

---

"Are we conscious between our reincarnations?"

We are. We are not conscious in the same manner as we are during life in the body. This world is the field of action. In it man lives and moves and thinks. Man is a composite being made up or composed of seven men or principles. At death the divine portion of man separates itself from the grossly material portion, and the divine principles or men then dwell in a state or condition which has been determined by the thoughts and actions through the entire life. These divine principles are the mind, soul, and spirit, which, with the higher desires, pass into the ideal condition which the life on earth has determined. This condition can be no higher than were the thoughts or ideals during life. As these principles are disconnected from the grossly material portion they are not conscious of the evil of the life. But they are conscious, and live out the ideals which have been formed during the life just ended. This is a period of rest, which is as necessary to the soul's progress as a rest at night is necessary to fit the body and mind for the activities of the coming day.

At death, the separation of the divine from the mortal principles allows the bliss of the living out of ideals to be experienced. This is a conscious state between reincarnations.

---

"What are the theosophical views of Adam's and Eve's reincarnations?"

Whenever this question has been asked of a theosophist it has caused a smile, for even though the idea of Adam and Eve being the first two human beings who lived in this world has been shown in its absurdities by modern scientific investigations, yet the question quite frequently comes up.

The well informed man will at once say that evolution shows this tale to be a fable. The theosophist agrees with this, but saying that the early history of the human race has been preserved in this myth or fable. The Secret Doctrine shows that the human family in its early and primeval state were not as they are now, made up of men and women, but that in fact there was no sex. That gradually in the natural development a dual sex or hermaphroditism, was developed in each human being. That still later were developed the sexes, into which humanity at present is divided.

Adam and Eve does not mean one man and one woman, but the whole humanity. You and I have been Adam and Eve. The reincarnations of Adam and Eve is the reincarnation of the human soul in many different bodies, in many lands, and through many races.

---

"What is the length of the time appointed between reincarnations, if there is any specified time?"

It has been said that the period between incarnations, or from the time of the death of one body until the soul takes up its abode in another which is born into the world, is about fifteen hundred years. But this by no means applies to all people, and especially not to the active-minded modern western man.

The good man who longs for heaven, who performs good works in this world and has ideals and a vivid imagination, one who longs for an eternity in heaven, may have a heaven for an immense period, but it is safe to say that such is not the average man in the present day.

Life in this world is the field of action in which seeds are sown. Heaven is a state or condition of rest where the mind rests from its labors and works in life that it may be again reincarnated. The period after which the mind is drawn back depends on what it has done in life and where it has placed its thought, for wherever the thought or the aspiration is to that place or condition the mind will go. The period is not to be measured by our years, but rather by the mind's capacity for enjoyment in activity or rest. A moment at one time seems to be an eternity. Another moment passes like a flash. Our measurement of time, therefore, is not in the days and years which come and go, but in the capacity for making these days or years long or short.

The time is appointed for our stay in heaven between reincarnations. Each one appoints it himself. Each human being lives his own life. Inasmuch as each differs in detail from every other no definite statement as to time can be made other than that each makes his time himself by his own thoughts and actions, and it is long or short as he makes it. It is possible for one to reincarnate in less than a year, though this is unusual, or to extend the period for thousands of years.

---

"Do we change our personality when we return to earth?"

We do in the same manner that we change a suit of clothes when it has served its purpose and no longer is necessary. The personality is made up of elemental matter combined into form, animated by the principle of life, directed and promoted by desire, with the lower phases of the mind acting therein through the five senses. This is the combination which we call the personality. It only exists for the term of years from birth to death; serving as the instrument with and through which the mind works, comes into contact with the world, and experiences life therein. At death, this personality is laid aside and returns into the occult elements of earth, water, air, and fire, from which it was drawn and combined. The human mind then passes on to its state of rest after the enjoyment of which it builds up and enters another personality to continue its education and experiences in the world. A FRIEND.

# FACSIMILE OF PERCIVAL'S LETTER
## TO THE READERS OF *THE WORD*

On the following two pages is a photographic reproduction of Harold W. Percival's letter to the Readers of *The Word*, which appeared in the last issue of *The Word*, dated September 1917. In this letter, he states that he authored the editorials and the answers to the questions posed in "Moments With Friends," all of which were originally unsigned.

To the Readers of *The Word:*

No further issues of *The Word* will be published for the present. But this number, which ends the Twenty-fifth Volume, is not expected to be the last. For the present, the publication of *The Word* will cease. The readers will be notified when *The Word* begins a new series.

Appreciation is due from all readers to the various contributors to *The Word.*

I have written an editorial for every published number of *The Word*, since my message was written in October, 1904, and have answered the questions in "Moments With Friends," which appeared from time to time. The editorials written by me were not signed with my name. Information not before given, so far as is known, will be found in these editorials and in some of the "Moments."

The main object of my writings was to bring the readers to an understanding and a valuation of the study of Consciousness, and to stimulate those who choose to become conscious of Consciousness. To that end a system has been made known by me. I have called it the Zodiac.

I would not state these facts, as to purpose and authorship, except that it is advisable, so as to guard against misrepresentation by some persons who have claimed and some who may claim to have found these teachings elsewhere than in *The Word,* and by some who attempt to change, distort or obscure what is stated in these Editorials. The information I have given in *The Word* is for those who will use it as a sacrifice to the plan of raising matter to Consciousness.

If *The Word* is taken up again it is my intention to write other articles. They will lead some of the Readers to know what it is to be Conscious of Consciousness.

HAROLD WALDWIN PERCIVAL.

New York, April 15th, 1918.

# INDEX

# The Word Foundation

### Declaration

The purpose of the Foundation is to make known the good news in the book *Thinking and Destiny* and other writings of the same author, that it is possible for the conscious self in the human body to nullify and abolish death by the regeneration and transformation of the structure of the human into a perfect and immortal physical body, in which the self will be consciously immortal.

### The Human Being

The conscious self in the human body enters this world in a hypnotic dream, forgetful of its origin; it dreams through human life without knowing who and what it is, awake or asleep; the body dies, and the self passes out of this world without knowing how or why it came, or where it goes when it leaves the body.

### Transformation

The good news is, to tell the conscious self in every human body what it is, how it hypnotized itself by thinking, and how, by thinking, it can dehypnotize and know itself as an immortal. In the doing of this it will change its mortal into a perfect physical body and, even while in this physical world, it will be consciously at one with its own Triune Self in the Realm of Permanence.

# Concerning The Word Foundation

This is the time, when the newspapers and books show that crime is rampant; when there continue to be "wars and rumors of wars"; this is the time while the nations are distraught, and death is in the air; yes, this is the time for the establishment of The Word Foundation.

As declared, the purpose of The Word Foundation is for the vanquishing of death by the rebuilding and transformation of the human physical body into a body of immortal life, in which one's conscious self will find itself and return to The Realm of Permanence in The Eternal Order of Progression, which it left in the long, long ago, to enter this man and woman world of time and death.

Not everybody will believe it, not everybody will want it, but everybody should know about it.

This book and other like writings are especially for the few who do want the information and who are willing to pay the price which is in or by the regenerating and transforming of their bodies.

No human being can have conscious immortality after death. Each one must immortalize his or her own physical body to have immortal life; no other inducement is offered; there are no shortcuts or bargains. The only thing that one can do for another is to tell that other that there is the Great Way, as shown in this book. If it does not appeal to the reader he can dismiss the thought of eternal life, and continue to suffer death. But there are some people in this world who are determined to know the truth and to live the life by finding The Way in their own bodies.

Always in this world there have been individuals who disappeared unnoticed, who were determined to reconstruct their human bodies and to find their way to The Realm of Permanence, from which they departed, to come into this man and woman world. Each such one knew that the weight of the world's thought would hinder the work.

By the "world's thought" is meant the mass of people, who ridicule or distrust any innovation for improvement until the method advocated is proven to be true.

But now that it is shown that the great work can be done properly and reasonably, and that others have responded and are engaged in the "Great Work," the world's thought will cease to be a hindrance because The Great Way will be for the good of mankind.

The Word Foundation is for the proving of Conscious Immortality.

H. W. Percival

# ABOUT THE AUTHOR

As Harold W. Percival pointed out in the Author's Foreword of *Thinking and Destiny*, he preferred to keep his authorship in the background. His intention was that the validity of his statements not be influenced by his personality, but be tested according to the degree of self-knowledge within each reader. Nevertheless, people do want to know something about an author of note, especially if they are involved with his writings.

So, a few facts about Mr. Percival are mentioned here, and more details are available at thewordfoundation.org. The Author's Foreword of *Thinking and Destiny* also contains additional information, including an account of his experiences of being conscious of Consciousness. It was because of this noetic enlightenment that he was later able to know about any subject through a mental process he referred to as *real thinking*.

In 1912 Percival began to outline material for a book to contain his complete system of thinking. Because his body had to be still while he thought, he dictated whenever assistance was available. In 1932 the first draft was completed and was called *The Law of Thought*. He did not give opinions or draw conclusions; rather, he reported that of which he was conscious through steady, focused thinking. The title was changed to *Thinking and Destiny*, and the book was finally printed in 1946. And so, the one-thousand-page masterpiece that provides crucial details on humankind and our relationship with the cosmos and beyond was produced over a period of thirty-four years. Subsequently, in 1951, he published *Man and Woman and Child* and, in 1952, *Masonry and Its Symbols*—In the Light of *Thinking and Destiny*, and *Democracy Is Self-Government*. These three smaller books on selected subjects of importance reflect the principles and information contained in *Thinking and Destiny*.

Mr. Percival also published a monthly magazine, *The Word,* from 1904–1917. His inspired editorials were featured in each of 156 issues and earned him a place in *Who's Who in America.* The Word Foundation started a second series of *The Word* in 1986 as a quarterly magazine that is available to its members.

Harold Waldwin Percival was born on April 15, 1868 in Bridgetown, Barbados and passed away of natural causes on March 6, 1953 in New York City. His body was cremated according to his wishes. It has been stated that no one could meet Percival without feeling that he or she had met a truly remarkable human being, and his power and authority could be felt. For all his wisdom, he remained genteel and modest, a gentleman of incorruptible honesty, a warm and sympathetic friend. He was always ready to be helpful to any seeker, but never trying to impose his philosophy on anyone. He was an avid reader on diversified subjects and had many interests, including current events, politics, economics, history, photography, horticulture and geology. Besides his talent for writing, Percival had a propensity for mathematics and languages, especially classical Greek and Hebrew; but it was said that he was always prevented from doing anything but that which he was evidently here to do.

# Other Books by Harold W. Percival

*Thinking and Destiny*

Many have found *Thinking and Destiny* to be unlike anything they have previously read. The author introduces us to the true meaning and purpose of Man, the Universe and Beyond. Provocative in its vast and detailed subject matter, the information may at first startle, or even elicit skepticism—until its contents have been absorbed. The statements made in this book are not based on speculation, dogma or religious authority. It was Percival's crucial experiences of the Presence of Consciousness as the Ultimate Reality that led to his ability to distill knowledge and truth from a process he called *real thinking*. Through this system of thinking he was able to provide sound answers to questions that heretofore have been considered by many to be unanswerable; such as, "Where did I come from?" and "Why am I here?" Mr. Percival stated that he was neither preacher nor teacher. He conveyed the information of which he was aware and left it to the individual to decide its veracity for him or herself. *Thinking and Destiny* is a guide for all humanity in a bewildering world. In print for over 75 years, this book is as relevant today as it will be for generations to come because the information is timeless and unaffected by prevalent thought. Reading this book may be one of your most profound and rewarding experiences.

*Man and Woman and Child*

This book, simply written, addresses humanity's descent into mortal bodies of birth and death. Here, you will learn the true identity of you—the conscious self in the body—and how you may break the hypnotic spell your senses and thinking have cast about you since childhood. Percival states: "These assertions are not based on fanciful hopes. They are substantiated by the anatomical, physiological, biological and psychological evidences given herein, which you can if you will, examine, consider and judge; and, then do what you think best."

*Democracy Is Self-Government*

Mr. Percival provides an original concept of "True" Democracy, where personal and national affairs are brought under the spotlight of eternal truths. This is not a political book. It sheds light on the direct connection between the conscious self in every human body and the affairs of the world in which we live. Percival tells us that we each have an opportunity, as well as a duty, to bring eternal Law, Justice, and Harmony to the world. This begins with learning to govern ourselves—our passions, vices, appetites, and behavior. "The purpose of this book is to point the way."—H. W. Percival

*Masonry and Its Symbols*

*Masonry and Its Symbols* casts a new light on the age-old teachings and exalted purposes of Freemasonry. This ancient Order has existed under one name or another long before the building of the oldest pyramid. It is older than any religion known today! The author points out that Masonry is for humanity—for the conscious self in every human body. This book illuminates how any one of us can choose to prepare for the highest purposes of mankind—Self-knowledge, Regeneration and Conscious Immortality.

*Monthly Editorials From THE WORD 1904–1917 Part I*
*Monthly Editorials From THE WORD 1904–1917 Part II*

From 1904 to 1917, H. W. Percival published *The Word,* a monthly magazine of a philosophical nature that had a worldwide circulation. Over this thirteen-year period, each of the 156 issues contained one of his editorials. These two books contain the complete collection.

৵

Thinking and Destiny, Man and Woman and Child,
Democracy Is Self-Government *and* Masonry and Its Symbols
*are also available as e-books from major booksellers.*

*To learn more about Harold W. Percival's books and other writings,
membership in The Word Foundation,
and our quarterly magazine,* The Word, *please visit:*

thewordfoundation.org

Made in the USA
Middletown, DE
06 June 2022

66615565R00195